THE STRENGTH SWITCH

Professor Lea Waters is a psychology researcher at the University of Melbourne, where she has worked for over 20 years. She is the founding Director of the Centre for Positive Psychology, holds the Gerry Higgins Chair in Positive Psychology, and is a registered psychologist and a member of the Australian Psychological Society. She is recognised as a world expert on positive parenting, positive education, and positive organisations, and has affiliate research positions with Cambridge University and the University of Michigan.

THE STRENGTH SWITCH

HOW THE NEW SCIENCE OF STRENGTH-BASED PARENTING HELPS YOUR CHILD AND YOUR TEEN FLOURISH

DR LEA WATERS

SCRIBE
Melbourne • London

Scribe Publications
2 John Street, Clerkenwell, London, WC1N 2ES, United Kingdom
18–20 Edward St, Brunswick, Victoria 3056, Australia

This edition published by arrangement with Avery,
an imprint of Penguin Random House LLC, New York

Published by Scribe 2017
Reprinted 2018

Copyright © Lea Waters 2017

All rights reserved. Without limiting the rights under copyright reserved above,
no part of this publication may be reproduced, stored in or introduced into a retrieval
system, or transmitted, in any form or by any means (electronic, mechanical, photocopying,
recording or otherwise) without the prior written permission of the publishers of this book.

The moral right of the author has been asserted.

In some instances, names and identifying characteristics have been changed to protect
the privacy of the individuals involved.

Neither the publisher nor the author is engaged in rendering professional advice or services
to the individual reader. The ideas, procedures, and suggestions contained in this book are
not intended as a substitute for consulting with your physician. Neither the author nor the
publisher shall be liable or responsible for any loss or damage allegedly arising from any
information or suggestion in this book.

Text design by Avery, New York

Printed and bound in the UK by CPI Group (UK) Ltd, Croydon CR0 4YY

Scribe Publications is committed to the sustainable use of natural resources and the use
of paper products made responsibly from those resources.

9781911344346 (UK edition)
9781925548341 (e-book)

A CiP record for this title is available from the British Library.

scribepublications.co.uk
scribepublications.com.au

To Matthew, Nicholas, and Emily.

May your strengths continue to shine.

*And to the little soul who started your
journey with us but did not stay,
you're shining in a better place.*

The most responsible, the most challenging, and, in the sense of being true to yourself, the most honorable thing to do is face up to the strength potential inherent in your talents and then find ways to realize it.

—MARCUS BUCKINGHAM AND DONALD O. CLIFTON, PHD,
authors of *Now, Discover Your Strengths*

CONTENTS

A Note About Pronouns

Masculine and feminine pronouns have been used interchangeably throughout this book.

A Note About Citations

I am indebted to many scientists and researchers whose work helped me to formulate my ideas on strength-based parenting. Key citations appear in this book. Additional citations that informed the chapters can be found on my website: http://www.strengthswitch.com.

Part One

LAYING THE FOUNDATION

CHAPTER 1

Standing for Strength in a World Obsessed with Weakness

Sometimes we find our callings; other times our callings find us. I certainly didn't expect to be handed mine at a cocktail party. It was 2011 and I was in Philadelphia for the World Congress of Positive Psychology, sipping wine and mingling with a group of fellow positive psychology scientists from as far away as South Africa, Korea, and (in my case) Australia, at the gracious home of Martin Seligman, PhD, and his wife, Mandy.

Martin Seligman is widely known as a leading authority on positive psychology, a branch of psychology that scientifically studies how positive emotions, strengths, and virtues help us thrive. Since its inception in 1998, positive psychology has grown rapidly,[1] with tens of millions of dollars invested in research and thousands of members from more than seventy countries joining the International Positive Psychology Association. Through Marty's many appointments and activities, including as director of the Penn Positive Psychology Center, and his best-selling books such as *Learned Optimism*, *Authentic Happiness*, and *Flourish*, he is passionate about making positive psychology a global movement. So this evening's informal gathering, which brought together professionals from around the world to connect and cross-fertilize ideas, felt very "Marty" to me.

I had met Marty when he came to Australia to establish a positive psychology approach at a school near the University of Melbourne, where I work. I had just transferred to the Melbourne Graduate School of Education from the School of Business and Economics, where as an organizational psychologist I'd been studying and consulting for organizations on integrating positive psychology into the workplace, particularly on how focusing on strengths as opposed to weaknesses could improve performance. Basically, I'd swapped offices for classrooms, senior execs for teachers, and workers for school kids. I was also leading the establishment of our Centre for Positive Psychology, a dedicated facility that was a first for Australia, for the university, and for me.

Marty and I were talking about how effective school systems could be for introducing positive psychology to children so kids could do better in school, feel better about themselves, and become adults who will shape a society empowered by positive psychology.

But as a psychologist and parent of two children, I knew that, in the infinite ways parents connect with children every day, families are by far the most powerful positive psychology delivery system of all.

The question was how to reach them.

Our conversation went something like this:

Me: It's great that we're doing this in schools. But what happens when kids go home? I'm using a strength-based approach with my kids, and I've seen the benefits. Someone should do the research that would inform parents about this.

Marty: Why don't you do it?

Me: But I'm an organizational psychologist, not a parenting expert.

Marty: You're raising your children this way, you're a qualified psychologist, and you're working with kids in schools. So why not you?

I think that's when I suddenly noticed that my wineglass needed a refill!

Despite initially avoiding Marty's question, it followed me all the way home on the thirty-hour flight to Melbourne: *Why not me? Maybe I could do it. Maybe I should do it. If I do it, I'll be helping a lot of parents and kids.* By the time the plane landed, I knew that bringing strength principles into families' lives was something I had to do.

Parents: 24/7 CEOs of Our Kids' Lives

These days I run strength-based workshops for schools, workplaces, and parents around the world. I've found that no matter what country, continent, or culture they're from, two things unite all parents: the desire to help their children flourish *and* a sense of inadequacy for this task.

Parenting can feel overwhelming. We're the CEOs of our children's lives, responsible for all the different departments: cognitive, physical, social, emotional, moral, sexual, spiritual, cultural, and educational. The buck starts and stops with us.

Parents today have a lot more to worry about. My parents didn't have to think about screen time, cyberbullying, or sexting. Expectations of parents are growing, too. We're raising kids in an era ruthlessly focused on grades, college admission, earning potential, and social acceptance.

There also seems to be less and less consensus—and more scrutiny—on the "right" way to parent. We're bombarded by conflicting approaches to raising good, successful kids. It can lead to anxiety about whether we're doing what's best for our child. We may feel so pressured to help our children grow into the person society says they *should* be that we may not be allowing them to grow into the person they actually *are*.

I know these pressures well. It takes all my confidence to tell other parents that I would rather let Nick and Emily play than provide them extra academic tutoring to pump up their grades. Am I putting them at a disadvantage? While there are more opportunities like this than ever for our children, they come with more competition and incessant chatter about how to help our child get ahead. How do we know what is the best approach?

Based on my psychological research on well-being; my work with schools, workplaces, and parents; and my own experience as a parent, I think the best approach is one that supports your child's ability for self-development, so that over time your child has the tools to take on the mantle of CEO.

This approach is rooted in positive psychology and provides a child with two vital psychological tools:

1. Optimism: the force that motivates your child to create a positive future for herself[2]
2. Resilience: your child's capacity to bounce back when life throws a curve ball[3]

You may be thinking, *That sounds great in theory, but how do I help my child acquire and use these tools?*

Strength-Based Parenting: The Antidote to "Parent Overwhelm"

Most of us have heard the expression "Play to your strengths," but how many of us really do this in any systematic way? Instead, we tend to focus on our weaknesses: what we've done wrong or need to improve. We tend to do this with our children, too, thinking that fixing their weaknesses will make them strong and successful.

But maybe you've noticed that overemphasis on the negative makes life feel like a slog—dull, frustrating, or downright depressing—certainly nothing we want for ourselves or our kids. It doesn't make parenting easier, either.

Through my work and research, I've found that building the optimism and resilience children need for success can be a rewarding, joyful journey for you and your child—because the pathway to both involves growing the things that delight you most as a parent: your child's talents and positive qualities.[4]

Most parents tell me they want to prepare their kids to be optimistic and resilient. But, in my professional opinion, our society has a case of "right intention—wrong direction." We mistakenly believe that the way to make our kids optimistic and resilient is to weed out all their weaknesses. Strength-based science shows the opposite is true. It tells us to turn the bulk of our attention to expanding their strengths rather than reducing their weaknesses.

My strength-based approach gives parents a clear idea of what strengths are and how we can help our kids play to their strengths. I'll provide a detailed definition of strengths in later chapters, but here's a working definition. Strengths are:

- positive qualities that energize us, that we perform well and choose often
- used in productive ways to contribute to our goals and development
- built over time through our innate ability and dedicated effort
- qualities recognized by others as praiseworthy, and they contribute positively to the lives of others

Focusing on your child's strengths is the basis of what I call "strength-based parenting" (SBP).[5] My research, coupled with findings in strength-based science,[6] positive psychology,[7] and neuropsychology,[8] my work with parents around the world, and my own experiences as a parent have helped me formulate this positive approach. Testing and analysis have proved its efficacy. This book will help you implement it.

Why Focusing on Strengths Makes Sense Today

Our quest to define and live "the good life" goes back to the ancient philosophers, but only in recent decades have we started examining the question scientifically.[9] The strength-based approach gives us the power to live the good life by drawing on our most abundant inner resources.[10] When we use it with our children, they internalize the idea that they have strengths, and they learn to use them to take charge of their life.

Why, then, do we tend to focus on the negative? As many parents confide to me: "I love my kid, but I keep criticizing him. What's going on?"

I have two words for you: *old wiring*.

Our brains were shaped by the rigors of survival into becoming brilliant pattern detectors. For most of our evolution, we've survived by quickly alerting to disruptions in the patterns of daily life as clues to possible danger or to weaknesses that put us at a disadvantage: That unusual movement in the grass might be a lurking predator . . . That one unsmiling face around the tribal campfire might be an enemy . . . Our inability to run as fast as the others might mean we'll be left behind when fleeing danger . . . and so on. This primeval tendency to zoom in on what's "off" helped us size up our chances for survival and decide whether our world might be about to turn upside-down.

This negative bias[11] can be hugely helpful when your life's at stake. But most of us don't face such extremes. For the situations we encounter today—which usually demand complex reasoning and problem solving, sophisticated cooperation and communication, reserves of persistence, or expert facility in a specific skill—the negative bias can put us at a disadvantage because it blinds us to opportunities, keeps us from seeing the larger picture, and bars access to the expansive thinking that unlocks innovation, collaboration, adaptability, growth, success, and fulfillment.

Attention on the negative helped us survive. Attention on the positive helps us *thrive.*

Three decades of research clearly shows the advantages of taking a strength-based approach for children and adults alike, including:

* greater levels of happiness and engagement at school[12]
* smoother transitions from kindergarten to elementary school and from elementary to middle school[13]
* higher levels of academic achievement (as found in high school and college students)[14]
* greater levels of happiness at work[15]
* greater likelihood of staying at work[16]
* better work performance[17]
* greater likelihood of staying married and being happy in your marriage[18]
* higher levels of physical fitness and of engaging in healthy behaviors (e.g., healthy eating, visiting the doctor)[19]
* better recovery after illness[20]
* increased levels of life satisfaction and self-esteem[21]
* reduced risk of depression[22]
* enhanced ability to cope with stress and adversity[23]

Rationally, we all know there are better tools than the "old" negative model. How many times have you inwardly cringed after you've snapped at your child, thinking, *Why didn't I handle that more constructively?* We just need to know exactly what those tools are and how to use them.

With this book in hand, you can feel confident that you're helping your child become his best self through strategies grounded in science, designed to support the innate desire of all children to reach their full potential, and backed up by millions of years of evolution selecting in favor of strengths.

In later chapters, you'll learn what strengths are and how they work to advance our children in life. You'll discover how to build the key capacities that will help your child find and grow his strengths, and how to communicate with—and discipline—your child in a strength-based way. You'll read inspiring and instructive stories from fellow parents, like Sharon's, later on in this chapter, who are successfully practicing strength-based parenting in everyday life and realizing just how powerful it is. You'll learn simple ways to train your brain to default to a more positive view and short-circuit the thought patterns leading to negative focus by using a technique that will help you switch instantly into strength mode—with your kids and with yourself. The result: a more harmonious, happy life.

So What Exactly Is Strength-Based Parenting?

Each of us has many strengths. We all have specific talents (e.g., physical, mental, social, technical, or creative)[24] as well as positive personality traits[25] (e.g., capacity for courage, kindness, or fairness), some in stronger doses than others. Strength-based parenting puts your kids in touch with their unique constellation of talents (which are performance based) and character (which is personality based). In the process, it changes your kids and it will change you.

It is never too late to start SBP, nor will it make your children arrogant or self-important. Last year, after giving a talk at a positive-psychology conference, a father from the audience approached me. He looked to be in his late fifties, with salt-and-pepper hair and the self-assured demeanor of a successful person—including a very direct style of conversation.

He skipped right past normal pleasantries and started with: "My oldest daughter suffered from anxiety during her senior year in high school, and I took her to see a psychologist. He helped her a lot, especially in coming to terms with her mother's and my divorce. So I can see the benefit of psychology in helping to fix problems. But I'm not convinced I should take this strength-based approach, especially with my two sons. If I focus on their strengths, does this mean I ignore their weaknesses? Isn't that a bit unrealistic? Won't they become overconfident?"

I'm asked these questions a lot, and they're ones we'll explore. But the short answer is: not at all.

A strong child is a child who can play to his strengths *while simultaneously working on his weaknesses* because his solid self-identity gives him the sturdy foundation necessary to acknowledge and address the areas he needs to improve. Being strength based doesn't mean we ignore weaknesses. It means we view and approach them from a different, larger context.

Let me be clear that strength-based parenting isn't about lavishing kids with the false and excessive praise that leads to big-headed narcissism.[26] It's about real praise based on your child's actual strengths. And since none of us is so perfect that we're showing our strengths all the time, rest assured you won't fall into a trap of excessive praise. There's no risk of creating a self-involved child who thinks she's the only special one in the world. If anything, SBP drives home the point that our strengths make us unique, but they don't make us special—because *everyone* has strengths. There's actually nothing special about having strengths. What *is* special is how we learn to use them in ways that are good for us and for others. That's what SBP achieves.

Let me also be clear that while strength-based parenting leads to greater levels of happiness in you and your kids, it's not about creating an artificially positive, saccharine-sweet environment where your kids face no challenges. SBP is as much about helping your kids use their strengths to grow during the bad times as it is about helping them thrive during the good times. Adversity, if supported in the right way, can build strengths in our kids. Connecting your child to her strengths during tough times is one of the most powerful things you can do as a parent.

As you can see, I've asked myself the questions this conscientious dad was asking. I love being a parent and I live the same dilemmas and worries of raising kids as everyone else, and so I truly enjoy talking these things through with other parents.

So after asking a few questions and learning a bit more about this refined man's concerns, on a hunch I asked him if he gardened. He did! I asked what he did to help grow his garden. He told me about his weeding regime, about the netting he uses to stop bugs from eating his roses, about the small fence he'd erected to protect some particularly special plants. This guy really gardened. And I'd hit the metaphor jackpot!

I asked what he did to ensure that his plants were in the best possible health. He talked about mulching, seasonal pruning, regular additions of quality topsoil, and an expensive fertilizer he absolutely swore by. He even suggested I write down the brand for my own garden. He obviously loved his garden and helping it grow.

We talked about how some of his actions reduced impediments to his garden's growth (for instance, removing weeds), while others enhanced growth (such as adding that superb fertilizer). It was a beautiful parallel to strength-based parenting: If we want to cultivate well-being in our children, we need to show them how to remove their weeds (weaknesses) *and* how to add fertilizer (strengths).

Seeking out a psychologist for his daughter was akin to the weeding process. But when I asked him to think back to a time when he had engaged in parenting that enhanced her strengths, he thought for a moment and then shook his head. "I see what you mean," he said. "And I'm sad to say I didn't do anything like that. I thought fixing her problems was enough."

When I suggested that he could still learn to grow his children's strengths by focusing as much on the fertilizer as on the weeding, a big smile spread across his face and he shook my hand warmly as we said good-bye.

Six months later, I received a letter from that gruff yet devoted gardener dad. He wrote that he had left the workshop with a new perspective on parenting. He spoke about initially feeling sad and guilty after my workshop that he'd not been a strength based parent. He wondered: Had he harmed his kids without realizing it? But he remembered my encouragement to start being strength based, and he moved forward. He discovered that being strength based didn't make his boys soft or self entitled, as he'd feared. He shared that this was the closest he had ever been to his daughter and that she was calling him from college to talk a lot more often these days. He had grown and felt better as a parent, too, writing that helping his kids see their strengths had helped him find what he could offer them—his own strengths—as a father. He also enclosed a photo: his three children and him, working together in his garden.

Being a strength-based parent changed the life of this family. It brought them together in a whole new way and helped each of them grow. It can happen in your family, too. I know because I've seen this happen time and again. SBP energizes parents and develops confidence in kids because it builds on what each person already has inside, rather than trying to "fix" or put in what was left out.

Most of us are doing the best we can as parents. And if you're not strength based, that doesn't mean you're not a good parent. What I do know, though, is that SBP helps us be better as parents. It helps us combine our love for our kids with the latest information in strength-based science, with the goal of giving our children the best possible start in life.

The Old Model

Our understanding of good parenting was developed in the 1960s by University of California, Berkeley, psychologist Diana Baumrind, PhD,[27] whose research has had a pivotal impact on parents for more than half a century. Open most parenting books and you'll see her ideas of warmth, attachment, boundaries, and autonomy.

Dr. Baumrind focused on two parenting dimensions:[28] "control" and "nurturance." Control refers to the extent to which parents supervise and set boundaries. Nurturance refers to the amount of affection and warmth parents provide. Dr. Baumrind used these two dimensions to classify parents into one of three parenting styles: punitive, permissive, and authoritative.[29]

At one end of the spectrum are "punitive parents" (control-cold). Punitive parents are strict, rigid, and unloving. Their focus is on gaining a child's obedience rather than on nurturing the child's needs.

At the other end are "permissive parents" (freedom-warmth). They're warm and loving but lack rules and discipline. Punitive parenting is too hard. Permissive parenting is too soft. Both are damaging.

Yet, as Goldilocks found, there's a "just right" middle ground: Authoritative parents (control-warmth) are sensitive to their children's feelings and needs without being overindulgent. They set clear rules and boundaries but are willing to be flexible and encourage independence.

Five decades of research show us that, of the three styles, authoritative parenting produces the best-adjusted, best-behaved, most resourceful, and highest-achieving kids.[30]

But why settle for "just right" parenting when we can now achieve so much more through what we're learning in positive psychology?

How I Developed Strength-Based Parenting

That question was running through my mind as I launched into motherhood in 2003. I'd received my PhD in organizational psychology and was busy applying the then-emerging science of positive psychology—especially strength-based team dynamics—to organizations through the School of Business and Economics at the University of Melbourne. Not only was it transforming performance at work, but it was also changing the personal lives of the high-powered (mostly male) executives I worked with. I lost count of how many told me, "This has transformed me as a boss, a person, and a parent." Their spouses confirmed it. I vividly recall one holiday party at a major global investment banking firm, when the wife of every one of these alpha-male bankers approached me and thanked me for the work I'd done, smiling broadly as they said, "He's changed so much."

Having experienced the power of focusing on strengths, many of these executives also asked, "Why didn't I learn this earlier in my career? It would have been really helpful."

As I pondered this question, my first thought was: *How do we start training new recruits, fresh out of college, in strength focus?*

Then, maybe because I had two young children who were thriving under the strength-based approach, my thought became: *Why start with twenty-year-olds when I could start with two-year-olds?*

And that's how one Friday night, over takeout in front of the TV, I told my husband, to his surprise, "I need to start working with schools."

Fortunately, I had developed a wonderful connection with the dean of the Melbourne Graduate School of Education, Field Rickards, PhD. We'd meet for coffee a few times a year, and it was a bit of a joke between us that pretty much every time he'd ask, "When are you coming to work for me?" "Never," I'd answer. "Schools aren't my specialty." I was having fun in the high-powered world of multinational corporations. This went on for years—until one day I said, "Well, if you find the right role, let's talk."

In what I like to think was a "cosmic coincidence," on the Monday after my takeout epiphany, the dean called. "I've found the role for you. I need someone to develop and direct a new leadership degree in partnership with the public education system to enhance leadership capacity in schools. What do you think?" I quickly calculated the pay cut I'd be taking and allowed myself a few moments to lament the perks I'd be leaving behind at the School of Business and Economics (*Good-bye, bonuses; farewell, travel stipend; au revoir, secretarial support; ciao, free cappuccinos. . .*). "Yes," I said, "but only if I can infuse positive psychology into this program and we can talk about building a center that brings strength work into schools. Is there any chance of it happening?" To my delight, he said, "I've been thinking the same thing." That's how the Center for Positive Psychology began in 2009.

By the time I had my fateful cocktail party conversation with Marty Seligman in 2011, I'd done intensive strength-based work with teachers and kids in many schools. Like the executives, the teachers were telling me what a difference it was making in their classrooms *and* at home, where they were using it with their own kids. I was presenting strength-based workshops to parents in evening sessions run by the schools and found they were hungry for it. I already knew from my research that a strength-based approach boosts student well-being.[31] Marty was right: Researching the effects of strength-based parenting was the logical next step for me.

I started with a simple enough idea. I wondered if effective (i.e., authoritative) parenting might be influenced by a third dimension beyond Baumrind's two dimensions of control and nurturance: "developmental focus." I reasoned that parents could either have a deficit focus or a strength focus. Parents with a deficit-based developmental focus implicitly believe that the best way to help their child become a happy and successful adult is to help them eradicate faults and flaws so their weaknesses won't limit them as adults. Parents with a strength-based developmental focus believe that the best way to foster development and raise a happy and successful adult is to identify and build their child's strengths and positive qualities.

How do you know which developmental focus you have? Here's the exercise I do with parents in my workshops, which will give you a glimpse into your own developmental focus:

Imagine your child is a lump of clay. Take some time to shape the clay into the form of your child, the same height and shape as your child. Now, step back. What you'll see is that some parts of the clay are already fully formed and beautifully sculpted. These are your child's strengths. Other parts are half formed or even not at all formed. These holes are your child's weaknesses.

Then I ask parents to think about their child and specifically label some of the strengths and weaknesses they see in this model of their child. "What would you do next," I ask them, "to help your child grow up so that he's a happy and successful adult?"

The natural temptation for many parents is to seek to fill the holes, because those are what grab our attention and because we think the form will collapse if we don't plug the holes. This is the deficit focus. A much smaller percentage of parents talk about building on and expanding the clay that's already there. This is the strength focus.

This exercise is a quick and useful way to help parents uncover whether their developmental focus is deficit based or strength based.

Here's the thing. We can spend a lot of our time and energy

plugging the holes, building the half-formed areas, and smoothing out the rough edges in our kids. When we focus on minimizing weaknesses, the holes do get smaller. But we haven't done anything to build our kids' strengths.

What would happen if, instead of filling in the holes, we spent that time and energy on refining the parts that are already there? As we contour, build up, and shape these areas—our child's strengths—the holes naturally get smaller and smaller. The clay you're building expands into the holes. Strengths grow into the space where the weaknesses used to be.

In my work with parents, I've seen well-meaning authoritative parents who were inadvertently blocking strength development in their children because they were being deficit based—albeit in a nurturing way. For example:

- focusing on the child's lower grades and ignoring the higher ones
- dwelling on the child's short attention span instead of noticing the activities that engross her
- reprimanding the child for rudeness but not noticing her when she is being polite
- commenting on the fact that the child colored outside the lines rather than on her interesting choice of colors

When I asked a sample of nearly ten thousand teenagers to rate the degree to which their parents were strength based, approximately 25 percent rated their parents as low in SBP and about 20 percent gave their parents just a moderate rating. Only a little over half rated their parents as being strength based. Yet my studies show that when teenagers do have strengths-focused parents, they report better psychological outcomes, including:

- higher levels of life satisfaction
- higher amounts of positive emotions such as joy and hope
- a better understanding of their own strengths
- using their strengths to help them meet homework deadlines
- using their strengths to help deal with friendship issues
- coping with stress in more proactive ways
- lower levels of day-to-day stress[32]

While these findings are a gratifying confirmation of my theories, I also had a very personal reason for my passionate interest in strength-based parenting. Like many children, I was conditioned to see myself for what I'm not—to focus on my weaknesses, flaws, and faults. To some degree that's just part of growing up in a world obsessed with weakness. But on top of that, I was deeply affected by my mom's mental illness. Mom's depression led to erratic behavior and extreme mood swings in her from sadness, to neediness, to emotional vacancy, to anger and rage. Her rage led to physical violence. Things were confusing and uncertain in my home. I didn't feel like I had solid ground. When she wasn't coping, she would say that we were the reason for her illness and that she was going to abandon us. I was always on the lookout for signs that she was leaving. As the oldest, I took on a lot of responsibility. I did my best to protect my younger brother and sister and try to make Mom happy. I failed. I grew up thinking there must be something deeply flawed in me to cause my mom's unhappiness and anger.

Without any support from Mom's psychiatrist about what to do, my parents decided that the best thing to do was to not talk about her depression. They meant well, but what happened was that my brother, sister, and I had no one to talk to when things got out of control or after her suicide attempts or when she went into hospital for treatments. Our loyalty was strong and we dared not speak to anyone outside of the family about what was going on. That meant we had no one to help us make sense of what was happening, to cry with, to tell us that it wasn't our fault. I felt very alone and I carried oceans of sadness and shame inside of me for such a long time.

Don't get me wrong—there were good times in my childhood. We had fun summer vacations, my mom and my dad were very active in my swim club and spent untold hours driving us to all our sporting events. They valued education and supported me to go to college—a gift for which I am forever grateful. My parents worked hard to earn money for our family, and they instilled a strong work ethic in me. They taught me to accept people's differences and to think outside the box. My childhood fueled my passion to become a psychologist, and I was determined to grow up and help people and families who were struggling.

If the hardship at home was not enough, I was also badly bullied at school when I was fifteen. Until then I'd never been a target for bullies, but I felt strong empathy for the kids who were bullied. Growing up the way I did, I knew what it was like to feel different from others, like an outsider. So one day when the bullies were at work on a student at the school lockers, something in me snapped and I thought, *This has to stop.* I stood between the bullies and their victim. I told them they needed to stop and foolishly added, "Why don't you pick on someone your own size?"

For the next eight months, they turned the full extent of their venom on me. From the minute I got on the school bus each morning until the minute I stepped off at night, their viciousness was relentless. Taunting me, yelling at me, pushing me, shoving me, pulling my hair, and ostracizing me. They started horrible rumors about me and they slipped threatening letters into my school bag. Sometimes they'd call my house in the middle of the night from a local phone booth (the only saving grace was that this was before the era of social media). The worst was when they said things about my mom. Growing up in a small town as we had, a few of the girls knew a little about my mom's illness. The absolute worst was when they started bullying my younger sister. It was the only time they saw me cry.

I tried to rise above it and not let them see that they were getting to me. That just escalated the bullying. After a series of physical attacks where they tried to burn my face with a cigarette, then ripped my earrings out and left my ears bleeding, my parents moved me to a new school.

The sadness at home and at school were too much to bear, and I became bulimic. When I was bingeing, all I thought about was food. With each bite, I would push my emotions deeper and deeper down inside. In those moments, I would become numb and my struggles would fade away. But soon self-disgust would creep in and I'd go through the painful process of purging. For seven years, all my energy went into thinking about when and how much I could secretly eat and then purge. It was all-consuming and exhausting.

One day, while pursuing my PhD in psychology, I was listening to one of my professors give a lecture on a brain disorder called Wernicke-Korsakoff Syndrome, which is caused by long-term vitamin B deficiency. It can happen to alcoholics, who lose the capacity over time to metabolize vitamin B. "By the way," he added, "this can also happen to people who are anorexic or bulimic, because they're not getting enough vitamin B."

That casual comment hit me hard. Despite all my struggles, my intellectual strength had gotten me through high school, college, and into this PhD program. I couldn't lose that to bulimia.

Wanting to save the only strength I thought I had, I sought professional help. The psychiatrist diagnosed me with post-traumatic stress disorder and explained how my suffering within my family was affecting my brain chemistry. We worked on my fear and sadness from my childhood. I overcame the bulimia. It was an important start to my healing journey, but the journey wasn't over. Now that I wasn't using food to suppress my feelings, my years of pent-up sadness and worry turned into full-blown depression and anxiety, which stayed with me for more than a decade. On the outside I was high functioning and high achieving. On the inside I was a wreck. An empty, shaky mess. I would overschedule myself to keep my anxiety at bay. Then I'd get overwhelmed with work and my brain chemistry would crash into depression. It was a roller coaster, to say the least.

When I got pregnant with my son at age thirty-two, I was determined not to let these issues affect my child. One day, I happened to be in a bookstore meeting some friends for coffee when I spotted Marty Seligman's books *The Optimistic Child* and *Authentic Happiness*. It was as if they were there waiting for me. I think I was the best student in the world, reading those books, because I was reading them on behalf of a new life as well as my own. In particular, *Authentic Happiness* spoke to me, with its message about this new field of positive psychology and how we should stop putting all of our emphasis on what's wrong with us and start supporting what's right with us.

I found a strength-based therapist who helped me to see that, in addition to intelligence, I had many strengths—including kindness, compassion, curiosity, willpower, and humor, among other things—that had kept me going for years, through getting my PhD, meeting and marrying my husband, continuing to take care of my ill mother,[33] and making a circle of lovely long-term friends. I came to understand that my strengths were the life raft that had stopped me from sinking and had allowed me to function productively despite struggling with mental health issues.

Discovering and accepting that I had strengths brought a deep sense of calm. Knowing I had these inner resources available to me at all times in any situation helped me find self-security for the first time in my life. I realized that my strengths weren't just a life raft when the sea was choppy; they were also the oars that could help me row toward a more positive shore. In particular, my strengths were going to help me to be a good mom.

It was a hugely empowering way to understand myself and my life. And I was determined to support, from day one, the inherent strengths that this little boy I was carrying would bring into the world with him.

In the years since, my strength-based approach has grounded my kids and me. It has made my parenting more intentional, coherent, and consistent. I don't do everything right. But when I do, it's not accidental. SBP gives me the power to replicate my successes and, let's hope, minimize my mistakes. I want other parents to have the same experience.

Discoveries in Store

In the years since, I've taken the practices I first used with Nick and Emily and tested them with thousands of other children.[34] That brought me to my work today with families—and to the book you're reading right now. In the chapters that follow, you'll learn:

- exactly what strengths are (they're fascinating and have had researchers scratching their heads for years)
- how the latest findings from strength-based science, neuroscience, genetics, and positive psychology can be used to support your use of strength-based parenting
- a clear way to identify strengths in your child and know the difference between a core (true) strength, a growth strength, and a learned behavior
- how to see and support your child's strengths as they flicker, glow, and ignite
- a powerful technique for bypassing the old habits that keep us focused on the negative

- how to deal with children's weaknesses and other troubleshooting tips
- strategies and stories from my own and other parents' experiences showing how the strength-based approach has changed their lives and helped them raise strong, secure, good-hearted, capable children

Could SBP be the antidote to the sense of inadequacy that so many parents—like the gardener father you met earlier—tell me they're feeling? I vote yes. In one of my studies, parents who went through a four-week strength-based parenting program felt more engaged and more confident as parents and experienced more positive emotions about their children.[35] This was certainly true for Sharon, one of the parents who shared her story with me for this book:

Although Sammy is twenty-one now, when she was much younger I often worried about her propensity to be a "perfectionist." She used to spend a lot of time organizing things and getting very upset if things were not perfect. I often feared she had obsessive-compulsive disorder or would struggle when life's complexity and challenges increased. Unfortunately, it wasn't until she was well into her teen years that I became aware of the strengths approach and I found out she had an appreciation of beauty and excellence as her top strength. Suddenly it all made sense! When she became frustrated about her environment, commented on the mess of toys around our house or what others would think of our house (which of course with "mother guilt" I took on board as a personal failing), all she was doing was acting out of her appreciation for beauty and excellence. From then on, rather than taking her comments as personal rejections or judgments, I saw that she just appreciated things looking nice. Now I draw on her strengths when I'm preparing a presentation, cleaning the house, or giving a party. I also

know that one way to show my love for her is by making things attrac-
tive and organized when I can.

SBP also makes the family more of a team. Connecting kids with their strengths gives them a role in the family. That makes them feel important and valued—and it makes parents' jobs easier. You've just read how Sharon's daughter draws on her appreciation of beauty and excellence to help plan family parties. Then there's Marie's son, Finn, who's the family DJ for music and also the "humor ambulance," making the family laugh during tough times. There's Jo's organizer son who packs the school bags. And Ben's creative son who likes to cook meals. What strengths do you think your child can bring to your family life?

Finally, by helping your child realize her strengths—and discover new ones—you'll be cutting through the competing parenting advice out there. Confusion will be replaced with confidence because your child's inherent strengths will lead the way. You'll help your child learn how to transfer and expand her strengths across multiple domains, draw on them in times of struggle, and use them to create a positive future for herself. Finally, and maybe even most important, you'll help your child use her strengths in ways that enrich the lives of others.

Can a person be successful working from weakness or limits? Maybe. But is that person truly fulfilling her potential, and with resilience and optimism? Isn't that what we most want for our children?

Perhaps best of all, despite the complex science behind why it works so well, implementing SBP is relatively simple. In fact, I've boiled it down to two steps. First you see your child's strengths. Then you build on them.

In time, SBP will be your new default setting as you use your pattern-sensitive brain to find positive patterns in your child—just as the businessmen and teachers I was training were going home and seeing strengths in their wives, husbands, friends, family members, and kids.

Along the way, if you slip up, don't worry. Family life gives you lots of do-over opportunities. A key part of SBP is understanding that it's OK to make mistakes and it's never too late to start being strength based. Your kids are more resilient than you think. Compassion and forgiveness for yourself and others will help your journey. Like the gardener dad, there's no point holding on to guilt; the best thing to do is move forward positively. This book will give you the tools to do that.

One of my aims in writing this book and setting up the Strength Switch website is to create a community where we support and nurture each other as parents and where we celebrate and build the good qualities in our kids and ourselves. I invite you to visit the site at http://www.strengthswitch.com and join our strength-based parenting community by taking the strength-based parenting manifesto. I'll keep you up to date on new research, inspirational stories, and activities to do with your child.

Although the title of this chapter focuses on standing for strength in a world obsessed with weakness, when you take a closer look at our world, you may find that strength helpers are all around you—you just haven't seen them that way. My friend the dean, who repeatedly asked me to work for him, was seeing that I had the strengths to grow my leadership and professional expertise in a new direction. I denied his view of me for years, clinging to my business consulting role, which was rewarding but had become a little too comfortable, truth be told. Then there was Marty Seligman, who challenged me to undertake research I was convinced I somehow wasn't qualified to handle—and who more recently pushed my self-imposed boundaries again when he encouraged me to write this book.

We all have strength helpers in our lives. It might have been a beloved grandparent, aunt, or uncle who always believed in you. A teacher who "got" you. A coach who knew how to bring out your best. A boss or mentor who tapped you for a big project because he knew you could do it even if you didn't. Someone who took a chance on you, who saw something in you that you didn't (yet) see in yourself. It may even have been your parents.

Now it's your turn to become a strength helper to your child.

As my story shows, in one way or another, we all have hurdles we must overcome, and we are all works in progress. As long as we live, we have the potential to learn, develop, and become the best version of ourselves. The ability to focus on our strengths lights our path.

How to Use This Book

This book is for you as well as for your kids. There's no age limit to growth through strength. Some of the exercises in this book are intended for you as a person and a parent. Others are for you and your child to do together. Still others are just for your child to do. As you practice living a strength-based life, three benefits will occur for you:

1. You'll be a more effective parent and person because you'll be using your strengths.
2. You'll be modeling this new approach for your children and helping them to learn to be strength based.
3. You'll become a purposeful and intentional strength helper to your children and to others, leading to better relationships with those you love and care about.

Once you see your child's strengths and start to build on them, you'll see that operating within strengths is an effective, gratifying, and energizing parenting approach. You'll wonder why you ever did anything else, and maybe why you didn't try it sooner. What's important is that you're doing it now. It's never too late to make the shift to strength.

Let's begin!

Exercises: How Strength-Based Are You as a Parent?

Before starting a journey, we have to know where we are. These four exercises will give you an idea of the degree to which you may already be practicing some aspects of strength-based parenting. You can seek to build the areas you're already doing well (i.e., play to your strengths), and you can learn about the areas where you need work, which will help you make better use of the chapters to come. If your score on the survey below is low, don't worry. As you read this book, you'll be surprised by how quickly that will change.

EXERCISE: | Test Your Strength-Based Parenting

To what degree do you use strength-based parenting?

Below is the survey I use in my research studies. See how you score.

STEP 1: Read the statements below and think about how true they are for *you*. Then select the response that best corresponds to your experience.

1. I can easily see the strengths in my children (their personality, abilities, talents, and skills).

1	2	3	4	5
STRONGLY DISAGREE	SOMEWHAT DISAGREE	NEITHER AGREE NOR DISAGREE	SOMEWHAT AGREE	STRONGLY AGREE

2. I know what my kids enjoy doing.

1	2	3	4	5
STRONGLY DISAGREE	SOMEWHAT DISAGREE	NEITHER AGREE NOR DISAGREE	SOMEWHAT AGREE	STRONGLY AGREE

3. It's hard to tell what the strengths are in my children.

1	2	3	4	5
STRONGLY DISAGREE	SOMEWHAT DISAGREE	NEITHER AGREE NOR DISAGREE	SOMEWHAT AGREE	STRONGLY AGREE

4. I know the things my kids are good at doing.

1	2	3	4	5
STRONGLY DISAGREE	SOMEWHAT DISAGREE	NEITHER AGREE NOR DISAGREE	SOMEWHAT AGREE	STRONGLY AGREE

5. I'm aware of the key strengths in each of my children.

1	2	3	4	5
STRONGLY DISAGREE	SOMEWHAT DISAGREE	NEITHER AGREE NOR DISAGREE	SOMEWHAT AGREE	STRONGLY AGREE

6. I know what energizes my children.

1	2	3	4	5
STRONGLY DISAGREE	SOMEWHAT DISAGREE	NEITHER AGREE NOR DISAGREE	SOMEWHAT AGREE	STRONGLY AGREE

7. I can easily see the things my kids do best.

1	2	3	4	5
STRONGLY DISAGREE	SOMEWHAT DISAGREE	NEITHER AGREE NOR DISAGREE	SOMEWHAT AGREE	STRONGLY AGREE

8. I give my children opportunities to regularly use their strengths.

1	2	3	4	5
STRONGLY DISAGREE	SOMEWHAT DISAGREE	NEITHER AGREE NOR DISAGREE	SOMEWHAT AGREE	STRONGLY AGREE

9. I encourage my children to do the things they are good at.

1	2	3	4	5
STRONGLY DISAGREE	SOMEWHAT DISAGREE	NEITHER AGREE NOR DISAGREE	SOMEWHAT AGREE	STRONGLY AGREE

10. I suggest to my kids that they use their strengths every day.

1	2	3	4	5
STRONGLY DISAGREE	SOMEWHAT DISAGREE	NEITHER AGREE NOR DISAGREE	SOMEWHAT AGREE	STRONGLY AGREE

11. I actively show my children how to use their strengths in different situations.

1	2	3	4	5
STRONGLY DISAGREE	SOMEWHAT DISAGREE	NEITHER AGREE NOR DISAGREE	SOMEWHAT AGREE	STRONGLY AGREE

12. I encourage my kids to do the things that they enjoy.

1	2	3	4	5
STRONGLY DISAGREE	SOMEWHAT DISAGREE	NEITHER AGREE NOR DISAGREE	SOMEWHAT AGREE	STRONGLY AGREE

13. I think of ways to help my children use their strengths.

1	2	3	4	5
STRONGLY DISAGREE	SOMEWHAT DISAGREE	NEITHER AGREE NOR DISAGREE	SOMEWHAT AGREE	STRONGLY AGREE

14. I encourage my kids to do things that make them feel energized.

1	2	3	4	5
STRONGLY DISAGREE	SOMEWHAT DISAGREE	NEITHER AGREE NOR DISAGREE	SOMEWHAT AGREE	STRONGLY AGREE

STEP 2: Calculate your score according to the instructions below.

SEEING YOUR CHILD'S STRENGTHS

* Assign the following point values to your responses to items 1, 2, 4, 5, 6, and 7:
    1 = Strongly disagree
    2 = Somewhat disagree
    3 = Neither agree nor disagree
    4 = Somewhat agree
    5 = Strongly agree
* *REVERSE* the scoring for question 3 (i.e., if the score is 5, then make it 1. If it is 1, then make it 5. If it's 3, then it stays the same).
* Add the points for items 1–7.

QUESTION	YOUR SCORE OUT OF 5
1	
2	
3 (note reverse scored)	
4	
5	
6	
7	
Total score for seeing strengths	/35

BUILDING YOUR CHILD'S STRENGTHS

* Assign the following point values to your responses to items 8, 9, 10, 11, 12, 13, and 14:

    1 = Strongly disagree
    2 = Somewhat disagree
    3 = Neither agree nor disagree
    4 = Somewhat agree
    5 = Strongly agree

QUESTION	YOUR SCORE OUT OF 5
8	
9	
10	
11	
12	
13	
14	
Total score for building strengths	/35

COMBINED SCORE

- Add the scores from the two tables together for a combined score. The total should be somewhere between 7 and 70.

STEP 3: Interpret your score.

This survey divides your responses into two categories that reveal two key aspects of your parenting style: how much you know your kids' strengths and how much you encourage your kids to build their strengths. Let's take a closer look at each category:

Seeing Your Child's Strengths

You parent in ways that make an effort to notice and understand the things your children do well, enjoy doing, and find energizing. You make sure to tell your children that you're aware of their positive qualities. You help your children see their own strengths.

Building Your Child's Strengths

You parent in ways that actively encourage your children to spend time playing to their strengths. You encourage them to engage in activities in which they show high performance, high energy, and high use. For example, you may encourage your child to volunteer for a charity because you see your child's strengths of generosity and humanity, or you may suggest that your child sign up for the school band if you notice musical talent and enjoyment.

Understanding Your Score

Your score will range from 7 (no use of strength-based parenting) to 70 (a super-user of strength-based parenting). The key thing to remember, before you reflect on your scores, is that SBP is a skill set and you can build that skill set up no matter where you score on the survey.

0–20 = Low use of strength-based parenting. Don't worry if this is your score. Many of us have not learned how to focus on strengths. You may be surprised how focusing on your child's strengths just a little each day sparks a positive connection with your child. You'll learn quickly and you'll find lots of tips, techniques, and exercises in this book as well as on my website.

21–40 = Medium use of strength-based parenting. You've got a solid foundation of strength-based skills and are ready for a deeper dive into the process.

41–60 = High use of strength-based parenting. You probably are already seeing the benefits of the strength-based approach in your child and in your family life. Keep going and growing— more good adventures await!

61–70 = Super-user of strength-based parenting! Congratulations. You're blazing new paths in parenting and creating a strength-empowered world. Continue the great work!

This assessment is also available for free on my website: http://www.strengthswitch.com. You can let your friends know about it and if you would like to assist in ongoing research on strength-based parenting, you can sign up to take the assessment there. With your permission the results will go into a large database to help us further understand strength-based parenting.

EXERCISE: | Identify Your Own Strengths

Learning how to see and grow your child's strengths starts with you. In Chapter 3, you'll learn more about strengths and I'll point you to some specific surveys you can complete to systematically uncover your own specific talents and positive personal qualities, but for now we'll start more broadly. What are your strengths, and how do you use them in your role as a parent? Let's explore this in the activity below.

You at Your Parenting Best

Think of a time when you were parenting well. You felt great about what you said and did and how your kids responded. Now write the story below, describing it in detail. What did you do? How did you feel? What impact did this have on your kids?

The Story _____

_____

_____

_____

_____

_____

_____

_____

_____

_____

_____

_____

_____

_____

Now write down the strengths you used in that positive experience.

_____

_____

_____

_____

_____

_____

_____

_____

_____

_____

_____

_____

EXERCISE: | Identify Your Unique SBP Style

In the thousands of conversations I've had with parents all over the world, I've noticed three distinct patterns in the way parents enact the strength-based approach. Some parents do it through conversations with their kids. I call these parents Strengths Communicators. Others do it through coaching and directly helping their kids practice. I call these parents Strengths Activators. Still others do it by creating strength-based opportunities for their kids. I call them Strengths Creators.

I believe that these three patterns arise because, whether they know it or not, the parents are acting from their own strengths. Communicators will naturally use conversation as a way to connect their kids to strengths; practical, hands-on Activators will coach and directly help their kids; strategic, big-picture Creators will create enabling conditions that allow strengths to grow. I'm a Communicator and my husband, Matt, is an Activator. My guess is that the gardener dad was a Creator. Chances are you're using a blend of all three styles, but you'll have one style that's dominant. Where do you think you sit on all three styles? What is your unique combination? You can take the strengths parenting style survey as part of my online strength-based parenting course.

EXERCISE: | See How Other Parents Are Using SBP

One helpful way to start becoming a strength-based parent is to see how other parents have done it. That's why my Master of Applied Positive Psychology (MAPP) student, Lara Mossman, and I put together a website called The Strengths Exchange based on the Values in Action character strengths framework. There you'll find short videos from parents, kids, and teenagers talking about how they use their strengths. Watching these stories of character strengths in action will give you ideas for how to bring strengths into your family. The site includes resources and information on character strengths developed by two of my other MAPP students, Claire Fortune and Pamela Núñez Del Prado. Everything on the site is free. You will find the URLs to all of my websites at the end of this book.

CHAPTER 2

The Strength Switch

When Nick turned eight, we bought him a new bike. He loved it and rode it every day after school. Matt cleared a space at the side of our front deck for Nick to store his bike, but Nick seemed to forget this and left it by the front door more often than not, despite repeated reminders to put it away where it belonged.

One evening a couple of weeks after Nick's birthday, I came home from a long day at work to find Nick's bike leaning beside the front door as usual. *When will that boy ever learn?* I thought. Inside, in a not altogether nice way, I asked Nick to move his bike to the correct spot.

The next day, I pulled into the driveway to see the bike once again parked by the front door. *Wait—this again?* It felt like a scene out of *Groundhog Day.* I went inside. Nick came out of his room to greet me with a big smile on his face—but before he could say a word, I snapped: "You need to learn to put your bike where it BELONGS. I am getting tired of reminding you about this!"

His face fell, and I had one of those awful moments of classic parental guilt. I'd walked in the door and, before even saying hello, I'd pointed out something my son had failed to do. What should have been a happy homecoming after not seeing each other all day was instead a painful episode for both of us. Nick felt bad about not putting his bike away, and I felt bad for snapping at him. What kind of example was I setting about how to handle problems in relationships? Yep. Fail.

Why It Can Be Challenging to Shift to Strength

I laughed aloud during the Q & A at one of my parenting talks when a mother asked: "You talk about noticing our kids' strengths, but is there a parenting approach that's based on noticing their weaknesses? 'Cause I'm *really* good at seeing those!"

In Chapter 1, I mentioned our human facility for focusing on the negative. Unfortunately, the joy of becoming a parent and the love we feel for our children don't magically erase this capacity. We're supergood at seeing what our children do wrong and jumping onto the negativity train.

Psychologists have identified four thinking processes wired into our brain that predispose us to this default. Tune in to them and use the special tool I'll provide in this chapter, and you'll be on your way toward the more positive, productive default setting of strength-based parenting.

The Four Negative Defaults

Let's take a closer look at the four negative defaults.

Selective Attention

Imagine you're asked to watch a short video in which six people pass two basketballs between them. Three players are wearing white shirts; three are wearing black shirts. Your task is to mentally count the number of passes made by the team in the white shirts.

About thirty seconds into the game, a person dressed as a gorilla walks into the frame, faces the camera, thumps its chest, and walks offscreen.

This hairy beast is visible for a full nine seconds. Surely this would stand out. You might even lose count of the passes, right?

Not so. In fact, the researchers found that 50 percent of the people who watched the video and counted the passes didn't even notice the gorilla![1]

This phenomenon, known as "inattentional blindness,"[2] occurs because people are actively (i.e., selectively) placing their attention on something to the exclusion of much else. When I snapped at Nick about his bike the minute I got home, I was displaying selective attention: Blind to anything else Nick had done, I was seeing only the bike.

Selective attention is our brains' way of avoiding information overload by filtering incoming information. At any point in time, we get far more input than our brains can attend to. By selectively focusing on some aspects, our brain can make sense of the world, but it does this at the expense of noticing other aspects.

Let's run an experiment. For thirty seconds, hold this book (or tablet) but stop reading the words. Instead, focus your attention on what it feels like to hold the book or device. Bring your attention to your hands. What is the weight of what you're holding? Is it heavy or light? Does the surface feel warm or cool in your hands? Is it soft and malleable? Or sharp and unbending?

OK—time's up. Now come back to my words. You're probably feeling somewhat distracted, as your brain is still processing all the information I just asked you to pay attention to: weight, temperature, texture, and so forth. On some level, you're always aware of these things without realizing it. That's why you don't drop the book and it's also why you automatically shift hand positions every few minutes to keep the book stable and your hands from fatiguing. But your awareness of the book's physical properties is quickly fading into the background of your consciousness now as you focus your attention on my words. (Thanks, by the way!)

Selective attention is a smart evolutionary feature developed by our brains to ensure that we can function in a world constantly bombarding us with information. But the downside should now be clear. Our filtering system is fast but not perfect, so we often miss important information that could contribute to our assessment of what's happening around us.

The key thing about selective attention is just to be aware of it. If we are, we realize that we have power over it and can *choose* the focus of our attention—for example, on our child's strengths instead of on his weaknesses.

Selective attention isn't always negative, but it is always distorting. When I was trying to get pregnant, it seemed every other woman working at my university was pregnant. No, it wasn't because of some supernatural increase in the fertility of the area or because the genetics lab had slipped something into our drinking water. My attention was simply selecting pregnant women from the crowd because pregnancy was on my mind. Of course there was no baby boom at my university. It was just that my motivation to notice them had increased.

The good news, though, is that this motivation can be consciously directed.

Negativity Bias

The very architecture of the brain causes us to overlook our child's strengths. Simply put, we're programmed to see what's wrong faster and more frequently than what's right.[3] Indeed, this negativity bias is so automatic that it happens preconsciously. In a study at The Ohio State University, participants fitted with elastic head caps containing electrodes that recorded electrical activity in their scalps were shown a series of photos, some of which displayed positive images, some negative, and some neutral. The images flashed rapidly once on a computer screen. Electrical activity spiked dramatically when the negative pictures were shown. This reaction occurs even before people are aware of their own conscious thoughts about the image. Visual stimuli in particular are processed extremely rapidly, without any complex thought. In other words, our negativity bias happens before we're even aware of it.[4]

Negativity bias is universal. Even people with the sunniest personalities have what scientists call a "positive–negative asymmetry"[5] and will pay more attention to negative rather than positive information.

Because this bias happens at the fundamental information-processing level,[6] it's present in everything we do: how we react to events (good or bad), how we develop trust in relationships (or don't), and how we learn. When you first meet someone, you'll automatically place more weight on what you find wrong about him or her. This asymmetry endures: That person will have to do more good acts to undo a negative first impression than bad acts to undo a positive one. Bottom line: Bad impressions are easy to gain, and good reputations are easy to lose.

If it sounds to you like we're hardwired to be nitpickers, you're right. But as I've mentioned, there are good evolutionary reasons for this.[7] Negativity bias helped to keep us out of harm's way. Imagine your ancestors who lacked it. Oh, wait. You can't, because their genes didn't make it into the gene pool on account of their lives being unceremoniously cut short when they were chased to exhaustion, pounced upon, gored, poisonously stung, bitten, or otherwise eliminated by predators and dangers they failed to perceive. With their departure went their genes. And our negativity bias became increasingly ingrained.

Like selective attention, negativity bias has advantages, even though we no longer have to worry about saber-toothed beasts. Think of it as your personal built-in security camera system. It zooms in on potential threats and sounds the alarm. We've all had the experience of feeling uneasy without being able to put our finger on exactly why. This is our negativity bias alerting us to a threat in our environment.

But the downside, especially for parenting, is that it directs us to see our child's negative behaviors more readily than their positive behaviors. It fundamentally compromises our ability to see our children fully by only showing us a limited array of information instead of the whole picture.

Suppose a bright tenth grader comes home with this report card: A+, A, A, A, D. In other words, 80 percent of her grades are excellent and 20 percent are not. But which grade did you zero in on? And which of these grades do you think will occupy more of the dinner table conversation that night? In theory, that D should command about 20 percent of the conversation. Things are different in practice.

You might be thinking: *Well, of course we need to pay more attention to the D, because that's the grade that needs improvement and the one that's potentially stopping this girl from getting into a top college.* You're right. The question, though, is what happens when we place *disproportionate* attention on the D? Does so much attention on the lower grade help the girl improve? What if we addressed the D, but placed four times as much attention on the successes she's having? What if we helped her see how she might apply some of the abilities she's using to succeed in her other classes to assist her in the one where she's struggling?

A strength-based approach does just that. Focusing on the areas where the girl is strong opens opportunities to analyze her work in those high-performance subjects and see what patterns can be transferred to the class where she got the D. What was it about her work in those other classes that allowed her to get an A? Instead of asking what's going wrong, ask what's going right.

Now let's say a boy comes home with this report card: D, D, D, C, C. He is not gifted academically. He's not even all that interested in school. He doesn't intend to follow a long-term academic path. What he *is* excited about is fitness. He's interested in becoming a personal trainer. Let's suppose that in order to optimize his chances to get into a school to pursue that career path, he needs to get a C average—so he does need to lift his grade point average a bit. However, unlike the student in our first example, he doesn't have any high-performance classes from which we can apply his successes in studying and succeeding.

But he still has strengths. He's a good athlete, and he coaches a junior football team. With his teammates and his players, he's a strong leader. He's dedicated and disciplined. Arranging practices and developing game plans takes organization and perseverance. He puts long hours into training, and he follows a strict personal fitness routine. By helping him understand the strengths that allow him to accomplish all these things, you can also help him see how they can be applied to other areas of his life. He may not become an A student, but those Ds can definitely turn into Cs with effort, organization, and perseverance—which he has demonstrated he has in abundance.

That's not to say that rose-colored glasses are the key to success. But our negativity bias distorts reality in the opposite direction. What we're trying to do is cleave *closer* to reality: a blend of positive and negative. Too often the positive gets short shrift and doesn't get utilized for its power to enhance achievement.

Projection

Now for an interesting twist. While we see weakness in others more readily than strengths, we're very good at *not* seeing weakness in ourselves.

Naturally, positive self-views make us feel good and negative self-views make us feel bad. So our ego has developed ways to filter out the negative and amplify the positive in our sense of self. When confronted with information that challenges our positive self-view, our ego instantly seeks to restore the positive view, in a process psychologists call our "defense mechanisms."[8] Projection, also known as blame shifting, is a classic example.[9]

In projection, we subconsciously displace our weaknesses onto others. Similar to old movie projectors, where the film is passed over the light to send or project the image onto a screen, in psychological projection, we project the negative image of ourselves onto someone else. Thus we trick ourselves into viewing that negative quality in another person and restore our positive self-view.

Projection is common in everyday life, and if we aren't aware of our defense mechanisms (and most people aren't), it's an easy psychological trap for parents to fall into.[10] When we see our son or daughter displaying a quality we dislike in ourselves, we pounce. We think we're doing this to help our child, but the deeper truth is that we're also doing it because we don't want to hold a mirror up to ourselves and see our (ugly, we fear) reflections.

When I was growing up, I was unbelievably messy, forgetful, and disorganized. I used my floor as my wardrobe—my "floordrobe"—and was always losing homework, clothes, and keys. My schoolbooks once spent a whole semester in my best friend's locker (she was a very patient friend) because I lost my locker key so many times that the school refused to replace it. How I managed to get by with such a lack of organizational skills I'll never know.

Truthfully I never really grew out of being messy. When Matt and I were first married, our house was burgled. When the police entered our bedroom, the constable announced, "You've been ransacked." To my embarrassment, Matt had to smile and admit, "No, that's my wife's normal mess."

So I confess that when I see signs of my children showing messiness and disorganization—like Nick leaving his bike at the front door—it triggers a projection reaction. I react to disorganization more strongly than other parents might because it's a weakness in me.

Projection can also cause us to try to superimpose our strengths—or desired strengths—onto our children. We've all seen the "sideline parents" who try to live through their children's athletic feats, or stage parents who relentlessly push their kids' performance abilities.

Strength-based parenting gives us the tools to see our children for who they really are—not who we are trying to force them to be—because, as you'll learn in Chapter 3, it gives us clear, concrete criteria for defining a strength. Once you are able to identify *your child's* particular talents and character traits, you can take *your own* projections out of the equation.

Binary Thinking

"For years as an adult, I thought I was a flake," a friend of mine from college recently confided. This amazed and amused me, as I knew her as relentlessly studious and so organized that she underlined her textbooks in three colors. She pursued a fine arts degree in college, and during summer temp jobs she meticulously cataloged art at local galleries. In her first real job out of college, she moved to London and held a scattered boss together, seeing complex art restoration projects through to completion in a prestigious museum. But because she'd been cast in the "flake" role in her family, she couldn't see that she was creative, yes, but also disciplined and organized, with an impressive ability for structured thinking. Her older sister, a lawyer, occupied that role. For many years she did herself a disservice until she finally started to reconcile the idea that a person can be creative *and* logical. It happened gradually as she noticed her discipline and project management abilities bringing her success time and again at work, and as she saw the looks of total disbelief on her friends' faces when she confided in them about her supposed flakiness. As she began to see the full suite of her strengths, she got the courage to open her own business that purchases bespoke art for clients all over the world. My "creative flake" friend is an organized and successful businesswoman, and I'm so proud of her.

This is a classic example of binary thinking. It's all about either/or. Binary thinking is what we do when we describe our children like this: "He's the naughty one," "She's the serious one," or "He's the class clown." It's what we do when we place our children into categories.

Binary thinking fails to do justice to reality. People are never just one thing. But there's one aspect of binary thinking that particularly undermines strength-based parenting: It leads you to think that weakness and strength are polar opposites.[11] This has deep implications for how we raise our kids.

One of positive psychology's major contributions to parenting has been our understanding that strength and weakness are not polar opposites.[12] As just one example, take kindness and cruelty. We've all had days when we're running late and low on energy, and we simply don't feel up to being especially kind in situations where otherwise we almost certainly would be. On such days, we might only offer a nod of acknowledgment to the cashier instead of saying, "Thank you." But no one could say that we were being cruel. It's just that distraction, fatigue, or stress has put us in a different place than usual on the spectrum between kindness and cruelty. If kindness is a particular strength of yours, you may find that even when you are diminished by distraction, you're still kinder than others on their "good" days. Viewed this way, kindness and cruelty are not binary opposites. The absence of kindness does not mean the presence of cruelty. You aren't just one or the other.

A consequence of binary thinking for parents is that it leads us to think that our kids either have strengths or they don't. This just isn't true. Strengths sit along a continuum from high to low,[13] so a strength may be present and "grow-able" even if you don't see much outstanding evidence of it. We'll talk about growth strengths in later chapters.

A strength might also be manifesting in a way that you aren't yet prepared to see. Your child's drawing might not be museum-ready, but maybe she's pouring all her creativity into her fashion sense or how she decorates her bedroom. Some parents mistakenly think that if their child isn't doing well in school, it means she lacks knowledge or intelligence. Your child may not have traditional school intelligence, but I bet you anything there's a subject about which she is very knowledgeable. Maybe it's online gaming, music, movies, celebrities, cars, tools, fashion, or social media. A child fascinated by online gaming may be a child who could become interested in how those games are conceived, developed, coded, and marketed. A child who's always on the phone or into social media may be great at making friends and may become someone who knows how to build online communities that bond over common interests or help drive global movements. In the short term, she might be a skillful peacemaker in the family or your go-to partner for organizing family social events. A child who seems entranced by the latest fads could be an innovator, an early adopter, or a change agent in the making—someone adaptable and flexible with high levels of openness to new things—even though to the parent it might seem she blows with the wind.

And if it's simply something your child is passionate about that isn't going to change the world or become her career, so what? We adults have those, too—we call them hobbies or even guilty pleasures, and they range from fixing cars to crafting to crosswords to karaoke. You may or may not see these forms of knowledge as valuable per se, but what they do show is that your child has the ability to cultivate knowledge.

Bottom line: The negatively biased, projection-prone, binary approach to parenting doesn't let us see our children as they truly are.

But We Can Override
Our Negative Defaults

Let's take these insights back to that scene at my home after my long day at work. I've just spoken sharply to Nick about his bike and watched his welcoming smile fade, and now I'm wallowing in guilt.

It's hard to shift gears into strength-based parenting when we're tired or preoccupied. That's when our negative defaults kick in. Yes, chores must done, bikes put away, homework finished, and school stuff readied for tomorrow. But SBP helps you address those duties without nagging by helping a child apply a strength to something he doesn't really like or want to do, or tends to forget to do. You might still need to remind, but SBP can temper your temper. You'll be reminding in a task-focused way, without the spoken or implied negative view of the child's character (*When will that boy ever learn? Why can't he listen? Why doesn't he ever remember?*). Here's how it happened at my house.

In retrospect, I could see where my brain's negative defaults had derailed me. So the next day I decided to handle things differently. I was fairly confident, given Nick's track record, that I'd have another chance to speak to him about the bike. That would be my do-over opportunity to parent from strengths rather than from weaknesses.

Sure enough, when I pulled into the driveway, there was the bike, right next to the front door. I took a moment to acknowledge my frustration. Then I deliberately switched my attention to focus on positives rather than on negatives, and to actively seek the strengths in the situation.

First, upon entering the house, I greeted Nick warmly. Then, looking around, I noticed that he had unpacked his lunchbox and set it next to the sink. He also had put his school shoes away in the closet—which only a few months ago had been an "issue" just like the bike.

He's a good kid, I thought, *and I'm doing a good job as a parent. I can lighten up on both of us.* I hugged him and thanked him for emptying his lunchbox and putting away his shoes. I commented on how well his organizational skills were coming along. Then I calmly asked him to put his bike where it belonged and to please try to remember to do it again tomorrow.

And he did!

Introducing the Strength Switch: Your Tool for Short-Circuiting Negative Thoughts

What I was using was a technique I had recently developed called the Strength Switch—a small but powerful tool fundamental to SBP. It's a mental switch I flicked to shift my attention from Nick's weaknesses to his strengths.

I'd been getting better at seeing strengths in others—in my friends, my colleagues, my husband, and my kids, often thinking, *I wonder what underlying strength is motivating them to do that.*

I was doing it well when they were showing their strengths and when I was calm or in a good mood, but it all flew out the window when they weren't showing their strengths or when I was preoccupied or stressed. I realized I needed a strategy to help me take a strength-based approach when strengths aren't readily apparent or when I'm not primed to be looking for them. I needed a way to quickly short-circuit my negative defaults in real-time, real-life situations with my kids. Although taking a couple of deep breaths might help calm me down so I don't go in and roar at my child, that by itself wouldn't help me see any strengths in play. I needed a mental trick to redirect my selective attention to strengths.

I knew from the research that just because I wasn't seeing my kids' strengths didn't mean they weren't there. I had to find a way to shine light on them. I started to work on being mindful of that moment when the knee-jerk negative default started to take over, and pausing to get between myself and my reaction. I would 1) take a couple of deep breaths, and 2) insert a thought: *The strengths are here, but they're hiding. Let me switch over to find them.* Thus the Strength Switch was born.

The Strength Switch acts like a circuit breaker. I literally picture a switch and watch it flick inside my head to turn the spotlight off the negative and turn it on the positive. Its power is in reminding me that in order to be a successful strength-based parent, I need to look at what my kids have done right *before* I look at what they've done wrong. I need to focus on their strengths *before* their short-comings.

And when I see the shortcomings first—as may happen when we're new to SBP—I can use the Strength Switch to short-circuit my nega-tive default mode to strength mode.

Think of the switch as a self-imposed mental pinch—a wake-up call for you to focus intensely for a moment on strengths. It reorients you from the negative to the positive. It allows you to see your child's strengths in a tense moment.

Where Attention Goes, Energy Flows

This small switch can produce radical results. It gives us more control over our selective attention. And what we pay attention to becomes our reality: Where attention goes, energy flows. The more we focus on one thing, the more real it is for us, sometimes at the expense of everything else. I had made Nick's bike delinquency very, very real— to the point where it crowded out my view of Nick as a good kid.

Flicking the Strength Switch before I walked in the door altered everything from the previous day. With my awareness focused on the positive, it took no time for me to see all the good things Nick had done. I saw his affection for me in wanting to welcome me home—how lovely. I saw his newly emerging organizational skills through his putting away his lunch box and shoes. I realized that he had probably done these things the day before, but I'd missed them because my attention and energy had been focused on the *one* thing he hadn't done.

If I had continued to fixate on Nick's bike delinquency instead of his strengths, I might have eventually won the bike battle, but it would have been exhausting and destructive. I would have lost the opportunity to use the situation to connect Nick with his organizational strengths and help him see how he could use them to remember where to park his bike.

Hitting the Strength Switch also helped me see how projection might have played a role in my annoyance with Nick. Not that I should let him off the hook about putting away his bike, but it made me more aware of how some of my negative reaction has to do with not wanting to be reminded of my own messiness.

The bike issue wasn't instantly fixed by that one exchange. But over the next few weeks, as I concentrated on using the Strength Switch more, Nick and I found a positive approach to dealing with it—one that didn't leave both of us hurt. I could remind him about the bike without it turning into a point of contention because I was also pointing out things he was doing well. In addition, I was connecting with him through his newly forming strength of organizational skills. The more I commented on his success in organizing his things, the more he understood himself to be a strong organizer, and therefore the more likely he was to remember to stow the bike.

Here's how another mother used the Strength Switch to short-circuit negative bias around a long-standing issue between her and her daughter:

The last few years have been a real struggle with my daughter. When she was younger we had a good relationship, but now that she's a teenager, we fight a lot. She's on the heavy side and I tell her not to worry, but I can see it's affected her confidence. She takes her bad moods out on me. Two months ago she joined the gym. Last week she came home from the gym in a bad mood and grabbed a can of Coke. I was about to tell her off. What's the point of sweating at the gym if she's going to ruin it afterward? But I knew that the last time I did this we had a screaming match, she told me to butt out of her life, and she drank a second can just to spite me.

So I took a deep breath and visualized turning on the Strength Switch. It worked and I realized that my negativity bias meant I was paying more attention to the Coke than to the fact that she'd been at the gym for the third time that week. Coke's not great, but she's exercising—and that's more important to focus on.

If you're motivated to see your child's strengths, you will. Let the Strength Switch help you, as it has many other parents. In short order, you'll be amazed at how many good qualities you start to see.

Tips for Getting Started

The four biases don't magically vanish. But you'll discover that your brain is bigger than your biases. You can override them. It's actually a small shift. With a little practice, you'll tune in and hit the switch faster every time. Life being what it is, you'll get lots of chances to practice!

Of course, there will still be the occasional misplaced bike. But now you won't have to yell about it. One of the joys of SBP is how energizing and rewarding it is for the parent, too. It helps you to connect to your own strengths as well as your child's. Here are some tips for learning to use your Strength Switch:

- *Start with low-stakes situations.* Try it in situations that don't annoy the heck out of you, and when you're not feeling stressed, tired, or hungry.
- *Progress to using the Strength Switch on those small issues that turn into big arguments.* You know what they are. It's often these minor things that fester between children and parents. The slow eating at the dinner table. The constant reluctance to do homework. The unending requests to play computer games. The obsession with texting. The moodiness!
- *When you feel your negative defaults start to cascade, STOP.* In those few seconds:
  - *Notice how you're feeling.* Annoyed? Furious? Frustrated? Disappointed? Acknowledge those feelings—they are legitimate—but don't attach to them.
  - *Select a strength.* Is there a strength you can remind your child to use in working through this situation? Ask yourself, *What strength does my child have that could help her handle this differently? How would it change what I do or say about this?* Ask yourself, *What strength do I have that could help me handle this situation differently?*
  - *Visualize the switch and tell yourself: "Flick the switch."* These visual and verbal cues help shift your attention.
  - *Speak to your child's strengths.* When you see a strength, call it. For example, if your children are sharing, you can thank them for their behavior and say how you see them using a strength: "Thanks for sharing with your sister. That's really kind [or fair] of you." You can call forward a strength that's needed in a given situation. If your kids are fighting,

instead of saying, "Stop fighting!" you can say, "Hey, how about some cooperation here?" If your son has lost motivation to study for exams, you can remind him, "Now's the time for your perseverance to come to the fore."

I encourage you to think clearly and deeply about where you place your attention with respect to your child. And when you don't have the time to think clearly or deeply, remember the Strength Switch. And flick it.

EXERCISE: | Notice Your Negative Defaults

Recall a recent time when you were annoyed by something your child did or didn't do. Which of the four negative defaults were in play? What preoccupied you? What was the binary thinking? Any projection? Then ask yourself what strengths you might have been blinded to in the situation. If you were to do it over again using the Strength Switch, what would you do and say differently?

EXERCISE: | Notice One Strength

Notice and choose one of your child's strengths. Set a goal to see this particular strength in your child over the next week and have a conversation with your child about it:

"I really admire the **strategic thinking** you showed in organizing that fund-raiser at school. You thought through who needed to be involved, set goals, and followed a plan. You showed great **teamwork** and I'm proud of your **humility** in making sure everyone involved got recognized."

"It's great that you're stopping to think before you decide what snack to eat. I wish I had your **self-awareness** and **self-control**."

"I loved watching you patch up that fight with your dad. Way to go on exercising **forgiveness** and **integrity**."

"When I see you working so hard on that school assignment, I'm in awe of your **love of learning, persistence, and work ethic**."

"Wow, that outfit you've put together is super-**creative**. You're a true **innovator**."

CHAPTER 3

Understanding Strengths

Let's try a quick experiment. Grab a sheet of paper and a pen and give yourself five minutes to jot down as many of your child's strengths as you can think of. If you have more than one child, try it for a minute each. Just write down the first things that come to mind. Ready? Go!

OK, time's up. Now review your list. If you easily came up with a fairly long list, congratulations! But if you're like most parents who do this exercise at the beginning of my workshops, it might have been a struggle to come up with more than five or six items. Often they are specific skills their child is good at, such as math, reading, art, music, or sports.

I love seeing parents' eyes light up when I then fill the presentation screen with words: first, the twenty-four strengths of character that every child has, some perhaps not very often on display, but all in a child's being somewhere. Then I place more words on more screens—ultimately more than one hundred strengths in all—that start to get them thinking in an exciting, expansive way about their children's ɛngths. Words like *connector, improver, activator, deliberative, futuristic, harmony, authenticity, curiosity, courage, zest, fairness, hope,* and *persistence.*

"And these," I say, "are just the ones we know how to measure."

That's when parents realize there's a whole universe of strengths they may have overlooked in their kids. Much as we adore our children, most of us have strength blindness about them, to one degree or another, partly because of the negative defaults we talked about in Chapter 2, and partly because, in general, our strengths are so deeply ingrained that they become invisible. Even when we do see them, we tend to treat them as "standard features" rather than as assets because we take our strengths for granted, like the talented cook who says of a delectable meal, "Oh, I just whipped it up from some things I had in the fridge," or the brave hero who tells reporters, "Anyone would have done what I did." Even parents who are experts in strength-based parenting hit blind spots, as this mother recounts:

> *A few years ago, my daughter Samantha asked me to give her a special birthday present. She wanted us to sit down together and do a formal strengths coaching session, the way I do with my clients. For several hours, we sat at a chicken take-out place and discussed how her strengths of humor, kindness, and teamwork were showing up in her life in positive ways. We went through her strengths and I shared my best thoughts about how she could use them effectively, and how to avoid overusing them to her detriment.*
>
> *To this day, she tells me it was one of the most powerful conversations of her life. I second that opinion. As much as I thought I knew about my daughter, and as self-aware as she is, our strengths conversation still surprised us. For example, she had no idea that humor was such a powerful top strength for her, and although everyone in our family is funny except for me, I didn't realize it, either. I'd taken for granted that she was just extremely funny, but I realized that it's a*

sparkling strength for her. I asked her a lot of questions about how others perceived her humor and benefited from it. She began to own that strength more boldly in subsequent years, and it shows up in her blogs, social media, choice of friends, and much more.

As a result of doing this strengths exercise with her and subsequently with my sons, I now see them very differently. This surprised me. As a longtime practitioner in positive psychology, I thought I knew everything I needed to know about my children, but these sessions were eye-opening because I, like so many others, had taken their strengths for granted.

Since then, our conversations have cycled back many times to their strengths, including during the college application process. I've seen that my children now more frequently rely on using their strengths in positive ways to interact with others and pursue their goals. I can also tell that this process has helped them to feel truly seen and understood by me. My children's friends and college roommates have called me numerous times over the last few years and have asked me to review their strengths with them and help them understand how to use them in the right ways for the right outcomes. If every parent knew how hungry kids are for conversations like these and how much they take away from those conversations that is truly life-changing, parents would start having these conversations immediately.

When we take our kids' strengths for granted or see only certain types of strengths, we miss the chance to help them capitalize on their full portfolio of strengths as pathways toward optimism, resilience, and achievement. In this chapter, you'll find a way of looking at strengths that will help you identify them more readily in your child, start to see how strength-based parenting works, and learn why strength building is so powerful.

Strengths Can Be Skills, Abilities, Interests, Characteristics, Traits, or Talents

First, let's talk terminology. Scientific literature is filled with research and writing that tease out the differences among these terms. For our purposes, strengths encompass them all. A strength can be a very specific talent, such as the ability to compute numbers, draw in perspective, play a musical instrument, or run fast. But it can also be a positive personality trait that a child has in abundance.

Trait strengths are the positive aspects of our personality that benefit us and others (e.g., kindness, gratitude, fairness).[1] Researchers have found a key group of positive traits (referred to as character strengths) that exist across a large range of nations as well as in remote tribes and indigenous cultures.[2] The six broad groupings for these positive traits are: courage, humanity, wisdom, sense of justice, ability for temperance/self-control, and capacity to find meaning in something beyond ourselves.[3] Because these strengths are universal, we all have them, but each of us has them in different degrees as part of our unique strengths profile.

Personality strengths—our character—play a big role in helping us build our performance strengths—our talents. Think about anyone who has built a talent and imagine if it could have been done without character. Imagine Einstein without curiosity, the Beatles without creativity, Mother Teresa without compassion, and Neil Armstrong without bravery.

Yet for decades, scientists were blind to character strengths. We focused on performance strengths, often on physical strength and skills. In fact, when I first ask young children what they think a strength is, they almost always point to their biceps or talk about being able to lift something heavy. It's true that physical abilities helped us survive. Yet science has begun to show that certain character strengths helped our species solve problems and cooperate to survive, and researchers have developed ways to measure them. Research by Dacher Keltner, PhD, has shown that our positive personality traits such as love, gratitude, and cooperation encouraged close bonds among families and friends, allowing them to band together to share food, find mates, and raise children.[4] This is why positive traits like empathy, for example, are hardwired into our brains.[5] Survival of the fittest was supported by survival of the kindest.[6]

We all perceive character intuitively every day. After meeting someone, we've got a sense of "I like that person" or "I don't like that person." What's driving that is a subconscious assessment of the person's character.

We also perceive degrees of character. We know some people are kinder than others, some are more grateful than others, some excel at assessing the fairness of a situation, and some are super courageous.

Once you get familiar with the language of strengths and the framework for seeing them, you'll see character strengths easily in your child. In fact, you may find your child calls on her character strengths more often than on performance skills to meet life's challenges:

Katie is quirky and creative. She loves humanities, art, and design, but struggles with science and math. She was getting stressed about an upcoming chemistry test on the periodic table. I suggested she try an approach to her exam study that played to her strength of creativity. We got out her arts and crafts box and she built models of the elements out of foam balls, pipe cleaners, and fabric. Her exam prep looked like a piece of art that could go in a contemporary art gallery. During the exam, she could remember the elements because she could visualize the

,odels she had made. For the first time in her life, she scored an A in science—thanks to her creative, unscientific mind.

|||||||||||

Emanuel has physical challenges in his balance and coordination that make him shy away from athletic activities at recess. This restricts his scope of friends. He and I have talked about the importance of doing the things that we find challenging. His strengths are that he is resilient, determined, and big-hearted. I am drawing on his "don't give up" attitude to persist with the things he finds difficult. His teachers tell me that he has begun to get involved in some of the ball games at school. I am so encouraged that he has started mentioning the names of boys he normally doesn't play with.

Not only do character strengths help kids handle big challenges, but they also help with the everyday situations that crop up all the time:

Jarrod was invited to go to a trampoline-jumping venue with his friend after school. Although his friend said that he would need to leave the venue after just forty minutes because he had to go someplace with his parents, Jarrod agreed to go. On reflection, he realized it wasn't going to be worth his while to travel there by train for only forty minutes of jumping together. So Jarrod, who is highly cre-ative, tried to come up with a good story he could use as an excuse to get out of going and asked my opinion about which was the better story to use.

I reminded Jarrod that normally he takes a lot of pride in being genuine, respectful, and honest (his strength of integrity). I told him what endearing qualities these were and encouraged him to consider using them in this situation.

Jarrod decided he wouldn't make up excuses. He chose to use his integrity to follow through with his commitment, even if the situation wasn't ideal. Making that commitment redirected his creativity: He arranged to get a lift from a parent who lives near the venue. The boys ended up spending more than ninety minutes jumping together and enjoying themselves. I know Jarrod was relieved he didn't end up making excuses to get out of going.

The Three Key Elements of a Strength

You've probably seen a child joylessly perform at a piano recital. She may hit all the right keys, but there's no energy or enthusiasm. It's as if she doesn't want to be there. On the flip side, we've seen the child onstage who's clearly motivated and energized and who fearlessly flails through every mistake—of which there are many.

It turns out that three elements come together to form a strength. For purposes of strength-based parenting, we need to keep our eye on all three:

1. Performance (being good at something)
2. Energy (feeling good doing it)
3. High use (choosing to do it)[7]

Neither child at our hypothetical piano recital would be classified by psychologists as having a strength for piano because neither is showing all three elements of a strength: The first child performs well but without energy and probably wouldn't do it if given a choice; the second, however energized and interested, isn't performing well.

Strengths are things we do well, often, and with energy. This tripart model makes it easy to discern your child's strengths by asking three simple questions.

.eing Strengths in Your Child: The Three Questions

Ask yourself these questions to tune in to your child's unique constellation of strengths as you observe his day-to-day behavior and language:

1. DO I SEE PERFORMANCE? Watch for when your child shows above-age levels of achievement, rapid learning, and a repeated pattern of success. Examples: The young child who, within a short time of picking up a baseball bat, is routinely making great hits. The grade-schooler who buries her nose in books and uses more complex words and sentence structures than her peers. The teenager who consistently displays a more sophisticated understanding of emotions than most adults.

2. DO I SEE ENERGY? Strengths are self-reinforcing: The more we use them, the more we get from them. They fill us with vigor. You'll notice your child has abundant energy when using a strength. Emily has a talent for art, and when she's drawing or painting, I notice that she has unusually big stores of energy. She rarely gets tired when she's being artistic.

3. DO I SEE HIGH USE? Finally, look for:
   - what your child chooses to do in his spare time
   - how often he engages in a particular activity
   - how he speaks about that activity[8]

The teenage daughter of a friend of mine is a relationship builder with the strengths of service, equality, and fairness. She's highly civic-minded and spends her spare time on social causes, which energize her because they draw on her strengths. She's full of the latest information on social movements and how we can each help. The way she chooses to spend her time is a clue to her underlying strengths.

For true strengths, these three elements form a beautiful feedback loop: Great performance provides the child with a shot of high energy, so the child naturally chooses to do more. In turn, high use—also known as effort or practice—improves performance levels.[9] So, for example, if you notice that your child is energized when she plays the piano, and you provide enjoyable opportunities for her to play, if she's mining a true strength she will likely practice more, which improves her performance, which then energizes her . . . and so the loop continues:

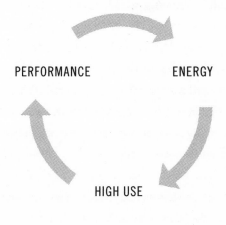

PERFORMANCE   ENERGY

HIGH USE

FIGURE I.
The Three Key Elements of a Strength

Keeping this triad in mind will help you avoid pushing your child into an area that *seems* like a strength just because your child is good at it. It will also help you differentiate between whether your child is bingeing on an activity in an escapist way or expressing a true strength. For example, parents have asked me, "My kid is great at computer games and wants to play all the time. Is that a sign of a strength?" I reply, "Observe his energy levels at the end. Is he drained and cranky?

Or energized and full of life? Are you seeing the full triad?" Computer games can tap into a child's strategic and problem-solving skills or stimulate creativity (in some games, you invent whole new worlds). Or they might just be about filling time. So look for all three signs. When you see your child do something well, with energy, and a lot—you'll know you've unearthed a strength.

Additional Clues to Your Child's Strengths

You also may see the following signs:

There's a Drive or Yearning

You can sometimes tell a strength by the yearning to use it. There's a sense of inevitability about it. A person thwarted in a strength won't feel like herself. Chances are, it will "leak" out somehow. The partner of a colleague shared this story with me:

> *In grade school I showed promise in music, so my parents enrolled me in voice lessons at the city's best conservatory. I loved singing but had crippling stage fright. The better I got, the more I was pushed to perform. Finally, in my teens, I quit, in a big tearful scene with my parents. I wouldn't sing when they were home, but when they'd go out, I'd sing for hours. Singing was when I felt most like myself. I joined the school chorus, enjoying choral singing through middle school, high school, college, and beyond. It was a way I could use my passion without having to perform solo. I taught myself the guitar. I started violin lessons (it was so technically difficult and I started so late that there was no risk of having to perform). After college, I took up dance—movement to music. And what's really incredible to me is that in my fifties I have*

come full circle to performing, participating in dance showcases with my fellow students. I still get pretty nervous, but I've always felt like music was in my veins, and I can't imagine my life without it.

When the yearning to express a core strength is blocked or frustrated, it creates a special kind of pain. A friend who is a professional writer told me:

In preschool, I had tantrums because I couldn't yet read. I grew up at a time when children weren't encouraged to read until grade school. When I saw my parents and older sister reading, it seemed like they were members of a special club I couldn't get into. It looked so easy, as if you just had to open the book and look at the page. But whenever I tried it, with a book I knew by heart from countless readings with my parents, nothing would happen. The words hovered just out of reach— indecipherable black squiggles. I was shut out, and I couldn't stand it. I was desperate to unlock the secrets of words.

My friend's tantrums arose because an early talent in her wasn't being nurtured. Her story makes me wonder what strengths parents simply overlook in their children because the child isn't "supposed" to develop a given ability until a certain time in life or schooling. Once my friend learned to read in grade school, she leaped ahead of her classmates. Her work was published in her high school and college literary magazines. It makes total sense that she ended up becoming a professional writer.

Your Child Naturally Displays It

You can learn a lot about your child's strengths just by observing what she naturally does and says. Emily is constantly doodling, seemingly without even realizing it. She'll be watching TV, but with a pencil in her hand. If cartoons are on, she draws the characters while watching. It's just part of who she is.

Strengths can show up in the most casual exchanges:

I have identical twin girls who completed a strengths assessment at school. In the car, they were having an afternoon snack and telling me about their top strengths. Zoe interrupted the conversation to exclaim, "This is the best apple ever! Just listen to that crunch!" Her top strength is appreciation of beauty and excellence, and there it was in action. Her twin sister (top strengths: leadership, teamwork, fairness, and humor) had already eaten her entire apple without noticing its crunch.

Part of the adventure of SBP is looking for clues like these, offering reasonable opportunities for the child to explore, and then assessing whether a particular trait or talent develops from "shows potential" to demonstrated achievement.[10] A friend of mine could bend his middle finger back to touch his wrist when he was a kid. It's an ability not many people have, but it wouldn't be classified as a strength because it didn't contribute to his development or lead to a productive outcome per se. However, his parents saw his finger-bending ability as a possible sign of deeper physical talents of flexibility and agility. They also saw that he was energized and motivated to use this physical flexibility, so they suggested he join the gymnastics team. Gymnastics helped my friend to develop his strength of flexibility and put it toward a productive use.

You don't have to respond to every strength clue—that would be exhausting for both you and your child, and not every bendy finger means a gymnast in the making. But it's fun to tune in to your child and take a step or two toward helping him experiment with interests and abilities and see where they lead. We do this instinctively when we buy Lego for a child who loves building with blocks, and puzzles for the child who's a whiz at sorting and assembling the pieces, when we present a library card to a child who burns through books, or encourage our teenager to volunteer at an animal shelter to build on his compassion and love of animals.

I look for ways to provide outlets for Emily's drawing skills. Every year, she's drawn her own birthday invitations. I scan her artwork, and we make the cards together. If I hear about an art competition, I ask if she wants to enter it. Often she does. Jenny, Matt's mom and Emily's grandmother, is a talented painter who exhibits her work internationally. We drop Emily off with Jenny, and they paint and talk happily together for hours. Emily comes home full of energy, with beautiful art to show us.

Sometimes a child's interest seems to come out of nowhere. A parent may wonder: *Is this a true strength—i.e., something that will last?* Here's how one family took a stepwise approach to explore that question:

When my daughter went horseback riding at age ten for a friend's birthday party, she fell totally in love with horses. She'd never even been on a horse and spent the whole time riding double with the friend's mom around the paddock on a big, gentle horse named Ringo while the other kids rode the trails. But she came home picking horsehair out of her socks and saying reverently, "Look! A Ringo hair!"

She kept talking about it and devouring horse books, so after a few months we enrolled her in weekly riding lessons. That was followed by Saddle Club—spending Saturdays learning how to care for a horse assigned by the stable. On Sunday nights she'd come to me while I was cooking dinner and say, "You know what?" "No, what?" I'd say. And she'd say, "I can't wait for next Saturday!"

After a few years of this, her interest and energy hadn't flagged—and we also felt she needed a nonschool activity and social outlet, since she only had a handful of friends at school, and they didn't live near us. So we purchased a (not too expensive!) horse, which she had complete responsibility to care for every day, and she contributed to his upkeep as much as she could from money earned doing odd jobs and working in her dad's store. She was a bit shy, so it was good practice in growing her bravery to call the vet and the farrier and make arrangements to have hay and grain delivered. And she loved the built-in social connections of being around others at the stables who shared her passion.

She had the time of her life throughout middle school and high school, and then in senior year she used her judgment and organization abilities to make the decision and all the arrangements to sell the horse before going away to college. She also used her love of animals to conceive an unusual senior project: volunteering in the children's zoo, where she put her animal handling skills to good use, caring for baby sheep, goats, monkeys, and more. She still looks back on those many hours at the stables as among the happiest of her life.

Your Child Loses Track of Time When Engaged in It

It's usually a sign of a strength if your child can sustain focus on it for long periods of time, with a tendency to become so deeply captivated that he loses track of time. This state has been described as "flow."[11] It's a good way to differentiate between a behavior that a child is good at but isn't really a strength and one that truly sustains him in that delicious feedback loop mentioned above. We generally don't lose track of time if we aren't energized by the activity.

We tend not to respect the flow experience as an important, valid signal of strengths. That's because we have a false idea that exhausting work leads to high performance. Actually, strengths do. When work is matched well to strengths, we're not working as hard because our strengths come naturally to us. Of course, we all face challenging, tiring tasks at times, but their effects can be tempered by other activities that put us in flow.

When Emily is bored, I'll say, "Why don't you do some artwork?"

Sometimes she says, "OK." Other times, she says she doesn't feel like it. Without forcing anything, I'll just suggest, "Well, how about just having it here in case you feel like it?" I might set out her favorite pencils and maybe new paper I've bought that she hasn't seen yet (to get her curious), put on the music she likes to draw to, or get out images we've downloaded from the Internet that she's said she'd like to draw or be inspired from. I might also suggest a reason to make some art, such as a friend's upcoming birthday and how much I bet her friend would love a special "Emily Artwork Card" (as kindness is also a strength of hers), or ways she could add to her school assignments with drawings. Then usually the problem becomes getting her to stop! She's so in flow that she doesn't even hear me when I tell her it's time to stop and wash her hands for dinner. Nick is the same when he's out back shooting hoops.

In later chapters, we'll look at strength-based ways to structure your child's day with sensitivity to building in "flow time" as a counterweight to activities your child finds challenging.

It Can Be Put to Positive Use

Researchers talk about how strengths need to be used in ways that are socially or morally valuable.[12] If my physically flexible friend had used his hypermobility to evade the laser beam security system and steal the Crown Jewels, his gymnastic prowess would be productive—he's successfully stolen the jewels—but not positive.

A parent's role is to guide children in positive uses for their strengths—just as Jarrod's mom encouraged him to use his integrity to keep his commitment to meet his friend, which shifted his use of creativity from coming up with a white lie to cancel the date to solving the scheduling problem. It can be inspiring to see how children start using their strengths as forces for good:

Lewis, age twelve, had seen an antibullying video at school. In the video a girl sits next to an empty chair with a sign on it that says "Sit with me." We talked about how that was an opportunity for an act of kindness. A while later, he told me he saw a classmate sitting alone under a tree at lunchtime. He realized the boy's best friend had been out sick for a while. Lewis sat with him and chatted with him during the lunch break. Lewis commented that he notices moments like these now.

‖‖‖‖‖‖‖‖‖

I'm the parent coach of a rugby team. My after-game debrief with the kids isn't about who scored but about who showed character strengths like loyalty, self-control, and leadership, defusing conflict when things get heated on the field. Over the years my son Dom has become known for being the peacemaker. He's six foot four—a giant young man—but he's a hugger and all the kids know it. He's actually been nicknamed Cuddles because he's so loving toward everyone.

What I've seen, as I've continued to reinforce his kindness and compassion, is that he's always the kid who stops playing when someone is injured and provides care, regardless of which team the player's on. People often comment on it.

‖‖‖‖‖‖‖‖‖

Matt's a smart kid, but not as self-motivated as his older sister. He hasn't figured out what he wants to do after he graduates this year. Also, it can be difficult to get him to focus on studying rather than on computer games and the Internet. This leads to a lot of tension at home.

Matt's strengths are creativity, curiosity, humor, modesty, and citizenship. Although his curiosity doesn't often tend to extend to his school syllabus, his modesty and citizenship are always on display. Matt never tries to dominate any circumstance. He'll happily go with the flow (cracking jokes along the way) and always watches out for others. Matt often speaks up for someone whose interests aren't being met. Frequently when watching movies or TV shows, he'll express concern for a character who is left out. I think of these strengths together as compassion, and Matt has it in spades.

It's easy at times to worry that he'll do himself a disservice by underperforming in school. But it's reassuring to focus on his strengths, see them playing out effectively for him, and have some trust that if we let him be himself, he's going to be fine in the long term.

We still push Matt to engage with his schoolwork. But we also keep in mind that a creative, curious, humorous, modest, loyal team player is going to be OK in this world.

How Strong Is the Strength?

To help parents figure out if what they're seeing in their child is a strength, could be a strength, or is definitely not a strength, I use the four-part matrix developed at the Centre of Applied Positive Psychology (CAPP). This matrix classifies behavior into one of four types based on the triad we've been talking about: the interaction of performance, energy, and use. The four types are: realized strengths, unrealized strengths, learned behavior, and weakness.[13]

When talking with children about their strengths, however, I've found the terms *realized strengths* and *unrealized strengths* don't work so well. Instead, I use the terms *core strengths* (because the strength is a core part of who they are) and *growth strengths* (because the strength is something small that can grow big with practice).

Let's take a closer look at the four types:

1. Core Strengths (aka Our "Go-To" Strengths)

Core strengths are the talents and traits that fuel high levels of performance, energy, and use. They're obvious to us and those who know us. You could say they're the essence of who we are, because if your core strengths were taken away, you wouldn't be you. Maybe your child has always been good at balance beam (physical ability), could hold a tune from a young age (musicality), or had an innate understanding of design and technology (spatial awareness). Maybe she's always been brave or compassionate or was born with a calm, serene nature (positive personality traits).

2. Growth Strengths

Growth strengths energize us and offer the potential for good performance, but use is typically low to medium. You may see only glimpses of them in your child, but they'll shine when given the opportunity to be developed. When your child is using a growth strength, you're likely to notice that she's energized and is showing early signs of good performance.

Growth strengths are fascinating because they don't look like strengths when they're still growing, but they can shoot up quickly when they are discovered. For most of his elementary school years, my son, Nick, avoided leadership roles. In fact, his first- and second-grade teachers both told me that when they asked who wanted to be the Class Captain, Nick was the only student who didn't raise his hand. But in the final years of elementary school, Nick discovered he was motivated by, was good at, and enjoyed leading his classmates. In team assignments, he learned he was skilled at seeing the bigger picture, and he got energy from fostering good relationships within the group. While he noticed his own energy levels and skill at these things, they were also pointed out to him by his peers, his teacher, Matt, and me. His experiences, reinforced by strength-based feedback, helped him to see and "own" his strength of leadership. This motivated him to participate in a leadership activity that organized and ran a charity car wash to sponsor endangered animals. His class raised enough money to sponsor a spotted leopard, a red panda, and a Tasmanian devil.

Following that leadership success, Nick campaigned to be School Captain in his final year. He didn't win but was proud to be the House/Sports Captain. And to his great surprise (and Matt's and my great delight) he was given a lead role in the school play. Most important, he entered middle school with greater optimism and resilience, thanks to his newfound strength in leadership.

You can encourage your child to use her growth strengths by:

- noticing the strength she's drawing on
- pointing out how her performance is improving
- letting her know that you see the positive energy she's exuding when she's using the strength
- offering low-pressure opportunities to use that strength
- praising her when she chooses to use it of her own accord (we'll talk about how to praise for maximum strength building in Chapter 8)

It takes a lot of energy to screw up your courage to use a growth strength. It took courage for Nick to run for School Captain. Think of the last thing you tried that gave you butterflies in your stomach, fitful sleep, or a lot of "what if" worry. But when you try, and it works, you get a huge shot of energy and you feel fantastic: *I did it!!!!* You're growing that particular strength muscle, and it feels great. That's the experience you want for your child.

Even very young children can be gently encouraged to experiment with growth strengths:

With our five-year-old son, we foster a growth mind-set by using the language of strengths and the idea that our body and brain muscles need to practice and practice before they get strong enough to be good at something. It helps to remind him of this when he is learning a new sport, riding his new two-wheeler, or learning to use scissors or other tools. Our intention is that when he transitions to school next year, he'll go knowing he has strengths and skills.

3. Learned Behavior

While our strengths reside within us, learned behaviors are things we need to "add in" from the outside. Most often we develop them through the requirements of parents, school, and others. As such, our motivation to perform them comes from our desire to please others, operate smoothly in the world, or gain external rewards. One of my graduate students has a talent for manuscript editing. She's really good at it (performance), but it doesn't give her high energy, and her motivation is simply to earn money to support herself through her PhD program. That's a perfectly valid use of a learned behavior, as long as she doesn't get pulled into doing it so much that it governs her time and attention for too long.

The best way to work with your learned behaviors is to know what they are and slot them into your life in ways that don't allow them to dominate for long stretches of time.

When I first took the CAPP survey years ago, I realized I was using a lot of learned behaviors at work. I have learned to become a strategic thinker as I've risen through the ranks of the university, and since I'm a good mediator, I'm skilled at chairing meetings and project management. But these aren't core strengths, so while some people come out of meetings charged up for action, for me the meetings are exhausting. I realized I had to dial down some of my learned behaviors and find ways to build in more of my strengths if I wanted to be less de-energized by the end of the day. Now I schedule team meetings right before lunch, so I get a break afterward. I put on my sneakers and go for a twenty-minute walk in the park near our offices, which feeds a core strength of mine: appreciation of beauty and excellence.

You can help your child develop learned behaviors, but do so knowing that they'll require a lot more effort and that it's unlikely your child will ever reach the level of performance that he will when using his strengths. Also, since he's unlikely to be energized when he's using this behavior, don't be surprised that you have to remind him a lot. Be patient and remember that your child's brain isn't wired to support this particular capacity—but that with practice, neural networks will grow and a new behavior will be formed.

Finally, there's the danger that overusing learned behaviors can sap a child's energy and motivation, thwarting our aims of building optimism and resilience.[14] Far better whenever possible is to encourage a child to identify and chart a course through her core strengths:

Over the last two years, we've been working with our seventeen-year-old daughter to help her navigate her college selection and course choices. She has a broad range of interests and academic strengths—including STEM (science, technology, engineering, and math)—and there was a subtle but firm expectation from the school guidance counselor that she continue to pursue these subjects. However, while she performs very well in STEM, she's not drawn to directly related courses or careers. In fact, her favorite subject is visual communication.

She had the opportunity to see STEM skills applied in a work setting with a medical researcher. While she enjoyed the work and it utilized a number of her signature strengths such as curiosity and love of learning, she didn't enjoy the experience as much as she expected and couldn't see herself working in that field.

When she struggled to articulate her mixed reaction to the experience, we helped her identify which of her strengths were being well utilized and which might not be getting drawn upon (her top signature strengths of love and humor). She came away understanding that it's not only the work itself that is important to her, but also the environment and the relationships that will enable her strengths to shine.

Since then, she has completed the VIA Survey and the Gallup StrengthsFinder 2.0 [see page 302], *among others. Her aha moment came when the VIA Survey showed that her top strengths are love, curiosity, humor, kindness, and love of learning.*

She's submitting her first round of university applications and we are brainstorming and researching potential careers that match her strengths to assist in determining which university courses may be the best options for her. The school has limited time and resources to be able to do this with every student, so we see this as a simple way to help her seek a career that will draw on her strengths and support her well-being.

4. Weakness

I define weakness similarly to what you'll find in the dictionary or after a quick Google search. Weaknesses are features regarded as disadvantages or flaws—specifically, a flaw that prevents us from being effective. We can be weak in certain skills, abilities, talents, and aspects of our personality/character.

We all have weaknesses, and it's important to be real with our kids about that. Strength-based parenting doesn't mean you ignore your child's weaknesses; it allows you to approach them from a new perspective. In fact, it supports more genuine, less defensive conversations with your child about their weaknesses, because your child knows that your focus is, first and foremost, on her strengths.

There are three important messages to give to your child about weakness:

1. Just as everyone has strengths, everyone has weaknesses.
2. Having weaknesses doesn't mean you're unworthy; it just means you're normal.
3. Avoid the trap of spending too much time focusing on your weaknesses.

In my workshops, I ask parents to write their child's name with their dominant hand. I talk about how each of us has a dominant hand. For me, it's my right hand. I didn't choose that. We're just born with our brain wired in a way that makes one hand easier to use than the other. We build on that propensity and further develop that neural network. We write with ease. Then I say, "OK. Swap hands." It takes them much longer to write their child's name with their nondominant hand. It's messy, even illegible. It's tiring and somewhat frustrating. When you constantly focus on getting your child to fix her weaknesses, it's like you're always asking her to use her nondominant hand. Her performance, energy, and use won't be nearly as high as when she works from her strengths.

Constantly working on weakness can be tiring, even demoralizing. This is why Alex Linley, PhD, CEO of CAPP, says, "We succeed by fixing our weaknesses *only when* we are also making the most of our strengths."[15] Noted leadership expert Peter Drucker tells us that exceptional leaders connect strengths with strengths in ways that make weaknesses become irrelevant.[16] He fully grants that we're all "abundantly endowed with weaknesses" but also that weaknesses are inconsequential to our performance if we are focusing on our strengths.

We'll talk more about how to take a strength-based approach to weakness in Chapter 9. Maybe the one thing more inspiring than watching your child play to her strengths is watching her draw on her strengths to address a weakness:

My daughter Mia told me she wanted to apply to the School for Student Leadership, where she'd be away from home for nine weeks of ninth grade. Only three boys and three girls from her year level were to be selected. My daughter wasn't an obvious pick, as she's not a high academic achiever and had some difficulties with literacy.

I took her through the VIA Survey to show her that her strengths are as much about her character as they are about academics. This changed Mia's view of herself. After learning that leadership was one of her top strengths, Mia decided the camp would be a good opportunity for her to apply this strength. She highlighted her strengths in her application and interview to show qualities that went beyond an academic yardstick. She talked about how her leadership abilities would help her encourage others to achieve common goals and maintain good relationships within the group, how her perseverance and zest would help her through the activities, and how her humor would help cheer up other children if they were homesick and make her fun to spend the time away from home with. Finally, she told the interview panel that she has hope as a strength and that she hoped to make it into the School for Student Leadership. She was accepted and had an experience that enabled her to build her strengths as well as her confidence.

Ellie started falling behind in math in the third grade when we enrolled her at a more rigorous school. Math logic just eluded her. Homework often degenerated into tears and frustration. She managed to get B minuses and Cs until middle school, when a new "go at your own pace" model was introduced in her algebra class. She got hopelessly bogged down and failed. Fortunately, the teacher saw and appreciated Ellie for who she was. When she had to repeat the class, he tutored her tirelessly. He saw and reminded her of her core strength of persistence: "You've got enough persistence to give away half and still have more than most people." He appreciated her creativity that led her to overthink math: "The world isn't ready for your kind of logic." He praised her ability to grasp concepts: "You got the hard part right; you just stumbled on some computation details." It took several years and many hours of patient coaching, but by senior year she was getting Bs and even A minuses. And although there was a two-hundred-point difference between her math and verbal scores on her college board exams, she was very proud that when she took her graduate school exams four years later, after studying no math at all in college, her math score stayed exactly the same, thanks to her persistence as a teenager in learning the foundations.

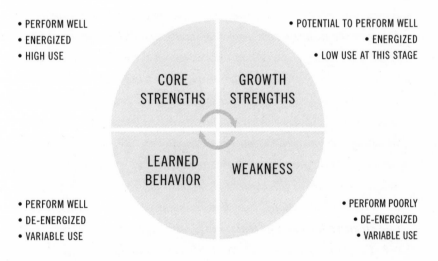

FIGURE 2.
This figure demonstrates how the three key elements of performance, energy, and use are displayed in the four different types of behaviors: core strengths, growth strengths, learned behavior, and weakness.

Nature *and* Nurture: Where Strengths Come From

Researchers view strengths as innate, suggesting that, to some extent, we're born with them. While core strengths will be more obvious and growth strengths might send weaker signals at first, both are deemed to have a genetic component. This means a child's core strengths will start to manifest at a very early age:

> *Breanna is strong in her appreciation of beauty and excellence. When she was just three years old, she wanted to show me how the vacuum cleaner cord was lying on the carpet in a heart shape. Now, at age eleven, whenever we go to someone's house, she always remembers the colors on the wall, the designs on the couch, and the patterns on the rugs.*

||||||||||||

> *My daughter has been curious from the day she was born. It began with her never wanting to sleep during the day. Once she started talking, there were endless questions. It could be very tiring. But I realized that all her talking was showing inquisitiveness and curiosity, and I wanted to encourage that.*

Studies on twins and children who have been adopted are particularly important in helping us determine the interplay of nature and nurture in strengths.[17] Twin studies compare identical twins (who share the same genes) and fraternal twins (who share only 50 percent of their genes) raised in their biological families to determine how much of a trait or talent is influenced by genetics. If identical twins show more similarity in a talent (e.g., musicality) than nonidentical twins, this suggests that the trait is shaped more heavily by our genes than by the environment. In adoption studies, scientists compare levels of similarity between adoptive parent and adopted child pairs (same environment, different genes) and the biological parent (different environment, same genes) to determine what we're born with.

Findings from twin and adoption studies support the idea of a genetic component to strengths—that's why they feel natural to us. For example, research at University of Western Ontario found a 50–50 split between genes and the environment on positive traits like altruism, empathy, and nurturance.[18] A similar finding came from the research of Michael Steger, PhD, at Colorado State University, where the genetic contributions to character strengths were, on average, 40 percent.[19] Traits like creativity, persistence, forgiveness, and self-control had an even stronger genetic contribution (between 50 and 60 percent). Heritability of our cognitive abilities ranges from roughly 50 to 70 percent, while the genetic contribution to our physical abilities ranges from 20 to 70 percent, depending on the aspect measured.

Evolutionary psychologists have demonstrated that the development of strengths is exactly what helped us advance as a species.[20] Although evolution primed us to be alert to threats and weakness (that negative bias we've talked about), atop that primal awareness were laid, over countless generations, the complex neural tracks that disposed us to use our strengths in ever more nuanced ways to overcome the negative:

- Athletic ability and physical strengths allowed us to hunt prey—and avoid becoming prey.
- Mental strengths like curiosity prompted us to seek out new food sources and new shelter materials.[21]
- Decision making and analytic skills helped us solve problems and make fire.
- Artistic talent helped our ancestors to transmit important lessons on cave walls.

The reality is that we have more strengths than weaknesses—if we didn't, we wouldn't have survived.

It makes sense, then, that humans are naturally motivated to develop strengths, according to prominent psychotherapists[22] such as Carl Rogers, Karen Horney, and Abraham Maslow (of the famous "hierarchy of needs" pyramid). Strength development happens throughout life, but it's especially rapid in childhood, when neuroplasticity—our brain's ability to change itself in positive or negative directions through a beautifully intricate and dynamic interaction with our environment—is happening at warp speed: In the first six months of life, as many as one hundred thousand neuronal connections are being made *per second*!

Your brain makes approximately ten thousand new cells every day and is constantly eliminating old brain cells. This phenomenon is known as "neurogenesis,"[23] and scientists have shown that the brain is always reorganizing itself. Most fascinating to me is that the process of reorganization is purposeful, not random: The brain delivers new cells to areas being stimulated by the environment and deletes old cells from areas no longer in use.

All experiences change the brain. You're changing your brain right now by reading my book. Even after a single activity (what scientists call short-term exposure) your brain changes,[24] prompting two neurons to connect temporarily—but if this experience is not repeated, the neurons will probably move apart again. For the brain to change and stay changed, repeated practice is key.

So if we want to build the brain areas that support our kids' strengths, we need to create environments and experiences where they frequently use them. The more a strength is practiced—be it solving sudoku puzzles or showing empathy—the more the neural chain for that strength is chemically bonded. These neural chains become linked in networks across different brain areas, connecting motor functions, sensory information, abstract thought, and emotions, thus further reinforcing the strength. Strength-based experiences shape strength-based networks.[25]

However, experiences can also eliminate neural networks. For example, when I was growing up, I learned the clarinet. With practice, my brain formed neural networks that allowed me to read sheet music and automatically shift my fingers to the keys needed to create the right note. But unlike the young woman I mentioned earlier whose strength in music "leaked out" everywhere, clarinet didn't turn out to be a strength of mine and I wasn't energized or motivated to continue, so I dropped it when I started high school. I figured I'd always know how to read sheet music, as I'd used that skill over so many years. But when Nick started music lessons, I discovered I had completely forgotten how to read music. Neuroscientists call this process of unlearning "synaptic elimination:"[26] When neurons no longer need to communicate, they drift apart. If they were on Facebook they'd "unfriend" each other.[27] The brain operates on the principle of "use it or lose it"[28] or, as Nick says to me: "You snooze, you lose."

Most of us intuitively understand our role in helping to build our child's abilities. It's why we play catch with our children, read with them, enroll them in sports, pay for music lessons, engage tutors, and so on. While it might seem daunting to teach less tangible strengths such as positive personality traits, it's not as hard as you think. It draws on the very same processes, inside and out: You make your child aware of when she's using the positive trait and help her practice it. With repeated practice, the brain is altered and the strength becomes ingrained.

At the University of Wisconsin–Madison, Richard J. Davidson, PhD, has done pioneering work on what we can do to make our brains happier, a field known as "affective neuroscience." Professor Davidson's research team has shown that we can actually build positive character in our brains with practice. In one study, after just thirty minutes per day of compassion meditation training (during which they envisioned someone suffering and wished relief for that person) over a period of two weeks, study participants showed greater activity in the neural systems associated with compassion.[29] And this study was conducted with twenty-two-year-olds, the age when neuroplasticity is starting to slow down. Imagine what can happen if you expose your children to daily opportunities to use their positive traits and talents during their most receptive ages of neuroplasticity (i.e., childhood and teenage years)!

Findings like these lead me to wonder: What would happen in our kids' brains if we spent as much time intentionally building their strengths as we do nagging them to work on their flaws? It takes practice and opportunity to build on our genetic potential. No strength is "fully made" at birth. Michael Jordan didn't make his first dunk until ninth grade. You can make a big difference in your child's strength development—and your child's brain is primed to soak it up.

My Formula for Strength Development

Adapting the ideas of Scott Kaufman, PhD, and Angela Duckworth, PhD,[30] from the University of Pennsylvania, whose work spans topics such as talent development, expertise, giftedness, creativity, and *grit*, I propose the following formula for strength development:

Strengths development = ability × effort

What starts as a slight genetic advantage (ability) allows for environmental gains that multiply over time as the child practices the ability (effort), resulting in the child reaching higher milestones sooner than other children. Psychologists call this the "multiplier effect." It's why your child will perform at higher levels when she puts effort into building her strengths rather than fixing her weaknesses.

This effect explains the story of a child who is a fast learner of social dynamics and develops his social intelligence more rapidly than others. He becomes known from an early age as a "people person," and his advanced understanding of others results in his being given positions of leadership and responsibility.

It's also the story of the child on the swim team who, while putting in no more hours of practice than the others, is gliding past them with ease. With each lap her stroke technique and muscle strength are built ever so slightly more than her peers in the next lane, causing her to inch farther and farther in front until she is laps ahead.

Given that your child is born with the broad brushstrokes of her strengths, your role as a strength-based parent is actually quite straight-forward. It's to help your child paint in the finer details of her strengths by putting her into environments that nurture her nature. In the ex-amples of the socially intelligent child and the swimmer, their genetic propensity kicked in only when they put in effort. You can help your child capitalize on the multiplier effect by encouraging effort. That will be easier for core strengths, but your child, like all of us, needs to work on growth strengths, learned behaviors, and weaknesses, too. That's why, in Chapter 7, we'll look at the importance of encouraging (and modeling) self-control.

Strength-based parenting relieves you from spending time and ef-fort taking a scattershot approach to figuring out your child's abilities, racing your child from one program to the next or enrolling her in something you think is "good" for her. Instead, by watching for signs of performance, energy, and use, you'll have concrete "data" to pin-point your child's strengths and help you decide what opportunities will be best.

The opportunities you provide will be different at different ages—something we'll discuss in Chapter 4. SBP is creative and dynamic and lets you and your child explore together, sharing feedback about what's working and what isn't. Take the joyless piano player I mentioned early in this chapter. She plays well (high performance) and was moti-vated enough to practice to achieve that level. She just doesn't seem to love it (de-energized). Maybe there's another way to look at this. Perhaps she doesn't like playing in front of an audience but *loves* to write music and practice. Maybe she's fully energized at the piano when it doesn't require her to be onstage and under pressure. In this case, we could look at helping her pursue her strength through other channels. Maybe she helps write the music for the school production and performs it from the music pit.

Paradoxically, your child's knowledge of his strengths also helps him deal with his limits. Your child may have a core strength in track and may be performing to the best of his ability, with full energy and use, but still not be chosen to anchor the relay. He may have a core strength of leadership and lead better than most kids his age, but that doesn't mean he'll end up being a CEO. What will a strength-based child end up with? Strong, developed areas of competence. A clear understanding of her strengths and weaknesses. A belief in herself. The satisfaction of pursuing her own best potential rather than chasing an external definition of "success." Self-assurance, so as not to be easily manipulated or swayed by others, whether a bullying peer, a belittling boss, or a controlling partner. The potential to be happy doing what she's good at *and* loves to do.

Viewed this way, a child's actual level of performance is sort of beside the point. The ultimate power of SBP lies in children internalizing the fact that they have strengths, that their strengths are what energize them, and that these strengths are their inner resources for developing optimism and resilience and pursuing what they want to achieve in life. What better outcome can there be for parent and child alike?

EXERCISE: | Assessing Strengths

On the Strength Switch website you'll find a list of 118 strengths presented across three different frameworks that have been developed by teams of psychologists.[31] The list classifies strengths based on qualities that are positive in nature and contribute to the individual and others in productive, socially valued ways. You'll see some overlap across the three lists and you'll also see some interesting differences. Undoubtedly, there are more strengths across the human race, but this list is a good place to begin as you start to use strength-based parenting.

This is an exercise that you can do on several levels. First, just read through the list and circle or write down the strengths you see in your child. My hunch is that you may discover your child has more strengths—things she does well, often, and with energy—than you realize. You might even discover some growth strengths: things you've glimpsed in your child that might be developed with some encouragement.

Next, depending on your child's age and interest level, you might decide to go through the list with your child and see what she picks out about herself. Some might be easy to spot. Others less so. You might need to explain or define some of the strengths for your child. Older children can go through the list on their own, and then you can talk about what they've found.

Finally, you might ask your child to go through the list and rate *your* strengths. That could start an interesting conversation about both your own and your child's strengths, and how each person in the family contributes unique strengths to the whole.

EXERCISE: | A Deeper Dive into Strength Assessment

If your child is enjoying the process of identifying her strengths, there are numerous surveys she can complete including the Values in Action Youth Survey or the Gallup Strengths Explorer or the Gallup StrengthsQuest. You can find the websites to these surveys in the Appendix.

Here again, there are multiple ways to approach this process: taking the surveys to discover your own personality traits, taking them to discover your child's traits, taking them with your child to help your child find his traits, or having an older child do the survey himself and discuss it with you afterward.

Identifying strengths in this way can help you build them. They might help you overcome strength blindness, but they shouldn't be used to pigeonhole you or your child.

Remember that these surveys are not the be-all and end-all. If your profile doesn't exactly match who you think you are, that's fine. If you think you're higher or lower on a particular strength than the survey has indicated, trust your judgment. Use the surveys as a starting point and a way to start conversations about strengths.

Once your child starts to see her strengths, she'll gain a better understanding of herself and others, and you'll gain a better understanding of your child—as these stories show:

Knowing their strengths has given my daughters confidence in their academic and aspirational choices. Zoe has gained confidence to choose subjects that support her in expressing her appreciation of beauty and excellence (art and design). Knowing her strengths also gave her confidence to step up and take a lead role in set design at the local youth theater. Because she understands her strengths, she has an authentic sense of who she is and what she is good at. Later, when the kids she was working with needed to be organized into action, painting and bringing the vision to life, she had no hesitation in moving back and letting her sister Matilda (strong in leadership and teamwork) step in to set up the workflow and assign tasks. From this I can see how my daughters' knowing their own and others' strengths helped them to take ownership of what they could contribute, and to allow others to do the same.

Breanna's top strengths are humor and appreciation of beauty and excellence. Talking with Breanna about her character strengths really helped her validate how she walks through each day, using her strengths in different situations. It has provided us with a framework and language around how she uses her character strengths, which has been helpful in deepening her understanding of her behaviors and how they affect various situations.

I first connected Jamie with his strengths at age seven or eight using the VIA strengths cards. We went out to a café (as a treat) to begin work on this. We laid the cards out on the table and I had him choose which cards he thought were most like him (I explained those he didn't understand). At the time, Jamie was in a new class at school, struggling with the teacher and getting in a lot of trouble. He selected his strengths easily (even though he was wandering around the café, zoning in and out of focus!).

Jamie also chose to think about his teacher's strengths. At first he said his teacher had no strengths, but then he realized his teacher had the strengths of fairness, forgiveness, honesty, and humor. He was able to recognize that, just like him, his teacher has things he is good at and not so good at.

Over the next week, we did the VIA Youth Survey. The process and the results were powerful, as listening to Jamie's answers gave me a lot of insight into how he viewed himself. I felt they were reflective of the situation we were dealing with at the time: his behavioral struggles at school and at home. At the time, he had a negative view of himself as not putting in or sustaining effort and only moderately feeling listened to and loved. Taking the survey changed his view.

EXERCISE: | Strength Stories

I've found this exercise works well after you and your child have identified his strengths. Ask your child to choose a strength and then say, "Tell a story of a time in your life where that strength was really, really evident." Telling Strength Stories makes children's strengths concrete and real to them. You can ask your child to tell you a story or you can start by telling him a story of the strengths you see in him. At the dinner table or in the car, you can talk about something positive you remember the child doing and the particular strength(s) it showed: "You know, I was thinking about how you organized the surprise birthday party for your BFF. You got everyone involved. You worked out a plan for making a big group "Happy Birthday" poster, baking a cake, and keeping everything a secret. You got it all done by the day you needed it. That really showed your strengths of leadership, organization, communication, and kindness."

If you think it would help your child to come up with ideas about her strengths, you might go first and tell a Strength Story about yourself. Here's a recent story I told Emily about Nick and me:

The other day as Nick and I left the shopping mall, we saw a young woman in the parking lot pushing a huge cart filled with baking supplies—baking powder, flour, fruit, etc.—and she had balanced the egg cartons on the very top.

You know where this story is going. We spotted her just as one of the egg cartons crashed to the ground and she was losing control of the cart. It was way too heavy and she hadn't balanced it properly.

Nick and I had an appointment and were running late. So I consciously had to think, OK. This is a person in need. Am I going to help her and be late to our appointment? Or should I let someone else help her? No, *I decided.* She needs help. *So I said to Nick, "We need to go and help this lady."*

It turned out it was her first day on the job at a café/bakery nearby, and she'd been told to go to their storage space and collect the baking ingredients. She was new to packing and pushing the cart.

We helped her pick up the eggs and repack some items. The cart was still way too heavy. So I said, "I'll help you take it to the store."

We pushed it together and Nick stayed beside the cart, ready to catch anything that fell. As we trundled along, I tried to reassure her, saying things like, "I'd have done the same thing. Don't worry about it. It's just twelve eggs. It's such an easy mistake to make. We all make mistakes."

By the time we got her to the bakery, I had a little "Oh my God" moment because I knew we were going to be late. But I felt good knowing we were helping her get through a bad patch on her first day on the job. She thanked us and I could see she felt less stressed. She told us, "You are both very kind people," and that made Nick smile.

You can also sneak in Strength Stories if you don't want it to seem like a formal exercise. You can bring these stories up in casual conversation just by sharing about your day: "X happened at work today, and this person got really annoyed and didn't want to call me back to talk about it. I don't like feeling that someone is upset with me. But I know I'm good at teamwork and empathy, so when I couldn't get her on the phone, I stopped by her office and said I probably would have felt the same way, but that she's hugely valuable on our team and we really need her in order to make a success of the project. It wasn't easy, but I'm glad I kept at it, because now we're communicating and I think in a few days we'll be going full steam ahead again."

CHAPTER 4

The Ages and Stages of Strength Growth

Now that you know how to define strengths and spot them in your child, let's look at how strengths develop from childhood to early adulthood. Different strengths come online at different times, connected to a child's physical, cognitive, and emotional development. Understanding the arc of children's development will help you know what to reasonably expect from your child at different ages. There are periods of explosive brain growth that seem almost chaotic in speed and pattern, and periods where growth is less rapid—and even declines. Starts, stops, side trips, and a certain degree of backtracking are to be expected. It's all part of what happens as your child's brain gradually takes on the distinctive configuration that makes her who she is.

You'll see these fluctuations reflected in how your child pursues, practices, and starts to specialize in certain strengths. Being a strength-based parent lets you enhance and appreciate your child's emerging uniqueness. Not only does this help your child become the best person she can be, but also it improves your relationship with your child:

Connecting my kids with their strengths has given me a way to relate to each of my children individually to express and build a deep sense of regard for each of them. For me it's about celebrating what is great about each child and about bringing them into casual conversations about a particular strength. Strengths conversations really are elevating conversations, as opposed to conversations about catching kids doing something wrong or misbehaving.

How and When Strengths Develop

In Chapter 3, we talked about how the brain supports our drive to grow our strengths throughout life and how the environment we create builds our child's strengths through neuroplasticity. Our brains are always changing, but for pure rate and scope of growth, nothing beats the first three years.[1] As I've mentioned, in the first six months alone, one hundred thousand new neural connections are formed every second. By the time your child is two years old, his brain has reached 80 percent of its adult weight—and did you know that the average two-and-a-half-year-old has about 50 percent *more* neural connections than an adult?[2] In childhood, the brain overproduces its quantity of gray matter, or "thinking matter," right through until the age of twelve.

This growth rate makes sense when you consider how much there is for babies and young children to learn. All of these neural connections help kids build their brain fast and develop basic abilities like hearing, rudimentary motor skills, language, simple relationship skills, and fundamental cognitive skills.[3]

Thanks to this neural proliferation, early childhood is a great time to build a child's strengths. You'll see many growth strengths popping forward if you've got your strengths radar turned on. Some show up very early:

What are my son's strengths? Resilience, persistence, and compassion. Most of these he demonstrated as a toddler and preschooler, and we continue to observe them today.

|||||||||||

Hamish loves taking a leadership role in playing with his fellow preschoolers—though he can let others take the lead, so he's not too bossy! His love for others shines through with loving words and hugs, particularly when his family and friends are sad or hurt. He can use his social intelligence to make connections and friends in just about any situation. He has a heartwarming appreciation of beauty, regularly commenting on sunrises, sunsets, flowers, insects, animals, buildings, cars—anything that he sees beauty in—with exclamations of wonder and awe. He has a boundless enthusiasm for life. Keeping up with him is invigorating and sometimes exhausting!

While this isn't the only time you'll have a chance to help your child find his growth strengths, it's a golden opportunity that extends over a period of years for exploration and experimentation.

To help you discover and build your child's core strengths and growth strengths from birth through the early to mid-teen years, try applying what psychologists who study talent development have learned about how strengths grow. Strengths unfold according to a pattern that Benjamin Bloom, PhD, has identified as having three broad phases.[4] Let's take a look at them, and at what's happening in the brain.

Romance Phase: The Early Years

In this phase, the child plays, explores, and has fun with potential strengths. It's the beginning of developing passions. You'll notice engagement and interest in certain activities and frequent displays of certain traits, with above-average learning and performance in these areas. Your role is to help your kids develop their passions by providing low-pressure opportunities to engage them and to reinforce their strengths by letting them know when you see the telltale signs: performance, energy, and use. Let them play.

Of course, the building of talents is happening right alongside the building of your child's brain. I like to think of the process of building the brain like building a house, with a child's talents like the contents of the house. In the early years, the shell of the house is built, and the foundations—the frame, plumbing, and wiring—are put in place. You might be surprised to know that the brain of your elementary school–aged child is almost as big as yours. In fact, by age six, a child's brain is only 5 percent smaller than an adult brain.[5]

But while the size of the brain doesn't grow much during the elementary school years, the *volume* and *density* of the brain grow swiftly, straight through to puberty[6] as your child gets busy filling the house with as much exciting stuff as she can: puzzles, games, music, sports equipment, projects, friends, pets, tools, crafts, bikes, boogie boards, books, and heaven knows what else. It's a fun, though kind of messy, place (a bit like my floordrobe).

This is happening thanks to that substantial growth in gray matter I mentioned that occurs as children try new experiences, develop new skills, and build their knowledge. Neuroscientists refer to this phase of brain development as an "overproduction" phase[7] because the brain produces far more cells and connections than it will actually need in adulthood. It's as if the brain is giving your child a taste of all the potential future pathways he can take. These brain changes are what underpin the romance phase of strengths development, when you want to encourage play, autonomy, and passion in your kids.

During this time, your child's limbic system, responsible for basic emotional responses, and his frontal lobe, responsible for rationality, are growing at about the same pace. They're both pretty small during infancy and preschool—that's when you get tantrums and impulsiveness as children learn to get their feeling and thinking processes more in sync and under control. In middle and later childhood, these brain areas grow at roughly the same ratio, so by the time the child is in grade school, the two brain areas are "talking" to each other more effectively. Sometimes one system overrides the other and there'll be a temper meltdown or an inappropriate decision, but you can see that most of the time there's conversation going on between the upstairs (frontal lobe) and the downstairs areas (limbic system) in your child's "house." This ratio changes again in the teen years, where we'll turn next.

Precision Phase: The Middle Years

In the phase during early to mid-adolescence, a child becomes clearer about his passions and chooses to more systematically develop particular strengths, starts to put in significant effort, and begins to display advanced learning. Your role is to provide resources in the form of opportunities and relationships to help your kids develop high-level skill in their strengths. These might include classes, clubs, camps, volunteer work, equipment, coaches, tutors, and more. Remember my friend's civic-minded teenage daughter from Chapter 3? My friend supported her daughter's strength by helping her daughter to choose social causes and plan and develop awareness-raising campaigns, driving her to charity activities, and connecting her with mentors knowledgeable about social activism.

You're also helping your child learn to use her strengths flexibly: calling on them when she needs them, using them to address weaknesses or handle challenges, and throttling them back or swapping them out when other strengths would work better in a given situation. More on all of this in later chapters.

This phase requires considerable time and effort from both you and your child, and probably money from you (not to mention that you may feel like slapping a "Mom's/Dad's Taxi" sticker on the back window of your car). It's a phase where our kids seek out increasingly complex experiences to pursue their passions. Being strength-based actually helps you be more selective about where you put your parenting energies as you zero in on a child's true abilities and interests. And it's not all up to you. You can enlist your child in the process of pursuing her passions by reading books, researching classes, and shopping for gear together. Maybe your child can contribute toward some of the costs by doing odd jobs around the house to earn extra allowance. Ultimately, using the three-part criteria for identifying strengths that you learned in Chapter 3 will help you distinguish true strengths from raw abilities.

The precision phase is marked by important underlying changes that begin in the brain in early to mid-adolescence.[8] The "house" of the teenage brain might look much the same on the outside, but it is undergoing major internal remodeling. In adolescence, the brain has another massive growth spurt, but it's different from the growth spurt of childhood.

For one thing, the brain's gray matter peaks at age twelve and then begins a long decline,[9] a process called neural pruning. This may sound ominous, but there's a good reason for it. The teenage brain is correcting the overproduction phase of late childhood[10] *and* preparing for the complex demands of adulthood. This long period of deep neural change allows the brain to become specialized,[11] more interconnected, and more efficient.[12] Another way to look at it is that the brain is deciding what strengths to carry forward into adulthood.

How does the brain know what gray matter to get rid of? That's determined partly by genes[13] and partly by neural competition. A type of survival-of-the-fittest endgame takes place where neural networks battle it out to secure their place in the remodeled adult brain. The neural networks your teenager uses more often become fitter and stronger and win the battle, while those that underlie less frequently used behaviors, thoughts, skills, and emotions are cut from the team.

At this time, teenagers get a more precise (you may occasionally say "an exaggerated") sense of their strengths. As the structure of the brain is refined through neural pruning, your teen gets better and more efficient at the things he does a lot. Basically, his strengths are strengthened. Your role is to help your child put more effort and time into systematically developing his strengths.

Also at this time, the roughly equal ratio of growth in the limbic system and frontal lobe is disrupted. The limbic system takes off with rapid growth, while the frontal lobe is slower in its maturation. In addition, the brain's white matter—the stuff that connects and enables different parts of the brain to "talk" to each other—is not yet connecting the limbic system and frontal lobe as strongly as we parents would like. Although there's a lot of white matter growth in the teen years, it starts in the more primitive areas of the brain and gradually moves up to the higher-level functioning areas[14] in a pattern neuroscientists call "back to front" brain development.[15]

All of this means that sometimes the emotion-driven limbic system overrides the logic-driven frontal lobe.[16] It's why the teen years are associated with emotional behavior, impulsivity, risk taking, and sensation-seeking behaviors.[17] Your child isn't doing this to annoy you. She really does see the world in terms of the here and now, because the parts of the brain that offer foresight aren't fully connected yet. It's also one reason why adolescence is a stage of greatest vulnerability to mental illness and we find high rates of mental illness in the teenage years.[18]

But the teenage brain is especially primed to learn during this growth spurt. As the white matter grows, it allows for more and stronger interconnections within and across brain areas, permitting sophisticated, smoother, faster communication.[19] You can remind yourself of this scientific fact next time you're exasperated with your teenager's poor communication skills. Things will get better. Things *are* getting better (even if your teenager isn't speaking to you right now!).

The best thing you can do is allow your teenager the freedom needed to build self-regulated, mature behavior while at the same time protecting your teen from physical, psychological, social, and emotional danger. Strength-based parenting can be a powerful way for you to connect with your teenager to let her know that you understand who she is, that you are there for her, and that you can help her use her strengths as anchors to guide her choices when her peers may be pressuring her into risky behaviors. This is also a time to be on the lookout for any hidden talents your child may wish to develop while the brain is deciding what stays and what gets cut.

Integration Phase: The Later Years

Fortunately, in the later teen years, the white matter connectivity has expanded and there's more upstairs–downstairs communication. Through this internal communication, teens learn how and when to bring their strengths to bear more consistently and appropriately in specific situations, be it their empathy, humor, organization skills, leadership ability, and more. You'll notice your child's emotional capacity improves in late adolescence, coinciding with the integration phase of strength development.

In this phase, the child achieves high performance or a level of mastery in certain strengths, and the strengths become fully owned and recognized as part of the child's identity.[20] Teenagers are able to see their strengths as resources they can use to plan a positive future for themselves, shape their life's purpose, and contribute to the lives of others. Teens who know their strengths may pursue and obtain interesting and relevant summer jobs, engage in community service, join or lead school clubs, participate in extracurricular activities, train with the more advanced sports team, shadow an expert in their chosen strength, and do other things that make their life full of interest and reward. All of this can become the basis of knockout college essays, scholarships from colleges or other organizations keyed to a child's strengths, and leads for internships and career choices later in your teen's life. These are hugely important payoffs. But even if your teen's strengths don't result in those things, the ultimate payoff is still there: an adult who is secure in what he knows, strong enough to admit what he doesn't know, and able to grow and learn as life unfolds.

Spotlight on Eight Strengths

It would be impossible to map the trajectory of 100-plus strengths, so I've chosen to spotlight the development of eight strengths that have the most research behind them. Below are profiles of four talents (music, creativity, athleticism, and intelligence) and four personality-based, or character, strengths (curiosity, wisdom, emotional intelligence or EI, and personality itself). While personality is a general construct, there's a great deal of research on it, and it's a clear example of how certain traits in children arise at different life stages.

Not all strengths come online at the same time, and researchers still don't have an exact map of the development of all the strengths. That's why, once again, it's best to look for the three signs of a strength—performance, energy, and use—as the everyday clues to an emerging strength.

The chart on the following page shows in general when we expect to see each of these strengths emerge and then most significantly develop. However, there will always be individual variations and pacing, and some stark exceptions, such as the fact that most "Big C" creative types (which refers to a very high level of creativity typically exhibited by acclaimed artists or people at the top of their fields who have produced something novel and adaptive, such as authors, scientists, inventors, composers, architects, and engineers) emerge in middle adulthood, despite examples of child prodigies who make Big C contributions to society in adolescence (e.g., Mozart). In addition, we can develop and improve our strengths to one degree or another throughout our life. For example, emotional intelligence starts in childhood but can be further developed in adults who take EI training at work; retirees can take up art and become quite talented; and so on.

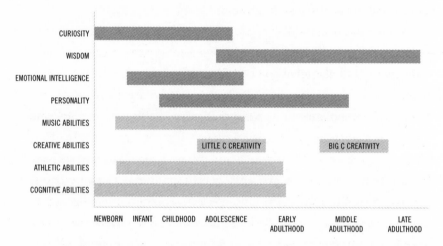

FIGURE 3.
This figure demonstrates the developmental trajectories of eight key strengths.

As you'll see from the figure above, some strengths are evident from birth. Curiosity, for example, is immediately identifiable in newborns in how responsive they are to their environment, particularly to the people around them. Intelligence researchers have also shown that babies are born with intelligence, and studies using indicators such as heart rate changes and eye movement tracking reveal that infants possess sophisticated cognitive responses to their environment. Infants have the intellectual capacity to discern most human speech sounds, discriminate between small numbers of objects, distinguish animate from inanimate objects, imitate facial gestures, form concepts and categories, and recall past events.

Musical ability is detectable from six months of age.[21] Infants have been shown to be able to detect musical frequency, timing, timbre, and melodic contour; remember melodies for up to fifteen seconds; and group tones on the basis of similarities in pitch, loudness, and timbre.

Empathy, a key aspect of EI, also starts in infancy and is developed somewhere between six months and two years.[22] Eight-month-olds can make facial expressions, vocalizations, and gestures that attempt to respond to the distress of others.[23]

Moving into the toddler years, you can expect to see early signs of sporting ability, which advances through the first seven years of life.[24] This phase will also give you a glimpse into your child's personality based on his temperament, including the capacity to regulate impulses, the level of caution or willingness and eagerness to explore new situations, their energy levels, and their comfort with new people.[25]

Around the ages of three or four we start to see clearer, more consistent signs of a child's personality, including levels of agreeableness, emotional stability, conscientiousness, extroversion-introversion tendencies, and openness to experience.[26] You'll also see an increase in EI at this age, when kids start to have knowledge of their emotions. Researchers test this by asking children to match a hypothetical situation (e.g., receiving a gift) with an emotion (e.g., happiness) and the appropriate facial expression (e.g., a person smiling).[27] The degree to which a child shows the ability to match the correct emotion and expression for the situation is used to assess the range of emotional intelligence in children of this age.

Around the age of eight, we start to see kids display the more mature type of EI and empathy involving the intellectual understanding of another person's situation (as compared to simply responding emotionally to another's distress), because this is when a child's brain develops the capacities to see something from the point of view of another, such as advanced reasoning ability and perspective taking.[28]

In the later childhood years, you'll also see further signs of sporting ability and music ability. For example, harmony and tonality are thought to develop mainly between the ages of six to nine, but continue up to age twelve.[29]

Although intelligence begins at birth and is cultivated throughout childhood, cognitive capacity expands again in the teenage years, as teens have faster information processing, can think more systematically and abstractly, and can separate information into more complex categories (e.g., a preschooler has a category of "car"; an adolescent has subcategories: "van," "utility," "sedan," "four-wheel drive," "hatchback").[30] Little creativity, or "Little C," and daily ingenuity, marked by the ability to think of new, different, adaptive, and meaningful ideas, becomes evident in the teen years.[31]

Unlike intelligence, which "lights up" early, wisdom—the way we use and apply our knowledge—is a "slow burn" strength.[32] You may well start to see signs in childhood through behaviors such as learning how to settle disputes and asking deeper questions, but adolescence is really the time of rapid wisdom growth as teens' brains drive them to seek new sensations, separate from parents, explore the world, and gather others' perspectives, leading to deeper moral, intellectual, and social understandings. Girls tend to develop wisdom faster than boys, which is consistent with most character strengths.[33]

As parents, it's useful for us to know these broad developmental patterns of various strengths for three reasons. First, it helps us know when to expect early signs of talent such as musical or sporting ability. Second, knowing the developmental trends helps us gauge the performance aspect of a strength and know if we are seeing higher levels of, for example, empathy than what would be the developmental norm (but don't forget we're also looking for energy and use). Third, it ensures we don't push our kids too hard and expect them to show strengths that have not yet started to develop.

How to Encourage Strength Development as Your Child Matures

As your child grows, you'll see some strengths rise to the fore, others recede, some seem to come out of nowhere, and others seem to drop out of sight. It can be difficult to know whether strengths that diminish or drop away did so because they weren't true strengths, or because the environment didn't support them.

Try not to overthink this too much. Your touchstones for identifying and nurturing a true strength should always be the three identifiers we discussed in Chapter 3: Strengths are *energizing, performed well, and performed often.* If all three elements aren't there, then it is not a strength, and the fact that you see it diminish through lack of use is not of great concern.

Brains are always turned on, so you'll have many opportunities to work on strengths quite naturally during daily life with your child. It shouldn't feel forced to either of you. Given the brain differences described above, strength-based parenting does look different in younger and elementary-aged children compared to teenagers.

Spotting strengths in younger kids can be very direct (e.g., "I can see that you love telling stories. You've got the narrator strength in you"). With younger kids you can actively point out to your child when he's doing something he is good at, feels good doing, and chooses to do. You can also talk with him about how to use certain strengths in relationships, in schoolwork, in sports, or in his other activities: Relationships need the strength of kindness, schoolwork needs diligence, and sports need fairness—and all three need persistence.

With teenagers, your strengths coaching will be subtler. While you actively take the lead with younger kids to detect, direct, and cultivate strengths, with teenagers you're best off taking a step back and acting more as a "strength antenna" for how they can apply strengths in their activities. Their brains love novelty. So prompt them to experiment with using a host of strengths across different situations. Give them environments that help them learn what happens when they combine the strengths of love of learning and creativity. Help them draw on their strength of social intelligence to make sure their strength of humor doesn't offend anyone. Ask them to think about whether they have certain relationships where different strengths are required: Maybe one friend responds to zest while another responds to stillness. Maybe one teacher wants pride and another wants humility.

In the chapters that follow, we'll explore many ways to help children discover and use their strengths, as well as cultivate the underlying abilities needed for applying them (such as self-control). But the four key parenting strategies below will give you a solid foundation for being a good strength-based parent.

The Four Key Strength-Based Parenting Strategies

Here are four foundational psychological processes you can use to support strengths development in your children. They influence how your child perceives her ability to develop her strengths, how your child learns strengths management from you, and how your child will eventually internalize the capacity to build and apply her strengths. They are as follows:

* mind-set management
* role modeling
* scaffolding
* proximal development practices

Mind-Set Management

Each of us has a mind-set, including about ourselves. Whether you know it or not, you carry around a set of beliefs about every aspect of yourself, including your intelligence, talents, skills, character, and relational abilities.[34]

Carol Dweck, PhD, has identified two types of mind-set: growth and fixed.[35] A person with a growth mind-set sees herself as having qualities that can be changed, while someone with a fixed mind-set sees personal qualities as being static and unchangeable.

You and I might have opposing mind-sets about the same thing. The same is true for kids. For example, two children can have exactly the same level of intelligence but have different beliefs about the nature of that intelligence. One child might believe that intelligence is static and unchangeable, that there's nothing that can be done to make her smarter. The other child may believe that intelligence is changeable, that she can become smarter with effort and practice. Even though both students have the same level of intelligence, the student who believes that intelligence can grow will do better on academic tests.[36]

These two mind-sets create radically different mental worlds that are then played out in a person's life journey. Below are some examples of fixed versus growth mind-set. Feel free to add your own:

FIXED MIND-SET	GROWTH MIND-SET
"I'm a klutz."	"It takes me longer to learn physical activities than other things."
"I'm terrible at figuring out computer problems."	"I get tense when my computer freezes, but I take a deep breath, do some online research, call my tech-savvy friends, and get the help I need to fix the problem."

"I'm a slow reader."	"I would like to read faster, so I'm learning about speed-reading techniques to see if they can work for me."
"I have a short fuse."	"I am working on managing my temper."
"I'm too old to change careers."	"I am not sure about changing careers, but I'm looking into some new career directions to see what would be involved in retooling and retraining."

Although strengths are genetic predispositions, they still need to be grown through effort and practice. That's why a growth mind-set optimizes your child's chances of reaching her strengths potential. Children with growth mind-sets do better academically, respond more resiliently to failure, take on more challenges, generate more effective strategies for improvement, and show greater creativity—all things that help them succeed in tasks.[37] A growth mind-set also helps children in their social lives. Since they believe that people are capable of change, they act more prosocially, make fewer stereotypical judgments, and resolve interpersonal conflict in more positive ways.[38]

If you have a fixed mind-set, chances are that your child will, too. In Chapter 8, we'll talk about how to communicate with your child in a way that fosters a growth mind-set. But realize also that your child takes his cue from your mind-set. Recent research shows that parents' mind-sets about failure (i.e., is failure a good thing and an opportunity to learn, or a bad thing?) affected whether their kids had a fixed or a growth mind-set about intelligence.[39]

My own research with teenagers shows that a teen with a growth mind-set is more receptive to strength-based messages from her parents and more likely to use her strengths, compared to a teen with a fixed mind-set.[40] It's almost as if a teen's fixed mind-set blocks the parent's strength-based messages. You could be talking about strengths, but if your child has a fixed mind-set she'll be subconsciously turning down the volume of your strength-based communication and the messages won't be getting through. That's why a key part of SBP is to encourage a growth mind-set about strengths by helping your kids see that strengths can grow with effort.

Bottom line: Kids learn their mind-set from you, and from the moment they try and fail at something—which they'll do many times—they're taking away messages from you about 1) how to view and respond to failure and 2) whether strengths can be developed.

So what is your mind-set about strengths? Do you believe that strengths can be strengthened? Maybe you started this book with an idea that strengths are inborn (and that's partly true), so your kid either has a given strength or he doesn't. But by now you know that strengths have both a nature and a nurture aspect and that the brain is wired to help us build our strengths through practice. This means you can be confident in applying a growth mind-set to strengths. When you do, your kids will, too.

Role Modeling

Our discussion above about your mind-set is really about role modeling.[41] Children learn as much from what we do as from what we say. From mind-set to morality, practicality to persistence, leadership to loving kindness, children are always observing how we use our strengths, grow them, and handle challenges:

> My husband is a natural leader both at work and as a basketball coach. Our eldest son has drawn on his father's role modeling and leadership strength to referee at basketball and now coaches basketball himself.

As a teacher, I have a love of learning, and I also completed a second master's degree. I encouraged my sons to put in a big effort at school and in college. I remember our eldest son saying, "I could never work as hard as you do." I felt a little odd yet also pleased that I had been a good role model. His results, however, demonstrated that he had far greater ability than I. I knew that if he applied himself, with his innate ability, he would fly—and he has! This brings me great joy.

Emanuel has had plenty of tough times in his life. But true to his resilient nature, he hasn't let them stop him. One summer he was wheelchair-bound after he fell and broke his arm. Just prior to this accident, he had surgery on his foot. With plaster casts on his left foot and right arm, he was quite immobile. It was a blow, for him and for the rest of the family. But none of us ever gave up. We persisted with our summer plans. We traveled to the beach and enjoyed our summer as best we could. If something was difficult for him, we looked for ways to smooth his path. Not once did he seem down. Together we always looked at the brighter side of the situation.

What if you don't have or display the strengths your child has? Expose her to strength helpers who do. Take kids with artistic talent to museums and galleries so they can study the works of famous artists, read about them, and discover what character strengths helped the artist express his talent. Send math-loving kids to math camp. Find the teachers, tutors, trainers, and accomplished people who can help your children see how certain strengths look in action and begin to build their own.

Strength-Based Scaffolding

Take a look at the stories below and see if you can guess what they have in common:

I constantly reinforce what my son is doing well and what it shows me about his character.

||||||||||||

I'm working on supporting my son in a new habit: timely preparation for school in the morning. I have given him a checklist that we posted in a highly visible place, and I give him positive reinforcement when he uses it and puts the steps into practice. Now that I think about it, I could further encourage his use of the checklist and building this habit by tying his strengths to his success in following the steps.

||||||||||||

Jamie's teacher heard him talk about his sadness after reading books about refugees and got him to do a project on the topic. Using his strength of hope, Jamie became very engaged in looking for ways to help refugee children and grateful for his own life.

||||||||||||

I decided to look at how Lucy's strengths (bravery, forgiveness, fairness, gratitude, and perseverance) might help her get along better with others, and whether they might sometimes hinder her if she's overusing or underusing them.

I talked to Lucy about her strengths and gave examples of each. Then I asked her to think of examples of how her strengths might play out in her life. Her older sister was really helpful in making the language kid-friendly and explaining the impacts of various strengths. We made Lucy feel special, telling her that her strengths are like superpowers that can help others in times of need.

We decided she could use more of her forgiveness to "let things go" with her sisters. I reminded her that she knew the song "Let It Go" from the movie Frozen *and suggested that she sing it aloud or in her head when her sisters were getting to her and to remind herself that forgiveness is a superpower that she has. She added that she could go outside to jump on the trampoline and sing to get away and forget the conflict. We spoke about how she could use her fairness to help her see others' perspectives, including what her sisters were thinking and feeling.*

I told Lucy that we would talk every Wednesday to see how she was doing with using her strengths to be at her best with her friends and with her sisters.

What's the common thread? Every adult in these examples is using a technique called "scaffolding."[42] This simply means they're making sure that children have the resources and support they need to build their strengths. They affirm the child's abilities, help her tune in to her unique constellation of strengths, and then offer ideas and suggestions for how she can take her strengths to new levels in her life by applying them in challenging situations to change habits or to learn and grow as a person.

Going back to our house analogy, through scaffolding you're providing a structure to support children's growth until they can internalize and apply these processes to support themselves. It may take the form of insights, strategies, tips, techniques, lists, schedules, systems, reminders, encouragement, and pretty much anything else parents do to help children grow up to be independent, accomplished adults. As part of the process, you coach your child along, assisting without taking over, staying close without hovering, checking in for a "how's it going?" conversation, and working with your child to set targeted goals and formulate a plan for achieving them.

A scaffold builder can be anyone who:

- has the child's interests at heart
- knows the child's capabilities
- has something valuable to teach the child about her capabilities
- knows how to nudge the child forward in a manner aligned with her capabilities

Scaffolding is easy for loving, supportive adults to do with children. You're no doubt already doing it a lot. I'm simply suggesting that you become more aware and systematic about it and add a strengths focus. Strength-based scaffolding focuses on providing the child with ways to build and apply her strengths in her life. You might provide it, but it can also be provided by teachers, coaches, or wise and beloved relatives—perhaps an aunt, uncle, or grandparent whom the child adores and respects as a role model.

Deliberate Practice Within the Zone of Proximal Development

My dismal softball performance in middle school just confirmed my teenage perception that I was clumsy and uncoordinated. I was always the last girl picked for practice. Mainly I was a terrible fielder: afraid of the ball, unable to judge distance and bounces, constantly missing catches and letting runners get on base and score. I was like a black hole in the outfield—balls just disappeared there.

So my dad decided to try and help me out. Most evenings after dinner, that spring found us in the backyard playing catch. In the beginning, he threw easy flies straight to me, until I got confident that I could catch those. Then he started mixing in grounders that had a bounce or two, still directly to me. Then a high pop-up so I had to judge how fast it was falling and get under it. Then a slow grounder a little distance from me. Then back to the easy flies for a bit. Then a grounder even farther away so I had to run for it and judge where the ball was going to be.

Eventually he started adding speed, more bounces, and spin, so the grounders went in unpredictable directions. It was always fun and low pressure, but we were definitely practicing so I could get better. And I did! I surprised myself, my teammates, and our phys ed teacher. Taking things gradually was key. If he'd just started throwing hard, spinning grounders, I'd have quickly given up and been even more convinced I couldn't do it. Instead, it was the first time I truly understood that I wasn't born clumsy. I just needed extra practice to improve.

I love this father-daughter story for two reasons. First, because it shows that if parents simply hang out with their kids, a kind of magic happens. And second, because it's a perfect example of a parent using what psychologist Lev Vygotsky called the zone of proximal development.[43]

That's a complicated-sounding term for a beautiful, natural type of scaffolding in which an adult helps a child reach a higher level of understanding than he could have reached alone, by engaging the child in practice and gradually increasing the challenge of a given task, keeping it *just slightly ahead* of what the child is able to do.

In this process, assistance to the child should be provided at the minimum possible level to encourage the child to advance on his own when he's able, with the adult offering encouragement, tips, hints, strategies, techniques, and equipment or materials—but only giving specific demonstrations or providing and explaining the answer as a last resort.

It's the adult's job to find that sweet spot where there's enough challenge to push the child, but not so much that the child reaches the point of complete frustration and gives up. It's also the adult's job to find that mix of specific praise and "positive push" that keeps the child pushing himself: "Good eye on that one—you watched the ball all the way into your glove." "You read the bounce right; you just need to push off faster to get there in time to catch it." "Keep your knees together when you crouch down, or it'll roll right between your legs."

Picture a friendly, wise, helping hand reaching down to you, helping you up to the next steep step on a hard hike. That's what we want to be for our children.

Working in the zone of proximal development is a wonderful way to help kids practice improving their strengths, grow new strengths, or address a weakness in low-stakes situations under the watchful, caring eye of a trusted adult who provides the resources the child needs for growth.

Of course, don't overdo this and pressure your child to operate in this zone all the time. There are times when you can just let kids do things to the degree of their current ability and enjoy it. You'll come to know when it's time to get in the proximal zone. An older child probably will, too, even if she doesn't say so. I think our kids look to us to use our strengths to help them get stronger, to give them a wise, loving push in what they know deep inside is the right direction:

> *Recently my thirteen-year-old daughter and I were driving to basket-ball practice. She had made the regional team, and this was the last training before the tournament started. During the practices she had felt left out, as all the other girls seemed to know each other and most had already played together or went to school together.*
>
> *The crying began as soon as I started the car and it lasted for the entire half-hour trip. My daughter isn't one to cry, so I knew she was*

really upset. She told me she didn't want to play basketball anymore . . . she hated it . . . and so on.

I asked her if there was a way she could reframe what she was feeling, such as, "I don't like it right now, but I made a commitment to play and I need to see it through." I also reminded her that the tournament was short and before long it would be over. I mentioned the importance of not quitting when things get really hard: "What would happen if you chose that action each time an obstacle was placed in front of you?"

With a massive dose of courage, she wiped away her tears as we pulled into the parking lot. We agreed that I would stay and watch her practice. And off she went. She showed great resilience.

Luckily she enjoyed the practice more than other times, and we were able to have a great conversation on the drive home about the rewards of showing grit!

It would have been easy to give in to her, turn the car around, and head home. I am sure that my determination to help her find a way to keep her commitment enabled her to make the right choice in this situation.

A happy by-product of this story is that her basketball skills have improved hugely, and she is now challenging herself more!

The goal doesn't have to be big. It might simply be an everyday habit the child is trying to change. Stretching toward a goal can pay off even if the aim falls short:

My daughter Suzie was talking about her dissatisfaction with her habit of snacking and how I should avoid buying ice cream because she eats too much of it. I told Suzie that it is fantastic that she is showing some self-care and that she deserves to be healthy and active. I brought up the compassion and kindness that are so characteristic of Suzie by commenting on how she always makes the effort to care about others, and that she should make the effort to care for herself, too. I reminded her how she had expressed concern about one of her friends eating candy for lunch at school virtually every day and how she had suggested to her friend that she could eat a salad instead.

I talked about how temptations are always going to be around, so some self-regulation was needed if she really didn't want to snack on sugary foods. I also asked Suzie to consider applying her kindness to herself by not just minimizing her eating of junk food but also by considering introducing more nutritious and varied foods into her diet— since in the past, Suzie has been reluctant to try new foods and eats a very limited selection of salad foods and an even more limited selection of vegetables.

Suzie decided she would aim to eat one regular salad or vegetable that she normally eats (tolerates) and one new salad or vegetable per day at dinner. This agreement lasted about a week, and then Suzie reverted to her previous ways. However, through this process, Suzie did learn to tolerate avocado in sushi rolls and is willing to eat green beans more often. That's progress.

You, Too, Can Bloom

At thirty-two, I decided to become an optimist. I was pregnant with Nick, and as I mentioned in Chapter 1, I wanted to make a different childhood for my baby than the one I'd had. I especially didn't want to put my child at risk of the depression and anxiety that had followed me into adulthood, and I knew the research showed that one's level of optimism or pessimism has a big impact on depression.[44] Reading Martin Seligman's books *The Optimistic Child* and *Authentic Happiness* gave me my lightbulb moment, when I said: "This is the work I want to do. And this is the kind of parent I want to be."

But of course I couldn't just snap my fingers and become an optimist. I had to put in consistent effort to change my thoughts, change how I reacted to my feelings, and change how I behaved in just about every life situation—because my default setting was to always see the cup half empty and to always see my weaknesses more easily than my strengths. I grew up thinking I was faulty and not good enough.

Martin Seligman said that we learn optimism or pessimism from our parents in childhood. So I figured, "Well, if you can learn pessimism, then you can unlearn it." That's what I set about doing.

I knew that if I had one strength, it was intelligence. I was a good learner. So I threw all my strength of learning into undoing my old, pessimistic way of thinking and learning a new, optimistic one.

While I was writing this book, Nick turned fourteen, and I can safely say that I have changed the way I view and explain events in my life. I view setbacks as feedback about things that need fixing, not as a verdict of failure. I see successes as reflections of ability, hard work, and good fortune rather than a fluke or something I don't deserve. I'm not always an optimist; sometimes I'm more like a recovering pessimist who backslides into negativity. But my default, most of the time, is toward optimism.

I have genuinely changed this aspect of my personality, and one way I know this is the high levels of optimism I see in Nick and Emily.

Just last week, Nick completed the VIA Survey of Character Strengths at school. Guess what his top strengths were?

Hope and optimism.

In the VIA test, these are described as "Expecting the best in the future and working to achieve it; believing that a good future is something that can be brought about."

I'm so happy for Nick that he is optimistic about his future. That wasn't how I felt growing up. But I've worked hard on developing my optimism so it can come easily to my kids.

Of course, both of my kids are very lucky to have been given a big dollop of optimism by their highly positive father. But I've also played a role.

I'm still a work in progress. Aren't we all? And isn't that the point? That we are these marvelous beings with these marvelous brains that allow us, at any age, to become better versions of ourselves. That there is always time for us to bloom.

And when we do, so do our children.

Part Two

BUILDING STRENGTHS

CHAPTER 5

Attention, Savoring, Gratitude, and Goofing Off

Last week, I brushed my teeth with sunscreen. I had my reasons. The sunscreen tube is the same shape as the toothpaste tube. The stuff squeezes out thick, like toothpaste. It was in the top drawer, where the toothpaste is kept. And my mind was on other, far more important things. So I grabbed the tube, squeezed out the goop, and started brushing. My mind quickly rejoined my body the instant my taste buds were assaulted with sunscreen.

Stuff like this happens when we don't pay attention. A friend of mine used hairspray as deodorant—talk about a sticky situation. Another used instant coffee to make gravy. Her kids said nothing because—even more worrying—they didn't notice.

Maybe you've never brushed your teeth with sunscreen, but I bet you've had the experience of your body engaging in actions while your mind was elsewhere. Perhaps you've reached the end of a page in this book only to realize that while your eyes scanned all the words, your mind didn't process their meaning (I forgive you). Maybe you've hopped in your car and driven to the end of your driveway—or down your street—before your mind registered you were driving.

In fact, the wandering mind is engaging in a particular type of attention, as is the focused one. Both are essential to getting us safely and wisely through life. We can actually train ourselves to maximize the benefits of each through enjoyable processes that can become treasured parts of our day and make us more effective, too. Teaching your child how to visit and dwell in both domains of attention is an important foundation you can provide as part of strength-based parenting. In this chapter, you'll learn how to help your child:

- *aim* his attention away from weaknesses and toward strengths
- *sustain* his attention in the focused way necessary to build strengths through practice
- *restore* his reserves of attention while learning from his life experiences and forming a firm, positive self-identity

The Two Types of Attention

Daily life on planet Earth is hugely complex for us humans. Just think about every action you take on any given day. Every word you speak. Every thought you have. Boggles the mind, doesn't it? Yet all of this, viewed in terms of where and how we place our attention, really boils down to two types of applied attention. At any given moment, we are engaged in one of them, and we constantly toggle between them.

Directed Attention

Directed attention is the process of deliberately and consciously focusing the mind on something. It's "top-down," as if your brain is acting as a company CEO, directing the workers (your neurons) to get busy on a task: *OK, time to fold the laundry/make school lunches/drive to work/write that memo/make that call*, et cetera.

You can think of directed attention as being made up of two dimensions: direction and maintenance,[1] which I call "aim and sustain." Directing or aiming our attention helps us focus on a specific task, idea, or challenge. Maintaining or sustaining our attention allows us to stay focused on it.

Directed attention involves effort. It's all about screening out other input that could be distracting—like paying attention to doing homework even though the TV is on in the background. Or making sure we brush our teeth with toothpaste even when we've got a lot on our mind.

Free-Form Attention

It might seem counterintuitive, but attention is also built through rest.[2] I'm talking about times when the mind simply wanders, without a fixed agenda. In contrast to the top-down nature of directed attention, free-form attention is undirected and bottom-up: insights, ideas, and solutions bubble up from the depths of the wandering mind in a fascinating process that has captivated spiritualists and scientists and still mystifies us all.

Our mind needs this state the way our body needs sleep: for restoration and renewal. It happens when we give ourselves what we think of as "downtime." A good example is when we're in that flow state I mentioned in Chapter 3. Strength-based parents know their kids need this time, and they build downtime into their child's life despite social pressure to hop on the overscheduling bandwagon.

Now that you know the two main types of attention, we'll take a deeper dive into each and what they mean for SBP.

Let's Get Real About Attention

Here's the truth: We're not very good at paying attention. Adults max out at somewhere between twenty to thirty-five minutes[3] (I couldn't write this page without thinking about checking my e-mail, remembering something we need from the grocery store, and being distracted by thoughts of a work project). Yet we expect hours of sustained attention from ourselves, and too often we expect far more than our kids can deliver.

You may be saying, "I can sit at my desk working for an entire morning." I know you're not lying. But it isn't true. You probably do sit for hours and work hard, but you, like me, are thinking about e-mails, to-do lists, weekend plans, errands, bills due, and so on.

We start out focused, but then after nine minutes or so, our vigilance declines[4] and our attention shifts, if only briefly, elsewhere before we aim it back on task again.[5] Rather than focusing for hours, we're actually constantly re-aiming and re-sustaining our attention.

When we ask our kids to pay directed attention, we're asking them to narrow and aim their field of attention to one thing. Then we're asking them to sustain their attention on that one thing and not get distracted by anything else. That's not so easy for us to do, so we need to ease up on our expectations of our kids.

Research results vary and there are potentially large differences between individuals, but here are a few ground rules and a reality check about human attention capacity:

- Young children, perhaps not surprisingly, aren't skilled at aiming and sustaining attention. Most three-year-olds can hold focused attention for approximately three to five minutes.[6]

- Between ages six and twelve there's a developmental spurt, and a child can sustain focus for about ten minutes.[7]
- At around age fifteen, there's another spurt in attention-aiming capacity[8] thanks to brain growth and increased myelination—the insulating coating on our neurons that facilitates speedy transmission. That puts us at around the twenty- to thirty-five-minute mark for sustained attention.[9]
- After that, our attentional ability levels off, so our ability as adults to aim attention isn't much better than when we were teenagers.[10]

This last point may seem pathetic to us today, but there's an evolutionary reason for it. Out on the savannah, it wouldn't have been safe to get engrossed in something for hours because then we wouldn't be flicking our attention around to see if there's a predator about to attack us.

These research results on attention span come from what are called Continuous Performance Tasks, which allow psychologists to measure how accurate we are about information that comes at us and how long we can sustain attention on it. The tasks usually involve watching a computer screen on which flash a series of letters, shapes, or numbers, and having to hit a button each time a particular pattern is seen—say, for example, seeing the number *9* immediately preceded by the number *1*. This entails 1) aiming attention at the screen, 2) sustaining attention after seeing the number *1* to see if it's followed by the number *9*, 3) hitting the button only when we see the number *9*, 4) screening out all other sequences, and 5) continuing this process while accuracy is measured over time. Six-year-olds have about a 71 percent hit rate (correct response). At age fifteen, that jumps to 96 percent.[11] Adults do about the same (actually, a little worse) at 94 percent.[12]

Attention Training Without Tears? (SBP to the Rescue)

How many of your frustrations and conflicts with your children come from their lack of attention? As I hope the section above shows, none of us has the corner on attention. But focusing on your child's strengths fosters the positive, engaged mood that enhances attention. This family used a toddler's strengths of perseverance and blossoming creativity to support his powers of attention:

> I had to leave my two-year-old son, Ari, at home to travel regularly over the course of a year. In the hope of lessening the impact of Mommy going away, Ari went home from the airport that first trip with his very first set of Lego. So the love affair began. His dad helped him at first, but after a couple of trips, Ari was building things on his own. This blew us away. At age three, he was doing "big boy" Lego and showing such perseverance: interpreting instructions, maintaining concentration, fixing his mistakes. Once when I called, the Lego session had been going on for four solid hours, with food consumed on the side. His perseverance certainly shone through, but the creativity he also showed was awesome to see. We really made an effort during this time to praise the process and reaffirm the strengths we could spot. It is so beautiful to see strengths evolve in your child and I'm so grateful I have the language of strengths to encourage and nurture his development in this way.

When we direct our child toward developing a core strength or a growth strength, we're helping her aim her attention. Sustaining attention enables our child to stay engaged in the activities that help her grow her strengths—or constructively address her weaknesses—such as effort, practice, problem solving, and the like.

Although children are born with a genetic predisposition for their strengths, it's only through sustained practice, which requires sustained attention, that their strengths will reach full potential. Helping your child exert directed attention helps him aim his attention on his strengths instead of veering into fixation on his weaknesses, as our evolutionary wiring predisposes us to do. It helps him tap his inborn strengths when addressing weaknesses. And it will help him sustain these efforts for longer periods of time.

SBP improves your attentional capacity, too. As you practice the Strength Switch—the simple yet powerful attention-aiming tool you learned in Chapter 2—you'll notice it gets easier to shift your attention away from your child's weaknesses and toward her strengths, and to model that shift to your child. She, too, will find it easier to see and act from her strengths.

In all of these ways, directed attention both builds and is built by strength-based parenting.

I'm often asked if strength-based parenting can help kids with attentional challenges.[13] What I can say is that, by helping the parent to focus on what the child does well, SBP creates a more positive, supportive parent-child relationship. That means less tension and frustration for both parent and child around the attention lapses. When the attentional problems no longer become the defining element for the child's identity or of the parent-child relationship, this frees up room for the child's strengths to take center stage.

June Pimm, PhD,[14] who has worked with parents and children with autism spectrum disorder (ASD) for more than two decades, is a big advocate for taking a strength-based, developmental parenting approach and for setting up situations and relationships where the child can be at his best. Her ideas align with the Early Start Denver Model, an approach to ASD that's based on the child's developmental level and unique pattern of strengths and weaknesses.[15] The program uses positive interpersonal relationships to build social skills and adaptability. In a trial of the program, 30 percent of children in the program achieved decreases in ASD symptoms, moving their diagnosis from ASD to the less serious diagnosis of Pervasive Developmental Disorder–Not Otherwise Specified.

Research on positive parenting with children who have attention deficit/hyperactivity disorder (ADHD) shows that while it doesn't change their deficit disorder, it does improve their behavior.[16] ADHD children whose parents use praise, positive emotions, physical affection, and positive engagement as regular features of their parenting have fewer conduct problems, fewer mood issues, fewer sociability problems, and less hyperactivity. The researchers haven't framed these positive parenting practices as strength-based parenting, but I would.

One mother describes how discovering the core strengths of her son, who has Asperger's syndrome, allowed her to see his powers of observation (attention) of others' emotions that hadn't been as noticeable before:

> Fin has Asperger's syndrome, so it was a surprise to me that he has social intelligence as a signature strength. I didn't really believe it until I asked others who know him well. His teachers said it made perfect sense to them—Fin notices details that others don't and is very perceptive of others' emotions, even though he may not always respond or know what to do with that emotion.
>
> Seeing that this was a strength for Fin helped me to understand that he could observe people's emotions but needed help on appropriate responses. Sometimes when he has a friend over, he'll tell me the friend feels "uncomfortable" and he'll explain what he sees in the friend's face. Then we talk and he can think about how to help resolve the situation.

Whether or not your child has these kinds of issues, if you know her strengths, you'll be better able to help her pay attention because you can more carefully calibrate the match between a particular task and her strengths. If a task is too easy or too hard, our mind wanders. Positive emotions, confidence levels about the task, interest in the task, and enjoyment of the task also affect the ability to aim and sustain attention.[17] Knowing your child's strengths improves your insight into what will satisfy those criteria and where she may struggle and need more breaks, downtime, or support from you.

A common scene of frustration in my household at the moment is encouraging nine-year-old Emily to put on her shoes before we go to school. The scene goes something like this: I let Emily know that Matt will be taking her to school in five minutes and ask her to please put her shoes on. Emily is an agreeable girl and says yes—but more often than not, no shoes are put on. It's not unusual for this scene to end with me raising my voice and Emily still barefooted, looking totally confused about why I've become so frustrated. After all, she said yes—and she fully intended to follow through.

When Emily says she's going to put her shoes on, she genuinely means it, but in the blink of an eye, her attention shifts elsewhere, and she promptly forgets about her shoes. With SBP, we can transform these moments of frustration into opportunities for attention training.

The first shift of attention has to be mine as the parent: I use the Strength Switch to flip my attention from frustration to seeing the opportunity to help Emily pay attention. The shoe request then becomes a moment for me to tap into her strengths of adherence, cooperation, and service, helping her stay focused on her task by connecting with her genuine desire to please me by doing what I ask. My request goes from "Em, can you please put your shoes on?" to "OK, Emmy-Bemmy, now's the time to show me how strong your attention muscle is getting by putting your shoes on without getting distracted. Do you think you can do that? How about we have some fun and I'll time how fast you can do it?"

Beyond that, it doesn't require anything more complicated than turning off the TV and staying near her to keep her focused. Each time she aims and sustains her attention on the shoes long enough to get them on, she's developing her capacity for attention. Soon enough, I'll be able to ask, "Em, can you please put your shoes on?" and she'll do it because her attention span has grown.

When your child engages in activities requiring dedicated focus like sports training or chess practice, these are actually forms of attention training. He's not only building his athletic or thinking skills; he's also developing his capacity to sustain attention on a task—a core skill needed for strengths development. Nick and Emily attend a weekly circus club, where they learn acrobatics and other circus skills. Juggling and swinging on the trapeze are lots of fun, but they also require intense focus. One tiny lapse of attention and my kids drop the ball . . . or themselves.

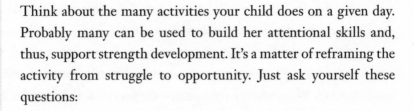

EXERCISE: | Activities for Attention Building

Think about the many activities your child does on a given day. Probably many can be used to build her attentional skills and, thus, support strength development. It's a matter of reframing the activity from struggle to opportunity. Just ask yourself these questions:

1. What is the strength that can be built here?
2. What should the expectations be?
3. How can I reframe this activity for my child in a way that makes it clear how it plays to her strengths?
4. How can I help my child use her strengths to complete the activity and better aim and sustain her attention?
5. If the activity calls for a growth strength, a learned behavior, or a weakness, how can I support my child's process?

The activities in the rest of this chapter will help both you and your child increase your attentional chops.

Savoring

Savoring is an enjoyable form of attentional training that captures moments of good experiences to build positivity in real time and create a "bank account" of goodness to draw on in tough times.[18] It involves concentrating attention on events and situations that make you feel good. When things are going great, there's plenty to savor. In tough times, being practiced at savoring lets you more easily switch gears to find and savor the positives in situations and in people—including your child and yourself.

I've made savoring a recommended practice for strength-based parenting because it teaches you and your children how to sidestep negative bias by aiming attention on positive things. Also, as it involves pausing to let our attention linger on what makes us feel good, it helps us sustain our attention.

Moments to savor are everywhere. For example, I love the smell of coffee. Luckily for me, there's a café on the ground floor of my university building. The aroma of coffee wafts into the lobby each morning, giving me the opportunity for a hit of olfactory pleasure as I come to work. The café also bakes its own cakes and pastries. The only thing better than the smell of a freshly baked blueberry muffin is the taste of a freshly baked blueberry muffin, don't you think?

Some days, I'm so preoccupied with work that although my nose registers the delectable smells, my mind doesn't notice. Before I know it, I'm in the elevator without even realizing I've passed the café, robbing myself of a small moment of pleasure.

Other days, I remember I can train my attention by savoring the aromas coming from the café. For just the moments I spend crossing the lobby, I switch my attention from work thoughts and place my full attention on my sense of smell. I try to guess what coffee bean has been brewing (Arabica? Robusta?) and what the fresh cake is (Blueberry? Cinnamon?). I relish the pleasure that just these aromas give me. It takes no time away from my busy schedule, but it helps me to aim and sustain my attention *and* it starts my day on a positive note.

You can build savoring moments into your day as games or activities with your kids. Nick, Emily, and I enjoy looking at the clouds and saying what we think the shapes look like. Savoring has become a big part of our everyday interactions. We luxuriate in the feel of sunshine on our backs, we appreciate the smell of pancakes that Matt sometimes cooks for us on Sunday mornings, we notice sunsets, and we literally stop to smell the roses in our neighborhood.

Savoring not only helps to train your child's attentional skills but it also boosts happiness, positive mood, and life satisfaction.[19] Your child's day is likely to have many little "moments of good" that, until now, have passed unnoticed. Once she learns how to focus on them, she can use them to build her positive bank account. And children with positive bank accounts have healthy reserves to draw from during challenging times:

> *My freshman year of college has been a huge adjustment for me. It's the longest I've been away from home and the most challenging academics I've ever had. The social scene is super exciting but also intimidating. Sometimes I'm really afraid I won't be able to perform up to the standards here. I've found that one way to help me stay calm is, before falling asleep, I'll picture summer evenings at home. I imagine being with my parents and going over to hang out with the neighbors on their back porch in the dark, looking out into the woods, listening to the sounds of the summer night, talking about this and that, with their springer spaniel lying underfoot for cuddles. This picture of home calms me so much. It reminds me that home will always be there for me, because I carry it in my mind.*

EXERCISE: | Make a Savoring List and a Pleasure Pact

On a sheet of paper, make a list of the things you savor. Don't spend too much time thinking about it; just write down things that always give you a lift, make you smile, inspire you, or otherwise bring you pleasure. It could be as simple as the smell of coffee, the sound of surf on the beach, greeting your pet when you get home, that first bite of a favorite food, or seeing your child laugh with delight. If you have trouble coming up with a list, no worries. It's a sign that some good savoring time should be in your future!

Next, talk with your child about the idea of savoring. Explain what it means. Together with your child, make a list of things your child savors. You might share your savoring list with your child. Together, make a pleasure pact to remind each other to remember to savor the things you listed. Look for things to add to your lists.

Five Ways to Strengthen Your Child's Ability to Savor

Here are some ways you can help your child learn to stop and savor the moment or the feeling:

1. *Noticing the environment.* Nature is full of beauty and wonders, providing endless opportunities for aiming and sustaining your child's attention. Emily has recently become interested in birds. She takes long walks with her grandfather, Rob, Matt's dad, a knowledgeable bird watcher, savoring the calls and colors of our beautiful Australian birds.

2. *Enjoying physical sensations.* Our bodies are like walking savoring devices. We can take pleasure in smells, sounds, and physical sensations. You can encourage your child to savor the taste of chocolate, the smell of dinner, the feel of warm water splashing on his back in the shower, the refreshment of a cool drink on a hot day, or a hug or a back rub. Next time you put fresh sheets on your child's bed, invite your child to notice what it feels like to slip under those crisp, clean covers.

3. *Creating family time.* The simple act of hanging out together as a family is something kids can savor. Watching a movie, cooking together, eating a meal, going for a walk, or exercising together are all activities to savor. One of my friends has a daughter who is a senior in high school, and the two of them have been going to the movies together. Not only is this a way for them to spend time together, but it's also an important way for her daughter to de-stress from school pressures and learn that she can turn her attention away from stress and toward something positive.

4. *Remembering happy times.* Savoring need not be focused on the present moment. You can encourage your children to

engage in what Fred Bryant, PhD, calls "reminiscent savoring,"[20] by thinking back to happy times in their lives, as the college freshman recounted, above. Try reminiscent savoring if your child has had a bad day. First, let him share with you about his day and the negative feelings he's having. Once things have settled down a bit, try reminiscent savoring to gently move your child out of unhappiness and back into happiness. Often with my own kids I talk to them about a funny incident from the past or dig into my memory for a time when they've had the opposite experience of what upset them. If they've had an argument with a friend, I let them get all their negative feelings out, we talk about a solution for moving forward, and then we talk about a time when they had a good time with that person. It always helps them to feel better, and they learn that they can direct their thoughts and attention away from something negative toward something positive.

Scrapbooking is one of my downtime activities and is also an effective form of savoring. As I look over the photos and assemble the pages depicting various significant family events, I reminisce about the event, and it makes me feel happy. Sometimes Nick and Emily join in and make a scrapbook page about events in their life, such as their birthday parties or family holidays. I love it when this happens, because we have wonderful conversations as they savor the moment aloud.

5. *Looking ahead.*[21] You can also encourage your children to think about something good planned for the future. For example, high school graduation, a family vacation, an upcoming trip, what they'll be having for dinner that night. This is called "anticipatory savoring." It teaches kids that they can take control of their attention and direct their own

mental time travel to the future if they want to find ways of making themselves happy. Some parents are reluctant to do this because they worry they might be setting up their child for disappointment. I don't believe that the potential of future disappointment should be a reason to stop the child from gaining the current benefits of anticipatory savoring. The key here is to help your child look forward to future joy and get the benefits of anticipatory savoring *now* while ensuring that when the moment does arise, the child actually stays in the moment rather than comparing it to an imagined ideal. If the moment doesn't match up to expectations, you can use disappointment as an opportunity to practice resilient thinking—from finding unexpected positives to calling on the child's strengths to move ahead despite disappointment to thinking up ways to improve the moment next time.

One night recently, Nick came into the kitchen and urged me outside to show me the sunset. It was a beautiful pink sky, shot with purple and orange. He had noticed it from his bedroom window. I savored that moment, and not just because the sunset was beautiful. Over the years, as we have practiced savoring, Nick's brain is now wired to notice and savor these moments of good. His positive bank account is well stocked. That's what I savored.

Whenever I feel like we're having a good moment, I've formed the habit of saying "Life's pretty good." It's a verbal cue for savoring that I use to highlight and extend the moment for all of us. Recently, I was bouncing on the trampoline in the backyard with Emily. She suggested we lie on the trampoline and do some cloud watching. As we told each other what we were seeing in the clouds, she spontaneously said, "Life's pretty good." My heart soared as high as the clouds we were looking at because both of my children are learning how to direct their attention toward positive experiences of their own accord. Mission accomplished.

Gratitude: The Super Strength Builder

You can probably see how savoring, by sharpening our powers of positive attention, gives rise to gratitude. As a positive psychologist, I have my pick of positive emotions to study, and I like them all. But after love, gratitude is my favorite for the huge wallop (now there's a scientific term) of positivity it brings.

A Two-fer and a Three-fer

Gratitude is about noticing and actively appreciating the good things in your life. It's a mash-up of attention and savoring—with an extra kick of action. Just noticing a good thing (*"Oh, there's steak for dinner"*) isn't gratitude. Noticing and savoring (*"Oh, there's steak for dinner and it smells great!"*) is the next level—the "two-fer" aspect of gratitude. But the extra kick—the three-fer—comes when you add action to the equation: You actively appreciate that good thing by expressing your appreciation. In this case, it's by saying to whoever's cooking that steak, "Wow, thank you for making that steak. It smells great!"

Think for a moment about what really happened here. You've turned your attention toward a positive focus and provided yourself with the cascade of neurochemistry that good feelings bring. But by expressing gratitude, you've created an environment where someone else can notice that good moment, savor it, and experience that same flood of positive sensation, too. Three-fer exchanges like these give both parties a huge shot of positive feelings. It's this pro-social aspect of gratitude that makes it so powerful for your family.

We can bring kids and parents into the lab, sit them in front of a computer, and do attentional training with them of the kind I described earlier in this chapter, every day for a month. They'd dutifully press the little red button every time they saw the number combination that they're supposed to focus on. And they'd get better and better at building their attentional muscle.

But it's no fun. Much more fun is to start practicing gratitude. Not only are we improving attention skills and boosting our positive emotions, but we're also spreading that improvement to others.

Gratitude can take the form of words—"thank you" being the most obvious and always effective—but you can be more elaborate in commenting on the particular strength a person is showing, be it cooking skills, thoughtfulness, creativity, or any of the 118 strengths developed by psychologists and listed on my website (www.strengthswitch .com). SBP itself is a way of raising your child in a manner that shows appreciation and gratitude for who she is and helps her appreciate the strengths in others, too.

Or your appreciation can take the form of an action: appreciating that a restaurant server has to clear hundreds of plates a day and as a family stacking up the plates on the restaurant table to help her clear them, bringing a coworker a cup of coffee because you notice he's having a super-busy day, saying hi to the new kid at school who's looking a bit forlorn, writing a thank-you note to an advisor for writing a college recommendation letter. These are little actions of gratitude that say "I see and appreciate you."

Practicing gratitude as you go about your daily life models appreciation in action for your child. Praising your child is a beautiful way to show him exactly how wonderful it feels to receive expressions of gratitude. We'll talk about the most effective way to praise in Chapter 8.

Gratitude is other-directed: We notice something, it stirs us, and we feel compelled to communicate that sensation to another—whether to a person, a spiritual entity, or the universe. When we feel appreciation without communicating it, we might call that awe or wonder. In a paper I wrote last year with one of my PhD students, together with Dianne Vella-Brodrick, PhD, we called it gratefulness, as distinct from the social quality of gratitude.[22]

We all want to feel noticed and appreciated. When we're truly experiencing gratitude, I feel that we are expressing our higher selves. It costs so little, but it means so much to so many.

Gratitude Is Good for You

Learning how to direct my attention toward gratitude played an important part in my own healing journey from anxiety and depression by helping me reframe events, find and appreciate the lessons, and discover benefits I might not otherwise have discovered.

There's a bucket load of research showing the importance of gratitude for our psychological health. It's linked to a host of positive indicators such as self-discipline, emotional warmth, altruism, positive mood, self-esteem, and life satisfaction.[23] People who practice gratitude report feeling less bitterness and depression over time (I dare you to try to feel bitter and grateful in exactly the same moment).

Alex Wood, PhD, of the University of Stirling has found that people who feel grateful just prior to sleep fall into slumber more quickly, stay asleep longer, and report better sleep quality.[24] For my family and me, that study was life-changing.

I used to go to bed with so many things on my mind that I'd repeatedly turn on the light to write items on a to-do list that I kept next to the bed, afraid I'd forget them by the next day. Going to sleep took hours. That was the "pre-gratitude Lea."

But after reading about Dr. Wood's work, I started doing a simple exercise to change what researchers call "pre-sleep cognition"—that is, what we think about just before we fall asleep. Instead of thinking about all the things I was worried about, I swapped in a pre-sleep cognition of gratitude by thinking of the many things I'm grateful for:

the hug Emily gave me that day . . . the joke Nick told that made the whole family laugh . . . a good conversation with Matt . . . the roof over my head. Instead of "I haven't done enough," the mental message is "Things are OK. Life's pretty good."

Aiming and sustaining my attention on things I'm grateful for calms my body and mind. Often I fall asleep in the middle of making my mental gratitude list! It feels lovely. But underneath it all, I'm changing my brain, building a new attentional pattern of noticing the good things. The more I train my brain to see the good, the easier it becomes to see my kids' strengths and my own.

For years, I've done this exercise with Nick and Emily at bedtime, inviting them to tell me some things that made them feel thankful during the day. I want them to be able to cultivate this strength of gratitude because it makes them better as people, and it makes them feel better about themselves.

Gratitude also builds our relationships.[25] Psychologists classify gratitude as a pro-social emotion: it has positive effects on you and others. It's deeply programmed into us because there was a primal evolutionary reason for it. Fear makes us flee the predator. Anger makes us fight back. Curiosity makes us search out a new food source. Love makes us bond, mate, and procreate to perpetuate the species. Why did gratitude get built into our emotional highway?

Evolutionary psychologists suggest that gratitude created a bond be-tween individuals who weren't in the same family/genetic circle,[26] build-ing a stronger community by fostering cooperative behavior. Suppose you and I are hanging out on the savannah and you offer me some tasty food you've gathered. You didn't have to do that, since I'm not related to you. If I get a warm glow of gratitude and am compelled to share that with you, whether through words or actions[27]—known as reciprocity, or returning the favor in some way—this exchange fosters positive feelings in both of us, making us likely to share resources again. The more we do that, the stronger and more effective our community becomes.

Perhaps that's why every major discipline that has studied society and humanity has mentioned the importance of gratitude. Every major religion preaches its importance, whether toward God or one another. Sociologists say we cannot function as a society without the cooperative behavior cemented by gratitude. Roman philosopher Cicero called it "the parent" of all the virtues.

EXERCISE: | Gateways to Gratitude

We can train ourselves and our children to be more grateful, and the process is as enjoyable as the results. It's simply training the brain to detect patterns—something our brains are very good at. It's strength-based training, too, because gratitude is a character strength. And, as I've said, showing appreciation for our child's strengths models gratitude.

What Went Well (WWW)

As I mentioned earlier, every night when Nick and Emily are tucked into bed, just before they go to sleep, I invite them to tell me three things that made them feel thankful that day. This is referred to as the "What Went Well" (WWW) technique. It's a popular exercise in many families:

> My nine-year-old daughter has core strengths of humility, bravery, forgiveness, fairness, gratitude, and perseverance. She often clashes with her older sisters, frequently ending up the odd one out and feeling overly sensitive about things. We talked about gratitude and I introduced her to WWW and suggested she do it every day so she could use this strength more often. We decided that she would lead WWW each day at family mealtimes. It's been four months, and she still asks to do WWW. She's much happier at school and her teacher is proud of how she's stepping up to help the younger kids.

> Jamie, age nine, has ADHD. He does WWW with me each night before bed. It exercises his strength of gratitude. It also allows me to reflect on his day with him and pull out which strengths he or others have used to help work through a situation. He asks me about my day, too. Of all three of my children, he is the one who loves this activity and asks to do it.

Thankful Thursdays

Each Thursday at our house we make time to talk about things we feel thankful for, from big items like completing assignments, winning awards, and getting support from others to everyday events like eating a meal together, having a laugh in the car, and enjoying good weather.

If you're short on ideas for what to say on Thankful Thursday, the website 1000 Awesome Things is really helpful[28] for reminding you of all the small things that put a smile on your face—like finding the chocolate with the particular filling you wanted in the chocolate box. I love looking at this site for a quick emotional pick-me-up.

Gratitude Jar/Graffiti Board

Set out an empty jar and ask your family to put in notes about the things they feel grateful for. Once the jar is full, you can thank your family by taking them to a café for a treat and tipping out all the notes to re-read and re-live the good times. This is a great exercise in reminiscent savoring. Or try a gratitude graffiti board: a whiteboard you can place in your kitchen or family room for all family members to write or draw the things they feel grateful for. You can also do this using a corkboard and sticky notes.

Gratitude Stickies and Letters

Speaking of sticky notes, in my house I use them as "gratitude surprises." When I feel thankful for something that Matt, Nick, or Emily have done or simply thankful for who they are, I leave a note for them on their pillow (the stickies don't really stick to the pillows, but I bend them a bit so they'll stay—and my family has learned to be on the lookout for them). In a lovely example of the value of role modeling, Emily recently left a gratitude sticky note on my pillow thanking me for helping her bake cookies, complete with a drawing of a cookie.

A longer form of the sticky note is the gratitude letter. You can encourage your children to write a thank-you letter to someone who has made a difference in her life. It might be a relative, friend, mentor, teacher, or someone else she knows. Ask her to really think about the unique thing that person did for her and to write about that specifically. Encourage your child to personally deliver the letter and read it to the other person (or read it on the phone or over Skype if the person lives far away).

Numerous studies have confirmed the power of the gratitude letter for increasing life satisfaction and positive feelings, including with teens and younger kids. Martin Seligman did the first such study; then Jeffrey Froh, PhD, repeated it with teenagers.[29] You will find guidance on how to write a gratitude letter from the Greater Good Science Center, University of California at Berkeley, in the Appendix.

For kids writing a thank-you letter, it's fine to keep it simple, specific, and heartfelt. It might start with saying thank you for whatever it was. Then with how the child felt when receiving the good thing from that person. Then something specific about why that thing was so wonderful. And ending with thank you again, with the child's signature.

Gratitude Journal

Think of a gratitude journal as an extended version of a gratitude letter but written for your eyes only, to put your attention on the things you are grateful for in your life. The Greater Good Center has tips to show you how to make the process both easier (don't worry, it's not about writing copious entries or taking lots of time—in fact, just the opposite) and maximally effective. And if words aren't your first choice for expression, get creative, as this teenager did:

> I did a photo gratitude journal for an art project at school. It started out just as a project, but I've kept it going for over a year now. It's made me realize what an amazing life I have.

Gratitude Walk

Go for a walk around your neighborhood with your kids and together point out the things you feel grateful for in the area where you live. The park where you picnic, jog, or play that is also home to songbirds, gardens, and beautiful trees; the stop for the bus that takes the family to work or school each day; the bakery that sells tasty cakes; the market with the friendly grocer; the lovely flowers in a neighbor's garden; your local school or church—all can trigger feelings of gratitude and thankfulness. Try this with your older children as a fifteen-minute study break to get the attention-sharpening benefits of moderate aerobic exercise[30] *and* to train their brain for gratitude. I also do this with Nick and Emily when we travel so we can remember the great places we've visited on our vacations.

Acts of Gratitude

We've talked about how gratitude can be actions as well as words of thanks. Talk with your children about things they can do to show appreciation for others:

> *Jess gets energized by acts of kindness, and it is something that we value as a family. I want the kids to know that doing kindness for others gives them a big boost in their own well-being. Jess decided she wanted to use her strengths of kindness and creativity more often. First we went to a café and bought a stranger a coffee (we sat back and watched—we used a kindness card from the Wake Up Project). Then Jess had the idea to do something more creative, also involving her brothers.*
>
> *We went to the flower shop and bought flowers. Jess wrapped her flowers individually and creatively and put them in a basket. Her brothers kept the flowers in one bunch. At first they left the flowers on neighbors' doorsteps, knocked, and ran away. But the impact wasn't there. We*

then went around the neighborhood and knocked on doors, giving residents flowers and saying, "These are to brighten up your day." The kids got such an amazing lift from people's comments and reactions.

When we got home, I wanted them to write down the comments so they could savor them a little longer and really let them sink in. One of the best was "My mother has died and I was sitting in my chair feeling so depressed—and you brought me these flowers to make me happy." Someone else said, "Just for nothing? For no money?!" Someone else said, "Thank you. Now I will go and do something kind for someone else!"

That night Jess told her friend (our neighbors) about the project. They got excited and wanted to do it. So the girls made cupcakes and delivered them to people in the neighborhood.

The kids still talk about this and the impact it had, and they want to do it again. I encourage everyday acts of kindness. Most weekends they walk to the bakery and I ask them to go in past Des, who's ninety-six years old. They ask him how he is and what cake he feels like today. Then they buy it for him and bring it to him. He tells them the same stories every time about his wife and the war, but they know it lifts his day.

Goofing Off Is Good. There. I Said It.

Savoring and gratitude are both forms of directed attention. But there's a second type of attention that I described early in this chapter. In contrast to the on-task focus of directed attention, free-form attention is what the brain defaults to when it's off-task, allowed to move in any direction it wants. It happens when the brain is in what scientists call the resting state. In the 1990s, neuropsychologists began to delve into free-form attention and found that it has many benefits. If you want to shift instantly into free-form attention, all you have to do is goof off.

Now I'm not talking about just any kind of goofing off. There's a constructive form of goofing off that is restorative to the brain and therefore important for our purposes of strength-based parenting. Let's call it "good goofing off."

Good goofing off has three characteristics:

1. The activity is not a passive activity—that is, your mind is not simply being "fed" stimulus.
2. The activity engages your mind in a way that simultaneously gives it free rein.
3. You're good enough at the activity that you don't have to focus closely on the process or the techniques.

This may sound complicated, but in fact good goofing off is the easiest, most fun state to slip into. We love going there. It happens when we're reading, doing artwork or crafts, cooking a recipe we know well, shooting baskets or pursuing other noncompetitive athletics, doing puzzles, tinkering enjoyably with something or building something, doing free-association writing, or simply daydreaming.

It's not making a recipe you've never made before for a houseful of dinner guests coming that night, zoning out in front of the TV or on the Internet, doing chores (unless you enjoy them), playing competitive sports or pursuing intense athletic training, or anything else that doesn't let your mind wander somewhere above the task while you're ably performing it. Sometimes activities begin by requiring focused attention and then become good goof-off activities as we get proficient at them.

What's Really Happening When We Goof Off, and Why Is It Good for Us?

As I said at the start of this chapter, we toggle between directed attention and free-form attention all day long. In fact, good goofing off acts as a bridge between directed attention, where we're laser focused on something specific, and mindfulness, where we actively notice the thoughts that arise during free-form attention—something we'll discuss in the next chapter.

Research now shows that when we're in this so-called resting state, our brain is still highly active.[31] Functional magnetic resonance imaging depicting the brain in a resting state reveals multiple brain regions lighting up, indicating activity. That's why I prefer to think of free-form attention not as a resting state, but as "deliberate rest." Although it might seem counterintuitive, deliberate rest plays an important role in building our powers of attention.

For one thing, deliberate rest refreshes and restores our capacity for directed attention, so when we shift back into directed attention, we can pay closer attention to whatever is happening. Downtime in the form of exercise may even help us aim our attention faster. It turns out there's a tiny lag time—about three hundred milliseconds— between when an event happens (your e-mail pings, your cat meows, or your child calls to you) and when you register that event in your brain, as seen by an electrical change in the brain. This measurement is called Event Related Potential (ERP). Essentially, it's our brain updating itself in response to reality. We're always a tiny bit behind. Scientists have found that ERP improves immediately after people engage in moderate aerobic exercise.[32] Perhaps evolution rewarded those whose brains got sharper at the same time that their bodies got fitter. What I do know is that when a teenager has three hours of homework but can only really sustain attention for about twenty minutes at a time, he's going to need breaks to help him attend to his work. Spending fifteen minutes every hour or so doing some physical activity he enjoys doesn't look like a time waster to me.

For another, our brain uses deliberate rest to consolidate learning and free up resources for new learning (including new strength development). Has your computer ever slowed down or crashed because you're running too many applications at once? The brain gets overloaded, too. So much information gets taken in through directed attention that it can result in "cerebral congestion"[33] as input competes for our neural connections. Our brains need downtime to process and sort through the information.

Researchers did an interesting study in which they tested electrical patterns in rats' brains while the rats explored a maze. Then they gave the rats some downtime and continued the electrical testing on their brains. The researchers observed that even while the rats were resting, the electrical patterns that were zipping around their brains were the same as while they were running the maze. The researchers concluded that what they were seeing was memory consolidation[34] (yep, goofing off even has benefits for rats).

Stepping up from rats in mazes, in another study on downtime processing, a group of university students in Amsterdam was given data on the size, mileage, maneuverability, and other features of a series of cars. Each student's task was to select the best car, based on analysis of this data. Half were given four minutes to review the specifications and make a decision in a focused way. The other half were given a little anagram puzzle to do for four minutes instead. It turned out that the students who were, in a sense, distracted from analysis of the specifications by doing the puzzle were more likely to choose the best car, compared to the students who had actively focused on the data. Their brains processed the information more effectively when they were goofing off. Once again, it seems there's something to be said for stepping away from the problem.[35]

We've all had the experience of having a sudden insight into a problem after we've literally gotten away from it for a while—in the shower, during a walk, after a workout, or while working on a hobby. Somehow, a solution filters up from our brain without our conscious effort. Downtime gives us the mental space that allows the brain to dive into itself and uncover what it knows.

Finally, our ability to toggle between directed attention and free-form attention improves with practice, making us maximally effective. We need to be able to snap to attention when necessary and then downshift to deliberate rest mode whenever we can, to maximize mental alertness, process what we've learned, and bring forward that knowledge to apply to the next attentive time.

These ideas are supported in the findings from a series of studies performed by Columbia University researchers, who partnered with schools to trial an unstructured play-based curriculum that involved activities such as computer games that progressively set tasks to build the child's working memory, noncomputerized games, aerobics, martial arts, yoga, and mindfulness for students ranging from four to thirteen years.[36] The researchers wanted to see what would happen if schools gave students a break from intense learning by injecting a play-based (i.e., downtime) curriculum. In a classic case of "less is more," the students showed significant improvements in attentional skills and cognitive functioning after the play curriculum, compared to having a full day of traditional academic classes. Attention is built through rest and play.[37]

Strength-Based Goofing Off

For all of these reasons, when parents seek my advice about what activities their child should be doing, they're often surprised when I pare down their proposed list and prescribe free time during the week for good goofing off.[38] It's not that kids aren't paying attention during this time, it's that their attention has shifted within. Important things are going on in there. We know that even adults can only pay attention for about twenty minutes at a time before getting less effective. We know that when your daughter has finished her math homework and is taking time between assignments to make a smoothie or read a chapter in a book, or when your son comes home after school and blows off steam by shooting baskets in the backyard for an hour before starting his homework, their brains are still processing information very effectively. They're sorting through what they've taken in, attaching emotional meaning to it, cementing it in memory, integrating it into their core selves. It's all part of building their identity, about learning who they are apart from what they do.[39]

Being a smart strength-based parent means holding firm against the pressure to constantly schedule your kids so they look busy on the outside. Rest assured (pun intended) they're always busy, even when they don't look it. Let your child press the pause button so she can reboot her attentional resources and come back strong to continue building her strengths. Fearlessly feature downtime in your kids' schedules. Encourage them to see good goofing off as an important part of becoming who they are:

> *My daughter Jasmine's core strength is appreciation of beauty and excellence. She now sees that taking the time to enjoy what she sees around her—and taking photos of sunsets, flowers, and animals—isn't "weird" or wasting time. She really enjoys doing this and has done a lot more photography in the last year, including enrolling in an elective subject at school.*

What should kids do during good goofing off? Anything that allows them to have softly focused inward attention. The key is that it's not about performance; they should feel relaxed while doing it. And just in case they ask: No, good goofing off is not texting or talking on the phone, which pulls us into the external world (one study found reduced empathic responses after just asking study participants—teens and young adults—to describe and draw an image of their cell phone!).[40]

EXERCISE: | Downtime Space

One way to assist strength-based goofing off is to create time in your child's routine and an actual physical space in the home. You don't need a separate room or a lot of space to create a downtime spot for your child. You just need an area a child can call his own. It might include a sturdy table and chair bought at a thrift shop, some shelves or cubbies to hold art supplies, games, and books, and maybe a big plastic drop cloth you can lay out so your kids can make a mess if they want to. Or maybe it's a reading nook with a lamp, beanbag chair, or comfy floor cushions. What you put in the space might depend on your child's strengths. Is it quiet? Or equipped with a device for playing music? Is it where you keep the family pet hamster or fish? Do musical instruments wait there? For a child with tech interests, what about a computer area where the child can make recordings or videos? More than physical space, toys, or tech, though, is the importance of providing mental space where your child's mind can roam free.

CHAPTER 6

Mindfulness

You might wonder, after reading the previous chapter, whether I'm suggesting that if we just focus on happy times and positive thoughts, life will be smooth sailing. But you and I know that while life includes scenic stretches of gentle waves that are fun to splash in, there are also storms that are no fun at all.

Savoring and gratitude help us and our children recognize the good times, intensify the juiciness of the moment, and do the strength building that happens when life is good. They're useful in difficult times, too, since developing our "positive attention muscle" helps us intentionally target and sustain focus on nuggets of the positive in the midst of challenge.

In downtime, which I also discussed in Chapter 5, our attention is not targeted but wanders freely, without our conscious control. This inward attention helps our brains integrate our experiences so we can summon what we've learned for future use. More important for our kids, research shows that it's the mental state in which we begin to process events and emotions, form memories, and develop our sense of who we are. You might say we're building wisdom without realizing it.

But it turns out that in the rough-and-tumble of daily life, we need more than the attentional practices I've outlined in Chapter 5 to keep us on an even keel.

In this chapter, we explore another kind of inward attention called mindfulness.[1] Unlike downtime, which is free-form and unfocused, mindfulness is an active, focused introspection that puts us in touch with our thoughts and feelings as they arise in response to life, allowing us to understand, work with, and direct them. As such, mindfulness holds tremendous power for strength-based parenting and living.

A Brief Definition of Mindfulness

Mindfulness can conjure up images of a yogi sitting in the lotus position "om-ming," but the way modern scientists and psychologists work with mindfulness is as a structured process of focusing the mind using three simple steps:

1. Focus your attention on a particular thing (for example, your own breathing, or the present moment).
2. Notice when your attention has wandered away.
3. Bring your attention back.

When you do this, you tune in to what's happening in your mind in real time, in the flow of life. This gives you awareness of your thoughts and feelings as they happen.

Most people who try mindfulness, especially at first, find that their mind jumps from thought to thought, feeling to feeling. That's OK.

Thinking fast is what minds do. Mindfulness helps your mind slow down a bit. When this happens, you gain the mental space to actually get some control over your thoughts and feelings. It helps you become aware that your thoughts are separate from you. It allows you to gently grab a thought and turn it this way and that, select another to examine, and so on. With practice, you can actually choose which thoughts and feelings to pay attention to and act on—including choosing to have more strength-based thoughts.

When I teach mindfulness, I use the metaphor of a helium balloon on a string. When you're mindful, the balloon is positioned directly above your head—fully present to your thoughts, feelings, and sensations in the moment. However, like your thoughts, the balloon slowly drifts away. When that happens, you'll feel a tug on the string. This lets you know your thoughts have wandered from the present moment (maybe you were thinking about a work problem or what you'll have for dinner). The tug reminds you to gently pull the balloon back over your head again, returning your awareness to the present moment.

When I started practicing mindfulness, I expressed frustration to my yoga teacher about how much my mind wandered. She gave me some wise and reassuring advice. She said that it doesn't matter how often the balloon drifts away. What matters is how much better you get at pulling it back.

"Bare Attention": The Heart of Mindfulness

At the center of mindfulness is what yogis refer to as "bare attention"[2]—experiencing all thoughts, emotions, and physical sensations *without interpretation or judgment*. That last part is tricky. Believe me, I know.

While I was writing this book, Matt and I took the kids on a vacation. The first few days were great, but toward the end Emily and Nick got sick of each other. Arguments broke out. Things came to a head one night when we sat down to watch a family movie. Emily decided to lie full-length on the couch so no one else (i.e., Nick) could sit on it. So what did Nick do? He burped in her face—something he finds hilarious, being a teenage boy, and she finds disgusting.

And it worked! She jumped off the couch. He jumped on. She had a fit, screaming that he's the meanest brother in the whole wide world. Meanwhile, he spread his body as wide as he could to occupy every inch of the couch.

I tried to tap into their positive personality traits, encouraging them both to use their perspective and see how much fun they'd been having together for most of the trip. No luck. Both were angry and neither wanted to admit that they do, generally, like each other's company. Next I tried their forgiveness capacity. Again, I struck out.

At that moment, bare attention became my friend. As the kids got louder and louder, I became aware of my physical sensations. I noticed my chest tightening and my breathing becoming shallow. I felt the urge to cover my ears and shove a handful of popcorn in my mouth. I tuned in to my thoughts and heard my inner critic—that negatively biased part of me—whispering weakness-focused taunts: *You're writing a parenting book and you can't even get your kids to stop fighting!* I became aware that I was holding up this unpleasant scene against a dazzling mental picture I'd created of the idyllic family vacation families are "supposed" to have.

All of this took just a few seconds. But thanks to bare attention, a little bubble of mindful space formed that gave me a small but blessed pause in which to think, not just react. I could tune in to the negative story I was telling myself about what was happening and see how that was only adding pressure to the situation. Although I knew I hadn't succeeded in getting my kids to use their strengths, in that mindful space I found the presence to summon *my* strengths:

- MY STRENGTHS OF REASON AND PERSPECTIVE: Kids fight sometimes. Fact of life. If a friend told me, "We went on vacation and the kids fought," would I think she was a bad parent? Ridiculous. Then a memory hit: *Remember when we all went to Disneyland and Nick and Emily were fighting because of jetlag? You didn't let it faze you. As the more experienced traveler, you used perseverance and kindness to help them handle their jetlag, and you showed confidence that it would pass and it did. You can use those strengths now.*
- MY STRENGTH OF HUMOR: My kids aren't allowed to fight because I'm writing a parenting book? Ba ha ha. That's hilarious!
- MY STRENGTHS OF COMPASSION AND KINDNESS: It makes me feel sad to speak to myself so critically. I'd feel bad if I heard a friend being so hard on herself. As a parent, I don't have to be perfect; I just have to be present.[3]

The mindfulness bubble saved me. I stayed calm. I didn't yell at the kids to shut them up so I could shut up the critic inside. I didn't shove the popcorn into my mouth for self-soothing. I weathered it with them, working on de-escalating things until they could become mindful enough of their strengths to get themselves under control. I said things like, "I know it's frustrating, but let's just take a minute and think about this . . . We've all been in each other's faces for too long. How about we go and do something else? . . . I know you're fighting right now, but actually, the rest of the time you've had a pretty good time together. Emily, I know you're telling Nick he's the meanest brother in the world. But most of the time you're pretty good friends, you know? Half an hour ago Nick was pushing you on the bike and the two of you were laughing your heads off."

With mindfulness, I can:

* *be present* to the situation and to the story I'm telling myself about it,
* *reframe* both,
* *choose* my actions, and
* *help my kids* learn to do the same

These are tremendous powers for us as parents.

The Proven Rewards of Mindfulness

Imagine someone gave you an app to download on your phone that beeped at you at random times for a week. Whenever it beeped, you'd complete a short survey that asked what you were paying attention to at that moment. Were you focused on what you were doing, or was your mind wandering into the past or toward something in the future?

This simple but telling study was actually conducted. It turned out that participants' minds were off-task 47 percent of the time. They might have been thinking about a conversation they had with someone, or about their plans for the weekend. This study found that our mood is best when we're present in the moment,[4] yet we're mindful only slightly more than half of the time.

Mindfulness has proven beneficial for children and teenagers. In a large-scale meta-review of mindfulness that I conducted in schools across the United States, Canada, the United Kingdom, Australia, and Taiwan, mindfulness was shown to boost optimism, resilience, self-acceptance, calmness, and general well-being as well as decrease stress, anger, and anxiety.[5] Students said things like, "If I meditate, I feel calm and feel like I don't have to argue with anybody" and "You are a lot more relaxed afterward, you get to clear your mind and it calms you down."

Teachers, too, reported feeling more settled and focused after mindfulness sessions.

Mindfulness also plays a role in raising positive emotions over time. Research by Richard Davidson, PhD, shows that people who undertake eight-week mindfulness courses have decreased activity in their right prefrontal cortex (the house of negative emotions) and increased activity in their left prefrontal cortex (the house of positive emotions).[6]

Can simply becoming aware of our thoughts be so powerful? Yes. Just thinking about an activity changes the brain. In one study, when people were asked to mentally rehearse playing a five-finger piano piece for one week, the brain area responsible for finger movement expanded—just from *thinking* about playing the piano.[7]

Mindful Parent, Mindful Child

Your mindfulness spills over onto your children. In one of my studies, I tested parents for their degree of mindfulness and then tested their children for their levels of mindfulness and stress. The results were staggeringly clear: the more mindful the parent, the more mindful the child—and the more mindful the child, the less stressed the child.[8] Parent mindfulness sets up a successful coping loop in kids. This is something they can take with them wherever they go.

As a mindful parent, you can pass three benefits to your children:

1. You'll do a better job of parenting your child in the moment.

2. You'll be modeling an effective way to handle interpersonal conflict and other stressors.
3. You can coach your child in becoming more mindful.

Mindful parents can help kids become less reactive. When the child is facing challenges or is caught up in negative emotions, parents can ask questions to identify the negative-bias thoughts the child may be having, such as, "What's the story you're telling yourself right now?" And, "How about we just take a pause? What are you thinking? Is that a helpful thought? Is it an accurate thought?"

So You're Mindful. Now What?

Most mindfulness experts use mindfulness to help people detach from negative thoughts and anxiety. But what do you replace these thoughts with? How do you move into positive action?

I propose using mindfulness to replace negative thoughts with strength-based thinking and work toward good outcomes in negative situations. You can teach your kids to do the same, whether it's dealing with a tough homework assignment, a tough teacher, a problem with a friend, or a transgression with consequences that must be faced.

Bringing strengths into my mindful moment on vacation gave me a path forward when Nick and Emily were fighting. I could stay calm and persist in appealing to their strengths of perspective, forgiveness, humor, and kindness to mend their rift.

I remember reading a mindfulness book in which the author likened our propensity for negative thinking to a radio tuned to a bad news channel 24/7. Why not use mindfulness to retune our frequency to the strengths channel—to ask, "What strengths can I draw on to handle this?" and help our children do the same? Remembering the mental-piano-playing study above, I wonder: What would happen if we asked our children to mentally rehearse their strengths every day?

How Mindfulness and Strength-Based Parenting Work Together

Every time your child practices the three steps of mindfulness I shared at the beginning of this chapter, she learns how to take more deliberate control over aiming and sustaining her inner awareness and redirecting it when it wanders. Over time, she'll improve at tuning out distractions and maintaining the sustained introspection that allows her to become aware of patterns in her thoughts and feelings.[9]

Mindfulness helps children understand the full range of their emotions, strengths, and weaknesses. This is highly useful in SBP because it prompts self-insight about unhelpful mental habits likely to block strengths development, such as procrastination, pessimism, and self-doubt. It gives your child a better chance of growing strengths through adversity.

Recently, Emily had a meltdown. When we talked afterward and I asked her how she was feeling, she said, "Mom, sometimes I get so angry that it feels like a bolt of lightning shoots through my body." The next time she seemed angry, I asked, "Do you have lightning inside you?" She paused and then said, "No, I'm not angry, just frustrated." In that mindful moment, she was able to label her feeling, differentiate between two types of negative emotions, and de-escalate herself from anger to frustration. Believe me when I say this was a happy ending for all of us!

Research shows that mindfulness, when practiced over time, fosters positive emotions,[10] which makes it easier to tap into strengths. For example, Emily tells me that when she's painting, she notices a "tingly feeling." Nick says he can tell when he's going to sink a shot in basketball because he gets tunnel vision. All distractions fade and the net seems bigger and wider. Mindfulness helps us to know how it feels when we're using our strengths and return to them more easily next time. As Ryan Niemiec, PsyD, so eloquently states, "Mindfulness opens the door of awareness to who we are, and character strengths are what is the behind the door."[11]

While mindfulness helps your children on their strength journey, it also helps you as a strength-based parent, getting you through those challenging moments when you're trying to hang on to your composure—as it did me during our vacation. It also helps in more enduring ways by allowing you to be emotionally present with your children, to really get to know who they are and what they're capable of. It helps you to open the door and see their strengths.

When you do, you'll be more likely to notice your child's strengths happening in the moment. You might detect a sudden shift in enthusiasm, a difference in your child's tone of voice, or a slight improvement in a skill—perhaps that's a growth strength to cultivate. You might see that your child is spending a lot of time on a certain interest—high use—a sign of a core strength.

Remember the mother from Chapter 2 who flipped the Strength Switch when she saw her daughter, who was "on the heavy side," grabbing a can of Coke after returning from the gym in a bad mood? Mindfulness of her emotions kept this mom from getting on her daughter's case by helping her notice her negativity bias (focusing on the can of Coke) and redirecting her attention to the fact that her daughter had gone to the gym three times that week. She describes how she used the positive attention tools we discussed in Chapter 5 to shift her attention to the positives. I would say she also used mindfulness to be aware of the negative story she was telling herself about her daughter and to create a new story about her daughter's maturity—a wonderful boost to her own state of mind and to her relationships, including with her daughter:

> *This week I've been paying attention to my positive emotions. I've been keeping a gratitude journal and focusing on savoring. I make sure I hug my daughter every day because it gives me positive emotions. I'm*

aware that my spirits have lifted and it seems easier to see the good things around me. I'm seeing the strengths of my husband and business partner more. I feel like I'm finding my old positive self again.

When my daughter came home from the gym last night, I thought about how much commitment she has been showing toward her goal, and I felt a burst of pride. For the first time, I actually noticed that she's lost weight and I saw that she's really starting to grow up and take responsibility for things. I didn't care about the Coke she was drinking, and I told her that I was proud of her. She gave me a hug and thanked me for supporting her. It was a complete turnaround.

Mindfulness helps you flick the Strength Switch. In Chapter 2, I told my story about Nick not putting his bike away for what seemed like the umpteenth time. When I sat in the car all those years ago and made the decision to turn on my Strength Switch, it was thanks to a moment of mindfulness. Just those few seconds:

- Allowed me to acknowledge my frustration but not get hooked by it.
- Gave me the mental space to see how I might be projecting my own weakness of messiness onto Nick, distorting my perceptions of him.
- Let me draw on my strength of perspective and think, *Hey, he's only eight. He's allowed to make mistakes. We're in this together. We worked for six months helping him get into the habit of putting away his shoes—now he does it all the time. This, too, will pass.*
- Helped me grab on to my strength of kindness: *He looked so crushed the last time I snapped at him about this. I want to find a more positive way to help him learn to do this. Let's try something different.* I was then able to use my self-control (which we'll look at in the next chapter) to override my impulse to tell him off and, instead, flip the Strength Switch.

Just as it doesn't matter how often you tug the helium balloon back to your present-moment thoughts when practicing mindfulness, it doesn't matter how many times you notice your Strength Switch is off. What matters is how much better you get at flicking it back on. And the better you get at mindfulness, the better you'll get at the Strength Switch.

Using Mindfulness to Help Your Child Work on Weaknesses

We all have things we're not good at. Mindfulness can help our kids deal with what comes hard for them. Suppose your child has problems with math. How would a mindful approach help? Here's how it might unfold:

1. BE PRESENT (BARE ATTENTION). Help your child tune in to the situation, his distressing emotions, and the story he's telling himself. How does he feel when he thinks about doing his math homework, opens the textbook, hits a problem he can't figure out (*frustration, anger, anxiety, helplessness*)? What's the story he's telling himself about it (*I'm stupid, I'll never get this, I'm just bad at this*)? You might ask, "What are the thoughts you're thinking when you sit down to do this? What voices are going on in your head?" Help him bring those thoughts to the surface and be patient if it takes him a while to articulate his negative thinking. Be there for him without judgment.

2. REFRAME. Help your child replace negative thoughts with strength-based ones by pointing out distortions in his thinking and strengths he could bring to bear. For example:

- "Do you think those thoughts are helpful? Do you think they're really true?"
- "Those are interesting thoughts, because I see you're actually *not* that way when you _____ [give examples of things the child does well and feels great about]."
- "Remember that math assignment where you did better than expected? That was amazing. What was different about your thinking that time?"
- "Tell me about a time when you got through your math homework without the negative feelings you've just shared with me. What were you doing or thinking then?"
- "I know math is hard. I used to feel that way about _____. You don't have the same ability for it as you do for _____. But you're making math harder because you're telling yourself these negative things. Let's see what else you could tell yourself that would help you get through it better."

Talk about strengths the child has that he could bring to the situation and that would change his self-talk. For example: *"Math isn't my ability, but I know I'm persistent. I can be goal focused. I'm organized. I can stick to the task. I'm curious and I can learn new things. I can ask for help or tutoring. I know I'll feel good when I master this. There are lots of other things I am good at, like English class, baseball, making videos, taking cars apart."*

3. CHOOSE ACTIONS. With SBP, you can get creative with your child about how to draw on his strengths to better handle the situation. For example, suggest that your child apply thinking from a strength angle:

* "English is a strong subject for you and you love it. Let's look at some of the ways you think when you're working on an English assignment. Let's do your English homework tonight and I'll set your phone to beep every ten minutes over the next hour. Each time it beeps, stop and check in with how you were feeling and what thoughts were going through your head. Write down your thoughts and feelings on this notepad beside you. At the end of the hour, review your notes. List your feelings and thoughts in one column and add a second column where you rate whether the thoughts and feelings were helpful or harmful to your homework."

The next night, take things a step further and try this:

* "Let's try an experiment. For the next thirty minutes, do your math the way you normally do. We'll set the phone to beep at you every ten minutes so you can record your thoughts and feelings. Then we'll rate them as helpful or harmful."
* "For the next thirty minutes after that, do your math, but try to substitute the more helpful thoughts and feelings that you have when you do your English homework. When the beeper goes off, stop and notice what you were thinking and feeling. Then look at your list from when you did your English homework and choose a more helpful thought to substitute."

Try other experiments keyed to the child's strengths:

* Agree to set a timer to work for X amount of time, or a goal to complete X number of problems. Then take a

fifteen-minute break to do some free-form mind activity your child really loves. Or let the child set a longer-term goal to enjoy an agreed-upon special treat if he gets a certain score on a test or exam (strength of goal setting).

- Do math homework first (when your child is feeling fresh and most able to draw on his strength of persistence).
- Do math homework after doing something the child loves, such as watching funny videos (strength of humor), playing sports (strength of athleticism), getting home from a club or group activity (strengths of sociability, leadership).
- Let the child organize how he'll do his math homework (strength of organization).
- Investigate having the child do math homework with a friend who's better at it and can explain the concepts (working from social strength—but make sure your child is really doing his own homework!).
- Help the child gain perspective or play to his strength of perspective: *I don't have to get the same grades in math that I get in English.* Or: *I don't need A's in math, but I do need a grade of ___ so my grade point average stays in range for the colleges I want to apply to.* Or: *I don't need math for the work I want to do after I graduate, but I have to do it now, and do well enough to get into the school I need for my job training.* Or: *I'll do my best, but not being good at math isn't the end of the world.*
- Help him have compassion for himself: "This is hard. Just stick it out for ten minutes, and then you can have a break and a snack. I'm proud of you for sticking this out. You've got persistence and you're gaining clarity about why this challenges you and how your negative thinking is making things worse. This is not as easy for you as other things, but you can get through this."

Initially, you'll need to walk your children through each step to help them name their feelings and suggest ideas for reframing their thinking and choosing actions from a strength perspective. You may have to stay close at first, sitting with the child as a comforting presence or checking in to see how things are going as your child's helium balloon keeps needing to be tugged back from wandering to the "old" ways of negativity. You'll need to ask, "What strength do you have that can help you here?" But as children get clearer about their strengths and learn how to tug on that balloon string themselves, they'll gradually internalize the mindfulness process, and you'll need to coach them only if they feel stuck.

Mindfulness and the Path to Resilience and Growth

I'm often asked whether being strength based means we can never have negative emotions or feel down when bad things are happening. Of course not. Being strength based doesn't mean we ignore bad times or falsely keep things positive for our children. We need to be real. And mindfulness is a great way to help your child build resilience.[12]

Highly resilient people experience negative feelings but still hold on to positive feelings. Resilience is strongest when, during great adversity, we can hold negative and positive emotions in tandem and make subtle distinctions between each emotion—something psychologists call emotional complexity.[13]

No matter how good a parent you are, your kids will face problems, have weaknesses, and be confronted with challenges. Your child can build resilience in the face of challenge only if she doesn't shrink away from it. Mindfulness wedded to strengths helps your child meet challenges because she knows she can sit with all of her feelings in the present moment, including discomfort, and call on her strengths to bounce back.

We can set this example for our children and assist them in finding these resources in themselves. John Gottman, PhD, calls this emotional coaching.[14] Children growing up with parents who are emotional coaches[15] learn that all emotions are acceptable. Psychologists and neuroscientists have found that these children have a calmer central nervous system, a lower resting heart rate, and a healthier emotional brain circuitry.[16] These are the kids who stay cool under pressure! They've learned how to capitalize on their positive emotions and feel negative emotions without letting them get the better of them.

I have a friend whose son is a gifted athlete specializing in the high jump. When he was seventeen, he landed a jump awkwardly and suffered a severe back injury. It took a full year for him to recover. Initially, he became depressed. A major part of his identity had been taken away. My friend knew her son had strengths such as persistence, motivation, focus, and sociability. Some of those were what had made him an excellent high jumper. She set about finding an outlet for those strengths.

Part of the physical therapy involved swimming, so my friend started swimming with her son every day. She used the commuting time to and from the pool and doctor visits to see and point out strengths in her son. She saw him apply his persistence, motivation, and focus to his rehab exercises. She also saw a level of patience and compassion emerge in her son that she hadn't seen before.

They entered an ocean swim event together that was to take place in nine months' time, and the boy decided to use his sociability, persistence, and newfound compassion to raise money for a charity supporting people with depression. He used the next nine months to prepare for the swim, recover from his injury, and develop new strengths. His depression lifted. He was motivated and energized by his quest, and he raised quite a lot of money. What could have been a very traumatic time turned into a mother-son bonding experience.

Through being mindful of her son's existing and emerging strengths, and helping him see them as well, my friend helped her teenager move through a challenge and arrive at a good place. Three years later, they still enter this annual ocean swim together.

Everyday issues like problems at school and with peers can create a lot of emotional pain for children, but these can be addressed productively through emotional coaching based on mindfulness and strengths. Here's how a fourth grader's mindful expression of emotion to a sensitive teacher led to a strength-based breakthrough at school:

During a conversation with Lauren, she shared her sadness about being excluded from her friendship group. I asked her to describe a time when she was doing what she loved and feeling her best. It soon became apparent to me that kindness might be a strength for her. I asked her what her kindness strength looked like. When she described her acts of kindness, I wondered how her friends might perceive them. With her permission, we met with a group of her friends and explored lots of the students' strengths. This is common practice at our school, so it was seen as just part of everyday learning. Her friends explained Lauren's kindness intruded at times on others' space and conversations. They enjoyed her company but respectfully explained that it could be a bit much! We chatted about how our strength can be overused. Later I asked Lauren how she thought the conversation with her friends had gone. She said how much she valued their honesty and kindness, so we decided to focus on being honest and kind. Before long, Lauren was being included in the group again. Knowledge of strengths and an associated shared language enabled this very authentic appreciation of others and of their differences.

We can also use mindfulness and strengths to take better care of ourselves as parents:

Reflecting on ten years as a step-parent, I find I used many strengths to nurture our sons and to maintain my personal well-being. It wasn't always an easy journey, particularly at the beginning. Observing, listening, questioning, using intuition, and managing emotions and perceptions have all been vital skills. I also learned to use my social intelligence to be more detached yet loving and light-hearted.

Five years ago, I started volunteering at a local hospital, as I wanted to help people and recognized that I needed a creative outlet. I remember my husband saying that I go to the hospital and talk to strangers when I could spend more energy interacting with our sons. At that time I found our sons preferred to interact with their father. It enhanced my well-being to interact with the patients and hospital staff who looked me in the eye, who engaged with me and talked to me. It also put me in touch with my gratitude that my family and I enjoyed good health. Happily, having my "bucket filled" gave me the emotional reserves I needed to interact more effectively at home. It is thrilling to see two flourishing young men and to enjoy our friendly and loving relationships today.

If you've grown up believing emotions should be suppressed and avoided (and if you did, it's not your fault; we generally learn how to handle emotions from our parents),[17] now's your chance to change that belief while helping your kids.

Emotional coaching is a skill you can learn quickly.[18] Sophie Havighurst, PhD, a colleague of mine at the University of Melbourne, has found that moms and dads of toddlers, preschoolers, children, and teens have done just that. After attending the "Tuning into Kids" program developed by Dr. Gottman—in which parents attended six weekly two-hour sessions at a local community center, with sessions involving group discussion and brainstorming, small group exercises, video examples, group leader demonstrations, and small group role-plays—parents in her studies were more encouraging of their children's emotional expression, increased their use of emotion labels, and were more skilled at discussing causes and consequences of emotions with their children. This had positive effects for both the parents and children.

One simple strategy is to get into the habit of regularly asking your child how he feels, using the strength-based mindfulness techniques we explored earlier. It's a great way to get feelings on the table and to help your child decide what to do about them by calling on his strengths. You're helping your child in the moment *and* helping him develop the emotional complexity he needs to grow his strengths in good times and bad. You can start tuning very young children in to feelings with games like guessing emotions in print ads or books, or with the TV on mute.

You may be surprised by how receptive your kids are to mindfulness. It means you're tuning in to them—and that makes them feel good!

In our house we try to practice mindfulness throughout the day using our breath to pay attention to our surroundings and calm our bodies. My hope is that the language and experience will become part of our family culture. We decided this summer to make a list of things that make us happy. Every night as we say good night, we see if we can add one or two new things to our list that may have happened during the day.

Last night, as my daughter Gracie (who is almost five) and I were snuggling and talking about the happy moments in our day, she said, "You know what makes me the most happy, Mommy? When we just lie on the grass together and stare at the clouds and practice listening for the birds. That's mindfulness, right, Mommy? That's my most happy thing."

Mindful moments can happen in even the unlikeliest of circumstances. A school once asked me to introduce mindfulness to a group of rowdy eighth-grade boys. The school had specifically targeted the need for these boys, who were in a remedial group, to be able to pay more attention to their schoolwork, and although they'd tried mindfulness before, it hadn't proved successful.

I was nervous since I was being asked to perform a task that had already failed once, but I went in with my strengths antenna up. What I saw was a room full of strengths. Vigor, humor, zest, energy, team spirit, playfulness, physical coordination, and athleticism were there in abundance. The group dynamic was all about competition and playfulness. Every second sentence was something to do with sports or genitals . . . but that latter part isn't relevant to my story.

I saw immediately that sitting still wouldn't work, so I decided to introduce mindfulness through their strengths by getting them to play mindful Frisbee.

The boys paired up and we went into the schoolyard. The only rule I set was that the boys had to do this exercise in silence. I started by getting them to pay attention to their hands and focus on the different ways the Frisbee felt in their hand when they threw it compared to when they caught it.

Next, I asked the boys to pay attention to the differences in the sounds made by the Frisbee depending on how fast, hard, and high it had been thrown. Our senses play a key role in the development of mindfulness because sensory input happens in the here and now. You cannot feel and hear after the fact.

After a few sessions of mindful Frisbee, the boys had experienced mindfulness: They could aim their attention at the sensations of the sound and feel of the Frisbee and block out distractions. Then we worked on developing awareness of the thoughts that ran through their heads when they made a good throw or catch versus a bad throw or catch. We talked about the harmful thoughts that occur when they missed a catch (*I'm hopeless; I'm a loser; I failed; I'm worthless; How embarrassing*) and how these thoughts also occur when they're learning new things in class. We made a list of strength-based thoughts and actions they could use to replace their negative thinking.

We were able to make the list because the boys had done their character strengths survey with me in class a few weeks earlier. After identifying his strengths and discussing them in class, each boy then did an assignment on how he had used his strengths to succeed at something in his life. Interestingly, most of the stories came from outside of school. I had to find a way to show these boys that their strengths could also help them with their academic learning. In class, we turned one wall into a Strengths Wall, where we listed all twenty-four VIA character strengths. Each student cut out a small photo of his head and stuck it onto a three-inch outline of his body that he made (you should have seen the bulging muscles and tattoos!). Whenever a classmate spotted a student using a strength, he had permission to leave his seat and go to the wall to place the mini-figure of that student on the character strength he was using. Soon the boys began to internalize their strengths.

Over the course of the program, I increased the physical stillness aspect of mindfulness, but we never let go of the movement aspects. We always stayed connected to their physical strengths. By the eighth session, the boys could sit in stillness, doing diaphragmatic breathing with their hands on their stomachs for fifteen minutes.

Their teacher was incredulous. She reported that the boys were more focused on their classwork and that when they got distracted, she simply stopped the class and did a two-minute breathing exercise. Through mindfulness they developed sharper focus and got better at tuning out distractions. Their strength-based thinking, born of their mindful awareness, helped them become a lot more optimistic about school and their academic future.

We ended our time together by sitting in a large circle out in the schoolyard with the Frisbee. I asked the boys to throw the Frisbee to someone in the circle and call out the name of a strength they saw in that person as the Frisbee flew toward him. This was how the game went until every boy had been thrown the Frisbee. It was an incredibly moving ending to my time with these boys, who all stood taller and prouder at the end of our eight weeks together.

Mindfulness and Children with Different Needs

As a psychologist who works a lot with young people, I've developed an interest in the effects that mindful parenting can have on children with autism spectrum disorder (ASD), attention deficit/hyperactivity disorder (ADHD), and oppositional defiant disorder (ODD). These young people face unique challenges, and their issues result in their frequently feeling intensely frustrated, which leads to anxiety, anger, aggression, and other challenging behaviors (e.g., kicking, biting, and hitting).[19] I often see these dynamics play out in the classroom when I'm consulting to schools, and whenever I see these students struggling, it stirs immense compassion in me.

Mindfulness has proven a much-needed balm for these children and their parents. In a study of the effects of mindful parenting for families of adolescents with ADHD, ODD, and ASD[20] over the course of eight sessions of mindfulness training for adolescents and eight sessions of mindfulness training for their parents, teenagers showed improvements in attention and reductions in aggressive behavior.

In a paper I published on this topic with my colleagues Rebekah Keenan-Mount and Nikki Albrecht, we found that mindfulness-based interventions helped not only children with spectrum disorders but also their parents.[21] When parents are shown how to pay attention to their child and their parenting intentionally—in the here and now, without judgment—it stops them from overreacting in automatic, negative ways to their child's behavior. The majority of parents in the research studies reported positive effects in their overall health and well-being, including feeling happier in their parenting role. By doing daily meditation practice, parents learned how to take care of themselves and bring calm into their family.

A common pattern in the studies we reviewed indicated that the parents' increased mindfulness also helped reduce their child's problem behaviors, particularly when mindfulness was combined with an education program providing parents with techniques for responding more empathetically to their child's frustrations (you might say strength-based programs). Bottom line: Mindfulness improves human relationships, making them more open and less reactive. This is a win for any family, but it is an especially poignant one for families whose children face these kinds of challenges:

> *Our ten-year-old son Jude was diagnosed with mild to moderate autism at age four. The first thing I noticed when entering this "autism world" was that it was full of stress and anxiety. Parents were worried about their children. Many were desperately looking for miracle cures or therapies.*
>
> *I was anxious, too. I didn't know anything about autism at the time and was not at all familiar with the therapies. So I started to learn and to look into education options for Jude.*
>
> *I attended one class where I felt the children with autism were being conditioned to answer or behave a certain way; another where kids' every move was recorded as if they were lab rats. I didn't want those situations for my child.*
>
> *I took Jude out of school. I wanted to spend time being alone with him without the noise, the stress, the anxiety. Just the two of us. To breathe.*
>
> *Later I found a place for him at a peaceful, accepting school—a good base to start from, for him and for us as his parents. I would then slowly learn about autism, and specifically about Jude's autism.*
>
> *When I was a teenager, I read a book about Mahatma Gandhi and India's independence. I was impressed not just by the concept of nonviolence but by the notion that one could consciously make such choices*

about one's thoughts and actions. Years later, I became interested in Buddhism and then discovered mindfulness.

I find being a parent overwhelming at times. Paying mindful attention to my thoughts, accepting change and uncertainty, choosing to act rather than react—these are precious tools for my role as a mother and for my own personal development.

Jude, like any other child, changes, learns, and grows. And like any other child, he does it at his own pace. When I feel worried about him and his future, I take a deep breath, hold him, kiss him, and tell him that I love him. He then tells me he loves me, too, with his big, big smile. The little knot in my stomach then goes away, and I am ready to go on!

Exercises for a Mindful Mind-Set

Some of the exercises below focus on mindfulness in general; others focus on becoming mindful of strengths. Most important, don't turn these into chores for yourself or your kids. Susan Kaiser Greenland, an expert on child mindfulness, rightly states that compulsory mindfulness is an oxymoron.[22] The trick to incorporating mindfulness into strength-based parenting is to keep it fun and playful.

If you're new to mindfulness, start with this simple exercise to strengthen your own neural circuitry for bare attention:

1. Focus your attention on your present-moment thoughts, feelings, and sensations.
2. Notice when your attention has wandered away.
3. Bring your attention back.

Expect and accept your mind's jumpiness. When your mind wanders, just gently bring it back to present-moment thoughts, feelings, and sensations.

EXERCISE: | Building Mindful Moments into Daily Life

There are lots of ways to build mindfulness into your family routine.

- MINDFUL SENSATIONS. Try mindful eating. Give your child something she likes to eat and ask her to eat it slowly, paying attention to the texture and shape of the food on her tongue. A friend tried this with her three-year-old using white chocolate. A few weeks later at the store, she was trying to decide between buying milk chocolate, dark chocolate, or white chocolate, and asked her son which one he thought she should buy. He pointed to the white chocolate, answering, "I think you should choose the mindfulness chocolate, Mommy, 'cause it makes your mouth and heart happy." Your kids can also be mindful of the sensations they experience when they brush their teeth, tie their shoelaces, take a bath or shower, and pack their schoolbag.
- MINDFUL MEDIA AND PEOPLE WATCHING. As I've mentioned, a fun way to help younger kids tune in to emotions is by muting the TV volume and guessing the emotions of the actors. You can play the same game while people watching with your kids when you're out and about, observing body language and facial expressions. Learning to read subtle emotional cues will also help your child to develop emotional intelligence.

You can weave in strength awareness by asking kids to guess at the strengths they see in characters on TV shows, in movies, and in books. Emily and I have identified bravery as a core strength in Harry Potter. We've had lots of conversations about how brave Harry was to go to a new school, learn wizardry, risk being bludgeoned in Quidditch, and, of course, fight Lord Voldemort. During that time Emily took a fall off the rings in her circus class. Her knee was bleeding and I could see that she was in pain because her face went bright red. I expected that she'd come over to me, but she took a deep breath, gritted her teeth, and got back on the rings. After class, I said to her, "I saw you hurt yourself. You were brave to keep going. What were you feeling in that moment?" She replied, "It really hurt and I wanted to stop, but then I thought, 'What would Harry Potter do if he fell off his broom in Quidditch?'"

Seeing strengths in others—teachers, coaches, relatives (including ancestors), and friends—can inspire your kids. It helps them to see the best in others and learn how to encourage and compliment others—not to mention putting them a step ahead of the game when writing thank-you notes, birthday cards, and gratitude letters (see Chapter 5).

- APPS. Using smartphone apps like Smiling Mind, Headspace, 1 Giant Mind, Happify, and Calm is an effective way to get tech-savvy kids into mindfulness. The graphics in Headspace are useful for older children (ages ten and older). The clouds and expanding breathing circle in Calm are great ways for teens to visualize calmness.
- MINDFUL COLORING. This has become a worldwide craze. There are many mindfulness coloring books available in stores, and you can also find free resources available to download and print at http://www.education.com/ worksheets/mandalas.

- MINDFUL MONDAYS. Most Monday evenings before my kids' bedtime, if they're into the idea, we do twenty minutes of mindfulness. Some activities we've enjoyed: Shake a snow globe and ask the kids to sit and watch the sparkles settle; turn out the lights and then shine a flashlight beam randomly at different locations around the room, asking them to keep alert so they can spot the location of the light as quickly as possible; give them a feather and guide them in placing the feather on different parts of their body, paying attention to how it feels. Sometimes I have them sit quietly and then raise a finger when they hear me softly ring a bell.

Mindful Breathing, Walking, and Listening

MINDFUL BREATHING EXERCISES

Breathing is one of the most reliable pathways to relaxing into mindfulness. Why not use this activity we do more than twenty thousand times each day to bring ourselves and our children respite?

Slow breathing reduces our heart rate, lowers our blood pressure, and tells our brain to stop the release of cortisol, the stress hormone. All lead to a relaxation response in the body.[23] Research shows that a relaxation response is triggered in our bodies after twelve slow, deep breaths. Since most people take approximately six breaths per minute, this means it will take about two minutes for us to get the relaxation response from deep breathing. Most people report that after two minutes of mindful breathing, they do indeed feel calmer and clearer. However, people who regularly practice deep breathing techniques are able to trigger the body's relaxation response in just six breaths.

Breath is always available. It's free. You don't need to purchase any fancy equipment and you don't even need much time. Just two minutes.

You can help your child take long, deep breaths anywhere and anytime—in the car, in the supermarket, or if you notice your child getting agitated. This is known as "in-the-moment mindfulness." You can also introduce structured mindfulness breathing exercises to your children at home such as the Traveling Breath, Breath Circuit, Abdominal Breathing, and Equal Breathing. You can find information about these and other breathing techniques by doing a quick Google search and in the mindfulness parenting books I've listed in the Appendix.

MINDFUL WALKING EXERCISES

How conscious are you of the beautiful and complex contact of your feet on the ground? Like breathing, we take walking for granted, yet just remember how long and hard your child worked to learn how to walk and you'll understand what an achievement it is. When we slow down those movements that we now hardly even think about, we can use them to become aware of the present moment.

When I find myself rushing from one meeting to another across the university campus, I remind myself to become mindful. I clear my thoughts of the last and next meeting and I concentrate on what my feet feel like as they take me to my next destination.

I love doing a mindful walking exercise with school kids. Here's one I learned from one of my yoga teachers called the "Silent Ninja."

EXERCISE: | Silent Ninja

Take off your shoes and start by standing tall.

Notice the way your feet feel against the ground. See if you can feel the specific parts of your feet as they make contact with the ground. Do you feel the weight more in the heels or in the balls of your feet?

Feel the way your body is slightly shifting from side to side and rocking back and forth in a way that keeps you balanced. Now focus on a point in front of you and gently roll your heels up to the sky. Balance on the balls of your feet. Pause for a moment and tune in to all the muscles in your body that are helping you stay balanced.

Now lower both feet and roll forward to push off with your right foot. S-l-o-w-l-y take a step with your left foot. Start by peeling the heel of your left foot off the ground, and notice how your sole arches up.

Lift the toe of your left foot off the floor. Feel how your leg moves through the air. Notice the sensation of impact as your left heel touches the ground. Continue the process of feeling your foot reconnecting with the ground, from the heel rolling through to the toe.

Repeat the process with your right foot.

Take five s-l-o-w, fluid steps like this.

While you walk, become aware of your thoughts. Observe any sensations or feelings you are having while you walk. When you become aware of any thoughts or sensations, simply notice them and let them float away. When a new thought or sensation comes, let that one go, too.

After you complete five slow steps, turn around and walk back in the same manner.

Continue this circuit for five minutes. When you finish, stand still for a minute and feel the sensations running through your mind and body.

Here are some other ways to have fun with mindful walking:

- Walk in slow motion, lifting your knees high, as if your feet are stuck in syrup.
- Pretend you are an Olympic marathon runner about to cross the finish line, running in slow motion.
- Pretend you are a model walking in slow motion down the catwalk. Walk, look . . . and s-l-o-w-l-y turn!
- March like a soldier, but in slow motion.

EXERCISE: | Mindful Listening Exercise

This is a good exercise for teens who love music and don't love to sit still!

1. Create a playlist of three of your favorite songs. Get comfortable and give yourself time and space where you won't be interrupted for the next twelve to fifteen minutes.
2. Listen to your playlist with your full attention and an attitude of open curiosity.
3. Do you notice anything new while listening to the songs in this way? For example, you might notice interesting rhythms, melodies, harmonies, or lyrics that you didn't pay attention to previously.
4. When your mind wanders, just notice that your mind has wandered. Observe your thoughts. Where did your mind wander to—the past or the future? What thoughts were you having?
5. Now bring your attention to the music again—catch the lyrics or the beat.
6. Notice the emotions you are experiencing. Do they change during the song or across the three songs? Do you feel happy or sad during some sections?
7. Observe how your body feels during different parts of the songs. For example, does your heart rate increase during louder parts? Do certain parts of your body feel heavier or lighter? Are you holding tension anywhere?

Mindful Moments with Friends

Once your child is more conversant with applying mindfulness to himself, talk about how he can use mindfulness to be a better friend—someone others love to be with. Some tips kids can use for getting started:

1. When hanging out with your friends, try to be present and accepting of them.
2. For example, if your friend is telling you about a problem, try putting your phone away and giving your friend your full attention. Let your friend talk, and do not interrupt or jump in with your thoughts. Wait at least three seconds before responding.
3. Be curious about your friends. Notice what's interesting about them, what you appreciate about them, and how you feel around them.

Mindful Strengths Exercises

EXERCISE: | A Better Question Than "How Was School Today?"

We know kids don't really answer that (unless you consider a grunt to be an answer). Instead of "How was school today?" I turn on my Strength Switch when I pick up Nick and Emily from school. On the way home, we share the strengths we've used during our day and give an example of a strength we saw in someone else that day. Over time, we've noticed patterns about what strengths we tend to use the most—a clue to core strengths. We also discover growth strengths to work on. And as they tell me about the situations where they used or noticed a strength, I learn what happened at school that day!

I never force this conversation, and there are certainly times where my kids are tired or grumpy and don't want to talk about strengths. One day, Nick hopped into the car all steamed up about a particular teacher. When I asked him what strengths he had used that day, he said, "I'm not in the mood, Mom." Fair enough. Then ten seconds later he exclaimed, "I'll tell you what strengths my teacher did *not* use today!" and went on to list about eight strengths he felt should have been used but hadn't been. He ended up speaking longer and more lucidly about strengths during that ride home than on other occasions. You know your kids really understand strengths when they can spot the *absence* of them.

EXERCISE: | Strengths Poster

One family exercise is to put up a strengths poster (a fancy term for a blank piece of paper) on the wall, and over the course of a week, ask family members to write on the poster when they spot others displaying strengths.

This exercise puts strengths mindfulness front and center for everyone because you must be in the present moment to notice the strength in the other person. It's also a bonding activity, allowing everyone to value the strengths of other family members. When my family did this exercise, we saw each other in a new light. At the end of the week Emily had the most examples of bravery recorded on the poster. It highlighted that Emily, the smallest of all of us, was also the bravest. Matt, Nick, and I saw that many of the things we do with ease (e.g., talking to grown-ups, counting the change we get from the cashier, staying upright when the dog jumps up on us) are tougher for Emily because she's younger. It was empowering for her to see herself through our eyes—as a brave person—whereas she'd previously thought of herself as the weakest because she was the smallest.

EXERCISE: | Strengths Silhouette

When Nick was four, I made him a "strengths silhouette." He lay on a large sheet of paper and I drew his outline. We stuck the silhouette on his bedroom wall, and over the next few months when we saw him use a strength, we'd write it in his silhouette— or he would; he was learning to write and this was also a good writing exercise. In time, he learned when his performance, energy, and use were high (the markers of a core strength).

That silhouette stayed on his wall for many years. Finally, when he was ten, he took it down. That day was bittersweet for me. I was sad to see the silhouette disappear, but I was glad that Nick had internalized the knowledge that he had strengths within. For Emily at age four, I made a "confidence cape" out of pink fabric and we followed the same idea as the strengths silhouette.

Strengths Games

With two of my past Master of Applied Positive Psychology students, Claire Fortune and Lara Mossman, I developed two games based on the VIA strengths model that parents can play with their kids to develop strengths mindfulness and become familiar with strengths language.

VIAINGO is based on BINGO, but instead of filling in a card containing numbers, you note the VIA character strengths on a sheet of strength words. You can post the sheet on the refrigerator and put a check mark next to a strength each time you see it during the course of, say, a week—signaling a family member's go-to or core strengths.

Strengths and Ladders, based on the game Chutes and Ladders, is a more structured game that you might save for a weekend or a family vacation. It's especially good for talking about overusing or underusing strengths—a potential downside of strengths we'll explore in Chapter 9.

Templates for both games can be downloaded for free from www.the-strengths-exchange.com.au.

EXERCISE: | Strengths Reflection

Keep a diary and at the end of the day mentally review what strengths you used and how you used them. Meditate on the feelings, thoughts, sensations, and emotions you got from each strength. How does humility, for example, feel in your body? At the end of your strengths reflection session, look at the list of strengths on my website to see if there were other strengths on the list that you used but were blind to. List these in your diary and think about them in your next reflection.

CHAPTER 7

Self-Control

It's around 11:00 p.m. The house is quiet. The kids are in bed, and all the things that happen with them in the evening—dinner, homework, together time—are over. Matt's reading or has gone to bed. The cat, dog, and even Blinky my chatty cockatiel are snoozing. I put on my favorite pale blue fleece hoodie PJs. Pad out to my study. Sit down at my desk and tap a key. The computer screen lights up.

I have night owl tendencies, so after a full day at the office, followed by home and family activities, I use the late-night hours to catch up on e-mails, review reports, prep for meetings, edit drafts of student papers or grant applications—and, for quite a while now, write this book.

It's been a long day of decisions, there's a lot of budget pressure around getting the grants we're applying for, and the manuscript deadline for the book is approaching. It all has to get done. I work steadily for a while. Then, suddenly, a thought about chocolate flashes through my mind. Specifically, Cadbury chocolate. More specifically, a Boost bar. I picture the dark blue and purple foil wrapper. My taste buds tingle at the memory of the crunchy biscuit pieces and caramel. I could really use some chocolate.

No. You don't need chocolate. You need to work.

Chocolate . . .

Work.

Cho-co-laaaaate!!!

WORK!!!!!

The tug-of-war between goal and impulse finally proves too distracting. I go out to the kitchen, to the cabinet where I've "hidden" the beckoning bar. It's way up at the top, in the back. I stretch on tiptoe, feeling around for the smooth, flat object of my desire.

It's not there.

Puzzlement. Then disappointment. Even a flash of childish rage. *Grrrrrrr! Who took my chocolate?*

Then I remember. I ate it last week during another late-night work session.

We've all lost battles with our impulses, though your irresistible impulse will likely be different from mine. Over the past seven years while building the Centre for Positive Psychology and becoming its first director, I've probably kept the Cadbury chocolate factory alive and kicking. But seriously, I've noticed that on the days when I work from home without the constant decisions and stressors of a typical day at the office, or when I'm not tired from trying to cram in another day's work at night after already putting in a full day at the center, those chocolate cravings don't overwhelm me. I still have impulses and distractions, but I'm better at staying on task and saying, "Later. Right now, it's time to work." My self-control is stronger.

So what's the difference between the times when an enticing impulse wins and when it doesn't? I used to think my chocolate cravings were the result of the need for comfort. But research indicates that the real cause is probably the erosion of self-control from making decisions all day long.

Making decisions is only one of several self-control sappers we'll talk about in this chapter. It's important to become aware of these factors as we seek to help our children call upon and maximize their strengths and work productively on their weaknesses. It's also important in helping us stay on track as strength-based parents.

Strength-based parenting actually helps kids build and maintain self-control. If you've been reading the previous chapters and helping your child build her capacities for attention and mindfulness, you're already priming your child to grow her capacity for self-control. In this chapter, we'll go a step further.

Self-Control Defined

Self-control is a key ingredient that allows human beings to single-mindedly manifest their potential in the world through ups and downs, thick and thin, slings and arrows, curve balls, s**t hitting the fan, or whatever else you want to call the rock and roll of daily life in human-land.

Minute by minute, hour by hour, every day of our lives, self-control helps us overcome internal conflict when we're confronted with choices.[1] Work or play? Hit the gym or take a nap? Fix a healthy dinner or veg out with a movie and a bag of chips? Put attention on strengths or on weaknesses? Self-control helps us make judicious choices.

But what is self-control, exactly? Where does it arise in the brain? Why is it sometimes so strong, other times lamentably absent?

Before we answer these questions, take a few moments now to assess your level of self-control:

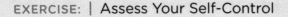

EXERCISE: | Assess Your Self-Control

Read each statement in Table 1 below and select how much the statement applies to you on a scale from 1 to 5, with 1 being "Not at all like me" and 5 being "Very much like me."[2]

It is easy for me to break bad habits.

1	2	3	4	5
NOT AT ALL LIKE ME	A LITTLE LIKE ME	SOMEWHAT LIKE ME	MOSTLY LIKE ME	VERY MUCH LIKE ME

I don't get distracted easily.

1	2	3	4	5
NOT AT ALL LIKE ME	A LITTLE LIKE ME	SOMEWHAT LIKE ME	MOSTLY LIKE ME	VERY MUCH LIKE ME

I don't say inappropriate things.

1	2	3	4	5
NOT AT ALL LIKE ME	A LITTLE LIKE ME	SOMEWHAT LIKE ME	MOSTLY LIKE ME	VERY MUCH LIKE ME

I refuse things that are bad for me, even if they are fun.

1	2	3	4	5
NOT AT ALL LIKE ME	A LITTLE LIKE ME	SOMEWHAT LIKE ME	MOSTLY LIKE ME	VERY MUCH LIKE ME

I'm good at resisting temptation.

1	2	3	4	5
NOT AT ALL LIKE ME	A LITTLE LIKE ME	SOMEWHAT LIKE ME	MOSTLY LIKE ME	VERY MUCH LIKE ME

People would say that I have very strong self-discipline.

1	2	3	4	5
NOT AT ALL LIKE ME	A LITTLE LIKE ME	SOMEWHAT LIKE ME	MOSTLY LIKE ME	VERY MUCH LIKE ME

Most of the time I put work before pleasure.

1	2	3	4	5
NOT AT ALL LIKE ME	A LITTLE LIKE ME	SOMEWHAT LIKE ME	MOSTLY LIKE ME	VERY MUCH LIKE ME

I never do things that feel good in the moment if I know I will regret them later on.

1	2	3	4	5
NOT AT ALL LIKE ME	A LITTLE LIKE ME	SOMEWHAT LIKE ME	MOSTLY LIKE ME	VERY MUCH LIKE ME

I rarely act without thinking through all the alternatives.

1	2	3	4	5
NOT AT ALL LIKE ME	A LITTLE LIKE ME	SOMEWHAT LIKE ME	MOSTLY LIKE ME	VERY MUCH LIKE ME

I can usually stop myself from doing things that I know are wrong.

1	2	3	4	5
NOT AT ALL LIKE ME	A LITTLE LIKE ME	SOMEWHAT LIKE ME	MOSTLY LIKE ME	VERY MUCH LIKE ME

John Wiley and Sons.

Table 1: Self-Control Scale

SCORING: Add your score for each item to arrive at a total score. The maximum score is 50, which indicates extreme levels of self-control. A mid-point score of 25 suggests moderate levels of self-control, and lower scores reflect lower levels of self-control.

Don't worry if you scored low. Research shows that self-control, despite being such an important quality, is often low.[3] More on that later.

A quick review of the statements in the self-assessment makes it clear that self-control, in essence, is about impulse control. It's the capacity we draw on when an inner conflict arises between an impulse and a goal. It's what allows us to rise above our needs and drives, exert our higher brain capacities, and control our emotions, thoughts, and actions in the service of a desired outcome. In lofty terms, it's the exercise of free will.

We have these moments of inner conflict constantly during a normal day. It may be about saying no to something we want to do (*No chocolate, Lea*). Or it might be saying yes to something we don't want to do (*Finish that report, Lea*).

The Connection Between Self-Control and Attention

Self-control isn't the same as attention (discussed in Chapter 5), although the two are interrelated. Attention is our capacity for vigilance, to stay focused on one particular thing. Self-control is our ability to stick to our plans and not be derailed by our impulses. Attention is needed for self-control: You have to be aware of something to control it. But self-control is useful in steering our attention toward one thing and away from another. The two go hand in hand.

Some psychologists here in Australia demonstrated this interconnection in a series of very cool studies in which participants went through one of three programs to build their self-control.[4] Individuals in the first study were tasked with setting the goal of becoming fit: joining a gym, constructing a plan for getting in shape, and sticking to it. In a second study, each participant had to devise and carry out a study plan. The third study had people set a goal to save money, which involved establishing and adhering to a budget. The ostensible object of these studies was to assess participants' success at meeting their assigned goals, but actually they were about assessing the workings of self-control.

Every couple of weeks, the participants came to the lab and took an attention test. In the test, they were shown a computer screen displaying a series of squares with one square of a particular color. When the squares jumbled around on-screen into a different order, the participants had to pay attention to that square as it moved and say where it ended up.

Now here's the twist. In the middle of the attention test, the researchers started playing an Eddie Murphy comedy movie on another screen. This was a test of self-control. Would the participants follow their impulse to watch Eddie Murphy and have a laugh? The moment they lost self-control, their attention would wander and they'd lose track of where the square went. The researchers found that, over time, participants in the three programs became more fit, adhered to the study program, or saved money, *and* they also got much better at not looking at Eddie Murphy and just paying attention to the square. In other words, their self-control improved, and so did their attention.

These researchers showed us that we can build self-control and attention by setting goals and sticking to them. They also showed that self-control and attention are mutually reinforcing. As you build one, you build the other. On the flip side, as you deplete one, you deplete the other.

Marketers know this relationship well: People are much more likely to engage in impulse spending when their attention is distracted.[5] That's why in many stores there's loud music, bright lights, screens with moving images, colorful displays, announcements, events, salespeople offering samples and special promotions, and so on. You may go in looking for one item and come out with that item plus a few more you didn't set out to buy.

The Roots and the Reach of Self-Control

In the Victorian era, self-control was seen as a psychological state. Being weak-willed was viewed as a mental failing at best, a character flaw at worst. More recently, we've learned that self-control isn't just in your mind. It's also in your body. In fact, it's a physiological capacity wired into our nervous systems.[6] A failure of self-control doesn't always mean you're weak-willed; it could mean your nervous system is overtaxed. That's why so many of us reach for junk food when we're stressed but can resist temptation in calmer moments. While some people have more innate self-control[7] than others, we all experience failures of self-control. Luckily it turns out that, like so many capacities, self-control can be strengthened.

Neuroscientists have located the brain area responsible for self-monitoring.[8] It's called the anterior cingulate cortex. In my parent workshops, I just refer to it as our self-monitoring system. Basically, its job is to detect when there's a mismatch between our intention (what we'd planned to do) and the action we're about to undertake (act on impulse or stick to our plan).

Suppose you're trying to lose five pounds and you're invited to brunch at a restaurant known for its incredible buffet. En route and even as you walk to the buffet table, you're thinking, *I'm going to go straight to the fruit display and have a bowl of fresh fruit.* But hang on. Are those hot waffles over there? Yep, with all the trimmings. You catch a delicious whiff. Your resolve wavers.

It's the anterior cingulate cortex that detects the dissonance: *Uh-oh! Intention in danger!* It sends out warning signals, in effect opening the door to the prefrontal cortex—our large, highly developed system of conscious choice, rational thinking, and future-oriented planning—which wedges in a foot and says, *Hey, I know you love waffles, but eating them won't get the scale to show the number you want. Remember how energized you felt yesterday after you ate fresh fruit and yogurt for breakfast? You can feel that again right now. And you'll feel great when you get on the scale next week without those waffles weighing you down.*

If our brain is designed to help us have self-control, why is it so hard to smack down our impulses?

It's because our impulses come from an ancient, powerful part of the brain called the limbic system. In the eons before we developed higher-level capacities, this was the original system that kept us safe, well fed instead of fed upon, and able to live to procreate another day. It still plays a vital role in keeping us in touch with core sensations of safety and comfort. It won't go away, so neither will our impulses. Research shows that we spend about 50 percent of our life having desires and impulses and three to four hours a day resisting tempta-tions. It's hard to do this, and we cave to our impulses about 60 per-cent of the time.[9]

Those statistics might seem depressing. But from an evolutionary standpoint, in a comparatively short time, we've gone from being or-ganisms largely governed by impulse to having a brain that actively helps us exert self-control. According to Suzanne Segerstrom, PhD, our central nervous system has evolved a self-control mechanism that she calls the "pause and plan response."[10]

Most of us know about the "fight or flight response," which hap-pens when one part of our nervous system, known as the sympathetic nervous system, goes on high alert in response to a perceived threat. It's all about revving up the body for action as our heart pounds and blood pours into our muscles in preparation for self-defense. The pause-and-plan response is a complementary response that occurs in a different part of the nervous system called the parasympathetic ner-vous system. In contrast, it triggers a sequence of coordinated changes to help us override that high-alert impulse. Blood goes to the prefron-tal cortex to bring its rational powers on board. It's all about slowing the body down. About taking a moment, a step back, a deep breath, a pause in which clear thought can emerge to plan a more rational re-sponse.[11]

We start to develop self-control even as infants.[12] By around eigh-teen months, babies start to be more cooperative when limits are set: They don't touch the trinket, even though they want to, if they are told "no" (some of the time, anyway). This shows the beginnings of im-pulse control and the ability to regulate desires/temptations. With toddlers, you start to see that they can resist the impulse to run across the road, begin to share their toys, and do a better job of waiting until everyone's seated before they start eating or ripping open their birth-day gifts. Here again, self-control is spotty, but you can see it develop-ing. Between four and six years of age, roughly a third of children show the capacity for delayed gratification.[13] They will use their self-control to forsake a treat now in order to get a bigger treat later on. For most kids, self-control comes online in a more stable way between the ages of seven and nine. Somewhere between nine and twelve, there's another small developmental spurt in our self-control capacity.[14]

Then in the teenage years, we backslide as the impulse and desire centers in the limbic system have a growth surge, temporarily outstripping the prefrontal cortex.[15] That accounts for the impulsivity and risk-taking behavior associated with teenagers. Here again, there may be evolutionary good reasons: We didn't live much longer than our teens in primeval times, and we likely needed what today we would consider foolhardy levels of courage to face off with predators, hunt down beasts for sustenance, head into uncharted territory for new food sources, and compete for the best mate in the tribe. *Sow your wild oats,* our ancient genes urge us. *You might die tomorrow. Actually, you probably will. PS: So have the waffles.*

Fortunately, as I mentioned in Chapter 4, the prefrontal cortex catches up and the connections between the two develop, with a particular spurt around the age of seventeen, so they can more effectively "talk" to each other and the cortex can put the brakes on some of that impulsivity.[16]

With such complexity wired deeply into us, rather than getting down on ourselves for our lack of self-control, I believe we should feel reassured to know that we have all of these internal regulating processes available to help us find our equilibrium as human beings and as parents. As we mature, then, self-control happens on two levels:

1. *Impulse control in the moment.* Examples: working on taxes despite wanting to watch TV, or your child practicing piano even though he'd love to have computer time instead.
2. *Longer-term self-control.* This entails the ability to both see and set patterns of attention over time. Examples: Noticing

that you're procrastinating on your taxes (seeing a pattern of inattention) and making a plan to work on them for a half hour every night before the deadline (setting a pattern), or noticing that your child isn't getting around to practicing piano because he's getting sucked into computer games (seeing a pattern of impulsivity) and making a plan with your child that he'll practice the piano for a half hour (setting a pattern) followed by a half hour of computer games.

Our kids are learning how to operate on both levels as their brain develops. It's intense and important. Self-control helps with many significant outcomes in a child's life. In research with middle school and university students, self-control is more important than IQ in predicting grade point average.[17] It builds confidence and caring behavior and reduces depression and risky behavior.[18]

Research shows that children with high self-control grow into adults with greater physical and mental health, greater education attainment, fewer substance-abuse problems, fewer criminal convictions, better savings behavior, and greater financial security.[19]

For all of these reasons, a big part of our role as parents and CEOs of our children's lives is to help them learn how to be aware of their impulses, access their pause-and-plan mode, and set up productive ways to manage their impulses, until they can internalize and perform these processes on their own.

Strength-based parenting primes your child to exercise self-control. Each time your child overcomes the urge to meet a short-term impulse and invests that energy into growing strengths instead (e.g., going to swimming practice instead of sleeping in), she's inching closer to realizing her full potential. Each time she remembers to draw on her patience and helpfulness in a team assignment at school even though the kids are being snarky, she's using her self-control to build positive personality traits. The impact of each small triumph of self-control compounds over time to take a child's strengths from the level of potential to forming the foundation of significant achievement.

The Top Four Self-Control Sappers

Roy Baumeister, PhD, and Mark Muraven, PhD, liken self-control to a muscle:[20] Like a muscle, it becomes fatigued with use. There are four major factors that deplete it:

- resisting impulses
- making decisions
- suppressing emotions
- stress

You can see how all of these can pile up over a day. Even when we start with strong self-control, as we repeatedly call upon it, our ability to apply it diminishes.[21] By the end of a typical day of work or school, we can expect self-control to be pretty low. No wonder tempers can get short by evening when the family's finally together—but there's dinner to make, homework to do, and myriad temptations to resist such as TV, computer games, movies, music, and talking and texting with friends.

Simply recognizing this can go a long way toward helping us hold on to our compassion for ourselves and for our kids when life over-taxes our brain and nervous system and self-control becomes an issue.

But the good news is that, like a muscle, self-control can be strengthened through the right kind of use. And SBP primes us and our kids to do just that.

How Strength Focus Helps the Development of Self-Control . . . and Vice Versa

In Chapter 3, we talked about the three key characteristics of a strength: high performance, high energy, and high use (also known as effort or practice). Self-control is critical to strength building because it's needed for the "effort" part of the equation: repeated practice, experimentation, trial and error, rehearsals, run-throughs, revisions, rewrites, retakes, and more. Our role as strength-based parents is to help our kids build the self-control they need to put in the effort required to develop their strengths.

SBP is less likely to cause the self-control sappers just listed above. My own research has found that children of strength-based parents experience less stress when making decisions.[22] And although children may work hard to develop their strengths, because they love what they're doing, they can push their self-control muscle harder for the sweet rewards of high performance and high energy.

Even when our children must deal with their weaknesses or with life's inevitable challenges (and we'll look at this in more detail in Chapter 9), they can apply their well-developed muscle of self-control and self-awareness gained from working mindfully through their strengths and anticipate better outcomes as a result.

It's also far less stressful for our children to operate from their core strengths than to slog forward using learned behavior and weaknesses. We all have to tap into our learned behaviors periodically, but when kids don't know the difference between learned behavior and core strengths, it can lead to study and career choices that put them at risk of dissatisfaction and burnout, draining them of the self-control needed to turn their lives around.

Five Strength-Based Strategies for Building and Sustaining Self-Control

Strategy #1: Assess the Structure of Your Child's Day (Yours, Too)

One defense against self-control depletion in our kids is to help them structure their day. Here are tips I suggest to parents to use at home:

- *Remember, they're kids.* If you think it's hard to put in a full day's work and then do more work at home at night, imagine how your child, whose brain is still developing self-control, may feel trying to manage a day at school, after-school lessons, tutoring, athletics, chores, and homework. That's a lot of decision making, stress, and impulse control. They're as depleted as you are, if not more.
- *Expect that your child will have less self-control at the end of the day.* Talk about what would help her rest and refresh her self-control muscle after school. A nap? A snack? Sports? A favorite "good goofing off" activity such as reading, making or building something, taking a walk or run or being outdoors, listening to or making music, or cuddling with the family pet?
- *Especially with young children, understand "toxic time."* This is what Matt and I used to call the hours between 4:00 p.m. and 6:00 p.m., when Nick and Emily were younger and it seemed they turned into tantrum monsters. I used to think they were tired—and they were—but now I understand that their self-control muscle was also depleted by day's end. They had less mental energy and their nervous systems were strung out. There was no physiological reserve for them to draw on

to stop the tantrum. Tiredness and self-control depletion are a double whammy.

* *Boost your child's positive mood through strength-based routines.* Make sure your child's routine regularly includes opportunities for her to flex her strengths. When we use our strengths, we feel positive. That alone is self-control enhancing. In a series of four studies conducted by Dr. Baumeister and his team at Florida State University, people in positive moods experienced less self-control depletion than people in neutral or sad moods.[23] In the first study, university students were primed to experience positive emotions either through receiving a gift of candy from the researcher or not. In the other three studies, students were primed to experience positive emotions by watching a funny video, primed into a neutral mood by watching a video of dolphin communication patterns, or primed into a sad mood by watching a movie of a dying mother saying good-bye to her son (talk about a tearjerker!). Then they were asked to engage in a task requiring impulse control, whether it was drinking a bad-tasting though healthy drink, persisting at a frustrating but achievable task, persevering in an attempt to solve an unsolvable puzzle, or continually squeezing a handgrip exercise tool until they gave up. In all four studies, the students primed into a positive mood persisted longer. They had more self-control as a result of feeling positive.

* *So talk with your child about how his strengths can come out during the school day.* It might happen while hanging out with his friends during lunch, finding a quiet spot to read, taking some photos, playing chess, joining a club, listening to music, working on a long-term project, or exercising.

* *Approach homework through an understanding of your child's core and growth strengths, learned behaviors, and weaknesses.*

Different approaches may work on different days, so don't be afraid to mix it up. You might have your child start with a strength subject that energizes her so she can bring those positive feelings to a subject she finds more difficult or draining. Or do the draining work first so that working on the energizing homework feels like a reward. Try breaking a challenging subject into timed increments that your child may be more likely to handle without succumbing to distractions, punctuated by working on strength subjects.

- *With older children, talk it over and agree on an approach to try.* It's a great way to exercise your child's mindfulness about how she is feeling and how she might handle subjects that aren't strengths for her. Another option: Sit down together and strategically map out a homework routine for the week based on upcoming tests, deadlines, and projects in process. You're setting your child up for success and getting her in the habit of tuning into her strengths, her self-control level, and her attention level as part of planning out her days.

- *Build in breaks.* Remember, attention is sustainable for only about twenty minutes on average. So when you see your child getting antsy or increasingly distracted, suggest a power break of about ten minutes[24] to do something appealing to his strengths—perhaps watch some funny videos, shoot baskets, read part of a chapter in a book, put on some music and dance, play with the family pet, do a crossword puzzle— basically, anything that allows your child to goof off.

- *Tap the restorative power of flow activities.* These are activities that use your child's core strength(s), often signaled by her joyfully losing track of time when she does them. Flow activities rest and refresh the brain.

- *Pare down busyness before big events.* If your child has a significant intense commitment on a given day—exams, rehearsals, intensive training, a major athletic event, a performance, or some other activity that will require strong focused attention—try to provide a less structured day or carve out some periods of "good goofing off" downtime. You want to make sure your child has reserves of self-control so he can learn and perform as effectively as possible during these big opportunities.

- *Invoke Dirty Sock Syndrome (or: Cut kids some slack when they're under extra pressure).* A study of college students' self-control found that during exam week, because all their mental resources were going toward studying, they didn't do any laundry. Think of it as Dirty Sock Syndrome.[25] So, during high-pressure times such as exams, playoff games, the run of a show they're in, a few days before a big project is due, or amid troubles with friends, give your kids a temporary pass on some of their chores, and go easy if they forget or lose things. This is especially true for teenagers, who, as mentioned, are neurologically growing in a way that can make it challenging for them to hang on to their self-control.

- *Be aware of your own ups and downs of self-control.* When you're starting out with strength-based parenting, don't expect to put it into action when your self-control is sapped by the factors I listed earlier. It takes mental and emotional effort to override our negativity biases and projections. I'd suggest practicing SBP first while doing activities you enjoy with your child. Your self-control will be higher because you're having a good time. Tell your child the strengths you notice him using during fun things you're doing together.

- Other tips: Practice the Strength Switch on the weekends, when you're not distracted or drained by work. Then try it on weekday mornings, when we tend to feel fresher and have more self-control. Expect that it'll be easier to flip the Strength Switch in low-stakes situations—over minor issues and annoyances—than in high-stakes ones at first. Finally, enjoy the positive-attention exercises of savoring, gratitude, and mindfulness we discussed in previous chapters. You'll feel happier and more replenished, and your self-control muscle will naturally strengthen—you won't even know it's happening!

Strategy #2: Have Routines and Make To-Do Lists

From getting school clothes ready the night before to always putting your keys away in the same spot to having a consistent wake-up time, routines are a fantastic way to conserve mental energy. Save your brain's decision-making resources for bigger and better things.

That's why making to-do lists is an excellent habit to get your kids into. Research shows that if you offload from your mind all the things you have to do into a list, the self-control that would have been needed to keep mental track of all those to-dos is freed for other purposes.[26] There are many apps to help, such as Todoist (en.todoist.com), Any.do (any.do/anydo), and Pocket Lists (pocketlistsapp.com).

Model the behavior by showing your kids how you keep yourself organized. I'm low-tech: I use sticky notes. On any given day I'll have somewhere between two and five stickies that list the things I have to do. My family knows this so well that if they want to remind me about something, they leave me a sticky note beside the kettle I use to make my tea. We're teaching Nick how to use a wall planner mounted on the wall over his desk and how to use the calendar on his computer.

Strategy #3: Practice Mindfulness

I mentioned earlier the two levels of self-control: self-control that happens in the moment and longer-term self-control in which we monitor our thoughts, feelings, and behaviors over time; notice patterns both positive and negative; and use that awareness to apply our self-control and attention to meet life goals. The more self-aware we are, the better we can see our patterns and control our behaviors. Self-awareness is fostered and supported by mindfulness.[27]

We explored mindfulness techniques in Chapter 6. Mindfulness hones the ability to tune in to the subtle signals from the anterior cingulate cortex when our self-control is wavering, which can be hard to hear and heed. Mindfulness provides that pause and prepare moment, when rational thought can step in and separate impulse from action.

Practiced over time, breathing exercises can actually reset the nervous system.[28] Often we're overtaxing our own and our children's biological reserves of self-control without even realizing it. Life gets busy and there's so much to do and deal with. It can be exhilarating but also exhausting. If you or your kids are having frequent breakdowns of self-control—maybe snapping at each other, giving in too often to unhealthy eating or lack of exercise, or feeling overwhelmed by too much on your plates—rather than getting down on yourselves, take it as a possible sign that the brain and nervous system need some TLC.

Just a few minutes of deep breathing or slipping into an activity that puts the mind into a restful free-roaming state can activate the calming effects of the parasympathetic nervous system so it starts to slow heart rate and blood pressure, telling our brain to stop the release of cortisol (the stress hormone). All of these physiological changes lead to a relaxation response that reduces stress, inducing a state where the quiet strength of self-control can reemerge.[29]

Last but not least, there's a purely practical benefit to mindfulness.[30] Every conscious thought requires energy. Imagine how quickly our self-control would be zapped if we attended to all the thoughts constantly bouncing around our brain. In mindfulness we learn that feelings, thoughts, and sensations can arise and pass without requiring our energy to evaluate or act upon them.[31] Thus mindfulness inoculates us against our impulses.[32] Teaching our children mindfulness gives them the power to allow unwanted impulses to pass and direct their mental energy toward their strengths and their goals instead.

I urge you to try mindfulness techniques yourself and, with your child, discover and cultivate reserves of calm, personal attunement, and greater command of the mind's powers.

Strategy #4: Be an Emotional Coach

Suppressing emotions depletes self-control. This was powerfully demonstrated by researchers at Toronto University who monitored the electrical activity in people's brains while they watched a video of animals suffering and dying.[33] You may be upset just thinking about this (I know I am), and if you'd been in this study you may have been randomly allocated to the 50 percent of participants who were told to stifle their emotions while watching this distressing video, with the other 50 percent permitted to express their feelings.

The researchers were specifically looking at activity in the anterior cingulate cortex, the "conflict-monitoring" region of the brain that, as I've mentioned, plays a big role in impulse control by alerting us to mismatches between our intentions (intending to skip dessert, finish chemistry homework, or see strengths) and our impulses (yearning for pecan pie, wanting to text a friend instead of doing homework, seeing weaknesses instead of strengths).

The researchers found that the energy required to suppress emotions robs us of energy needed for self-control: The people who had to stifle their emotions while watching the distressing film showed less activity in the anterior cingulate cortex compared to activity levels before watching the film, as well as in comparison to participants who were told not to stifle their emotions. In the next phase of the experiment, when participants were asked to solve a puzzle that involved self-control, those who'd been asked to suppress their emotions performed more poorly.

Interestingly, self-control depletion occurs when we stifle positive emotions, too. Todd Heatherton, PhD, a pioneer in social neuroscience at Dartmouth University, and his team looked at what happens inside the brain when people are asked to refrain from laughing at a funny video. Sure enough, the brain areas that assist with impulse control were weaker afterward.[34]

Along similar lines, Kathleen Vohs, PhD, teamed up with Roy Baumeister and had people watch a nine-minute clip of Robin Williams performing a stand-up comedy routine.[35] Half the group was instructed to suppress their emotions and remain completely neutral. To make sure they followed these instructions, they were videotaped for those nine minutes. (I can tell you straight up that I would have failed miserably.) The other half were allowed to respond with whatever emotions arose during the clip. Those people who had to suppress their emotions showed lower self-control at the end of the study. The way self-control was measured is interesting. It was done by looking at how much people disclosed about themselves to a stranger. People who suppressed laughter went on to be more "loose lipped" about themselves, whereas those who could express their emotions didn't "overshare."

We and our kids need to know how to feel and express the full range of emotions. For strength-based parents, this can mean voicing frustration and disappointment in our child's behavior: "I'm disappointed that you've been texting your friends for the past half hour instead of getting your chemistry homework done," but using self-control to flip the Strength Switch and let your child know the strengths she can bring to bear for a better outcome: "I know chemistry isn't your favorite subject, but you're organized and persistent. How about we work out a schedule to help you get your assignments done, and build in breaks for texting your friends?" Being strength based isn't about being artificially happy, ignoring your feelings, or letting your children get away with bad behavior; it's about using self-control to handle the feelings and bad behavior constructively.

You've got a head start on emotional coaching if you're using the mindfulness techniques in Chapter 6 to build your child's emotional complexity and to tune in to your own emotions as you practice strength-based parenting and living. Exploring and expressing emotions frees up self-control for better uses.

Strategy #5: Experiment with Habit Change

Working for just two weeks to change a habit can actually enlarge our capacity for self-control.[36]

One technique researchers have found effective is to spend two weeks reminding yourself to keep good posture. Each time you get the impulse to slump, you override the impulse and sit or stand up straight instead. Every time you succeed, your self-control muscle is strengthened. The habit itself seems a bit trivial, I know, but the point is really to strengthen self-control, which can happen even with this relatively straightforward change.[37] Researchers have actually found that study subjects can plunge their hand into a bucket of ice and exert the self-control to keep it there longer after doing just such an exercise.

See if your child feels like trying a habit-change experiment (leaving out the bucket of ice!) with something simple like improving posture, stopping nail-biting, or breaking the habit of saying "ummm," or some other small but pervasive habit. Better yet, each of you can pick a habit and support each other in changing it. A fun challenge that will probably get both of you laughing is to try using your non-dominant hand for routine tasks. From there, you and your child can "graduate" to all kinds of habit-change challenges to build your self-control muscles. And your child can apply her strengthened self-control to any number of important goals she wants to achieve.

Remember the Australian researchers' experiment I mentioned earlier, where they tested participants' self-control in attending to a computer task by playing an Eddie Murphy comedy film nearby? Well, those scientists discovered something remarkable quite by accident. You may recall that the participants were divided into groups, each tasked with a specific goal of losing weight, adhering to a study program, or sticking to a budget. The researchers found that not only did each group get better at the task the group was supposed to perform, but they also got better at the other tasks they *weren't* supposed to perform! That's right—the group losing weight also got better at budgeting and studying, and the same was true for the other groups.

Proof positive that the muscle of self-control knows no bounds. The ability to monitor and mobilize thoughts, emotions, and actions toward a goal is transferable and, apparently, can kick in without our even being aware of it. With proper care and management, it can throw its power behind any task. You and your child will be the winners.

CHAPTER 8

Communication

As your awareness of your child's strengths deepens, the conversations between you and your child will naturally begin to change, because you'll start communicating more from a strength-based perspective. Of course, you'll want to communicate your insights about your child's strengths to her as clearly as possible so she can develop her own awareness of them, cultivate them, and know when to call on them. One of the most powerful ways to do this is through praise.

Working with parents and teachers from many different walks of life in the United States, Canada, Europe, Australia, New Zealand, and Asia, I've heard many opinions about praise, most falling into one of two camps. Some worry: "Praise makes a child complacent, and he'll stop trying." Others take the opposite view: "Praise gives a child confidence, so he'll keep trying."

Indeed, research shows that there is praise that might keep kids from pushing themselves—but not because it makes them feel complacent. And there is praise that seems to spur kids to keep trying—but it's important to also help kids feel OK just the way they are.

I believe that, all too often, praise is either overlooked in the rush of everyday life and the pressure to handle problems, or it gets diminished into well-meant sound bites that don't really tell the child anything useful—and may even be counterproductive.

Fortunately, strength-based parenting naturally provides you with the perfect ingredients for nutritious, sustaining praise. With a few tweaks and adjustments to your communication patterns, your words can become tools that build your child's strengths. And, according to the data, these changes are desperately needed.

The High Price of Harsh Words

If you're reading this book, it's because you adore your child and want to do the best possible job as a parent—so you're probably talking with and praising your child a lot already. But the research shows that we don't communicate with our kids as much as we think we do—or as *well* as we think we do. For example, when teenagers and parents discuss topics such as chores, allowance, and homework, and are then asked separately by psychologists to guess what the other person was thinking, 93 percent of the parent-teen pairs guessed wrong.[1] Further gaps are seen when we ask about the communication style in the family. When teens, moms, and dads are asked to give their perspective on two types of communication: open communication (e.g., "My mother/father is always a good listener") and problem communication (e.g., "My mother/father has a tendency to say things to me that would be better left unsaid"), teens report less open communication and more problem communication than parents do.[2]

This apparent mismatch has implications for the strength development and psychological health of our children. In a longitudinal study testing the relationship between parent communication and brain development in upper elementary school kids as they grew into teens, high levels of positive communication (defined as a pattern of communication where the parent is approving, validating, affectionate, humorous, happy, pleasant, and caring) were associated with beneficial brain alterations that enhance capacity for learning, decision making, social skills, and emotional functioning. In contrast, children whose parents displayed low levels of positive communication had a greater risk of growing into the teen years with brain alterations that create a vulnerability for depression.

We tend to think that if we're not being negative toward our kids, then we're doing OK—but this study showed that even low levels of positive communication may adversely affect a child's brain.[3] Failing to do a bad job doesn't mean you're doing a great one. So while you may not be nasty, the absence or scarcity of affectionate, validating, and caring communication harms the brain. It's like depriving a young plant of the sunshine it needs to grow.

In research with fifth graders, psychologists assessed how the parents reacted to their children's display of emotions during difficult situations (e.g., a pet dying, the child not winning a contest).[4] Parents' reactions were categorized as being warm or cold. A warm response was coded when parents accepted and encouraged children to express their emotions by asking about, paraphrasing, and validating the child's feelings. A cold response was coded when parents actively discouraged the child's expression of feelings by invalidating the child's feelings (e.g., telling the child that it was wrong to feel that way or that there was no point in getting upset) or saying hurtful things (e.g., teasing or criticizing the child for being weak). Almost half of the moms (44 percent) and more than half of the dads responded coldly (64 percent).

We can blame some of this mismatch on our inherent negativity bias. Simply being clued in to this is hugely important, but it's a lesson we need to reinforce through mindfulness of our daily communication habits, drawing ourselves gently back to seeing positives in our kids when the world tends to fixate on weakness or when we focus more on what our kids are doing wrong than on what they're doing right. As I mentioned in Chapter 2: Where attention goes, energy flows. Mindfulness can shift us away from criticism and into strength supportiveness by shifting our attention to how we see and speak to our children, as this mother movingly describes:

> *My son is now thirteen and for many years he struggled academically. I was continually called to the school for meetings with psychologists, teachers, speech pathologists, and occupational therapists focused on "fixing" him. It was an awful time and I felt like a failure as a parent. Upon reflection, I believe one failure I did succumb to was focusing too much on what was wrong with him and not nearly enough on his many accomplishments. I remember the moment when I became mindful of this. I was with a friend, cataloging the range of specialists I had been to see and their perceptions of my son's weaknesses. When I finally paused for a breath, I noticed a tear running down her face. Whatever could it be? She reminded me what a thoughtful, gentle, generous, kind, funny child my son was. She told me how sad she felt because not once had I acknowledged this since she had arrived.*
>
> *It was a turning point and a trigger for me to listen more intuitively to the lessons I knew were true—that focusing on his abundant strengths was the path to growth. My son is still not going to win academic prizes, but my shift to a strength focus and moving my son to a school that similarly focused on strengths rather than on deficits have helped improve his progress. I'm thankful, too, that the school appreciates his humanity: He was recognized for his kindness on a school excursion when he volunteered (unprompted) to give his seat to an elderly gentleman. He's also now performing at the appropriate academic standard, which is great to see.*

Remember, our kids have the same negativity bias that we do. So unless we tell them quite specifically that they have strengths, the negativity bias can magnify the effects of criticism—or, worse, of harsh words—to the point of leading kids to think that they have no strengths, as this school administrator recounts:

Brad is sixteen and living in an unstable home environment. He also had significant struggles with mental health. He came to our school after being expelled from three other schools. His self-talk about his future was pervasively negative. His teacher took him through the usual academic assessments and then the VIA Youth Survey. When asked prior to the survey, "What are your strengths?" he answered, "I don't have any. That's why I'm at this school. My teachers and my old family weren't good, and I'm bad at most things, except some video games." When his teacher went through the VIA Survey with him, humor arose as his top strength. His teacher was startled, because his emotions and demeanor had been flat the entire time. She asked, "Do you want to retake the assessment? You may see other strengths coming forward, too." (She later told me that she thought she had administered the test incorrectly, because it seemed there was no way humor could have been his top strength.) He replied, "No. And you know what? The test is right. No one knows I'm funny. But I am. I see the world in funny ways, but I just don't tell anyone. I like that humor is at the top. No one ever told me I was good at anything, but this test did, and maybe at this school I'll share my funny ideas with people."

As these stories show, when children's strengths are recognized and affirmed, they have a better chance to bloom.

EXERCISE: | Your Memories of Wounding Words

We've all experienced the sting of wounding words. In my parent workshops, I ask the audience to reflect on how their parents communicated with them. Decades later, many still feel the pain of their parents' harsh words as if it happened yesterday. Some even experience the same physical and emotional reactions they had all those years ago. One woman developed an instant rash on the left side of her face as she recalled an argument where her mother had told her that she was ashamed of her and wanted to disown her because of the boy she was dating.

Take a few minutes of quiet time and think back to your childhood. In general, how were you spoken to? What was the ratio of criticism to praise? What words and phrases were used? How did these words affect your perception of yourself? Do they still affect you today? What do you wish you'd been told about your strengths growing up?

The Praise Puzzle

Praise can enhance all three elements of your child's strengths: performance, energy, and use. Science shows that in toddlers through adults, praise is related to task achievement (performance), task enjoyment (energy), and motivation (use).[5] Praise makes your child feel good and influences how he reacts to failure and recovers from setbacks, so it's an essential aspect of instilling optimism and resilience in your child.[6]

But all praise is not created equal. There are three types I'd like to talk about. Each has an important effect on a child's mind-set.[7] In fact, the most powerful outcome from the praise a child hears is the mind-set it cultivates.

As I explained in Chapter 4, our mind-set is our core belief about whether our qualities, such as intelligence, personality, and strengths, are fixed or can change. Dr. Carol Dweck and her colleagues have shown that praise plays a key role in shaping a child's mind-set. With this in mind, let's take a look at the three types of praise.

Generic Praise

The most common praise we hear (and tend to give) takes the form of general, sweeping positive statements, such as: "Great job!" "Good work!" "Awesome!" "Well done!" "Way to go!" "High five!"

When you say these things to your child, you're basically saying, "I love you, I care for you, I think well of you"—and that's great! But while these statements may help to affirm your child, they don't build the child's strengths, because they don't help the child identify the strength(s) he used to succeed.[8] "Good job" doesn't tell the child what he did that was good, so he can't figure out how to replicate his success and continue to receive your praise.[9] Thus, generic praise can leave kids in a state of uncertainty (and, in some cases, anxiety).[10] So while generic praise has a role in affirming your love for your child, it's not a powerful tool for building strengths.

Process Praise

Then there's praise for achievement, also known as process-praise. This is praise for what your child does. It focuses on the child's effort, improvement, technique, or strategy. Suppose your child brings home a painting from school. Generic praise would be: "That is beautiful!" Process-praise would be:

- "This looks great. You must have really stayed focused to produce such a detailed piece of art." (praising child's effort)
- "Interesting! It looks like you used brushes of different thicknesses to get in a lot of detail." (praising child's technique)

Or suppose your child gets a better grade on a test than on the previous test in that subject. Generic praise would be: "Good job! I knew you could do it." Process-praise would be:

- "You prepared for this test by spending extra time each night last week reviewing material. And it worked!" (praising child's strategy)
- "You pulled up your score by a full grade! What do you think you did that helped you improve?" (praising child's improvement)

According to Dweck's research, process-praise is the most effective way to promote a growth mind-set.[11] By focusing on the processes your child undertook to succeed, you give her a shot of good feelings while also helping her see what she did to succeed so she can "own" her success and, presumably, replicate it. It stands to reason that a person who understands the processes she's used to succeed will be more optimistic about future outcomes and better able to deal with challenges and setbacks (i.e., be more resilient).

But here's an interesting point. Sometimes process-praise can back-fire. If a child has to expend a great deal of effort to meet a challenge, and your process-praise is, in effect, telling the child, "Keep trying, keep trying," the child may conclude that if she has to use so much effort so much of the time, it must be because she has little or no innate ability.

After a parenting workshop last year in Hong Kong, a mom ap-proached me about precisely this problem. "What happens if process-praise demotivates a child?" she asked. She explained that she had recently read about the importance of process-praise and had been using it with her teenage son for his homework. It had totally back-fired. Her son was actually doing less and less homework! In fact, earlier that week he had yelled at her: "Stop saying stuff like that, Mom. I know you think I'm dumb."

Naturally, this mother was perplexed. So was I. How could this mom's well-meaning praise about her son's *process* end up being viewed by the son as a negative judgment about his *ability*? I promised her I'd do my best to find an answer to her question.

I thought about it all during the nine-hour flight back to Australia and hit the university library when I got home. After hours of searching, I found a study that gave me an answer. Curiously, the study had been conducted at the University of Hong Kong, a thirty-minute drive from the school where I'd delivered the workshop and met this worried mother.

The researchers at the University of Hong Kong[12] found that the way a child views the relationship between effort and ability is a key determinant in whether process-praise motivates or demotivates. Some children believe effort and ability are negatively, or inversely, related. In this belief, a person with high talent doesn't need to put in effort, whereas a person with low talent needs to put in a lot of effort. Thus high effort implies low ability. Children with this belief see effort as an indication of low talent and therefore feel embarrassed to put in effort because it shows everyone that they're not talented.

The teenage boy in Hong Kong probably had a belief that effort and ability are negatively related and had interpreted his mother's process-praise as a judgment of his incompetence. The message he heard was, "You need to put in extra effort because you're not smart enough." He reduced his effort because he wanted to prove to himself he could get good grades simply through his intelligence, not through having to try.

Praise for Character (Person-Praise)

In contrast to process-praise, which focuses on behavior, praise for character singles out and recognizes a person's innate qualities—thus the term "person-praise." Using our examples of the child bringing home a painting or a test with an improved score, here's what person-praise might sound like for those achievements:

- "Wow, that looks great. You must have artistic talent to produce such good art."
- "Keep it up! You've got the ability to ace this class."

There's evidence that person-praise can build moral qualities in children—for example, telling a child he's a "helpful person" rather than praising his helpful behavior spurs the child to greater levels of generosity—around the age of eight, when kids' sense of identity might be in a critical phase of development.[13] When you praise a child for his moral strengths and help him see that these strengths are assets and qualities *within* him, rather than just behaviors or processes he's decided to undertake, he's more likely to internalize these strengths and use them consistently.[14]

But when it comes to achievement, Dweck's research has found that person-praise is more likely to lead to a fixed mind-set in the classroom, which can be an impediment to performance.[15] How so? Because if a child identifies herself as having a specific quality such as intelligence, then experiences challenges or setbacks in that area, instead of viewing these events objectively as "hmm, this isn't working," she's more likely to take it as a personal message of "I'm no longer smart." Essentially, problems can become threats to identity. That can lead to a tendency to play it safe, to a reluctance to try, or to an unwillingness to take on new challenges.

Dweck has found that while person-praise might make kids feel good in their moment of success, it weakens their resilience when confronted with academic setbacks later on.[16] In fact, when faced with challenging tasks, children who receive person-praise rate the quality of their work and their ability lower, and report lower levels of task enjoyment and motivation and higher levels of negative emotion compared to children who receive process-praise.

As you can see, there appear to be two conflicting models here. Person-praise seems to encourage moral qualities in children, particularly within a certain age frame, but it can discourage achievement. And process-praise may encourage achievement but has less effect on moral development and can backfire if the child believes effort signals low ability. What's a parent to do?

Introducing Strength-Based Praise

I propose that strength-based praise can meld the best of both types of praise, neither overwhelming kids with the pressure of having to uphold their image to the point where they don't take risks (the potential downside of person-praise), nor undermining them with the idea that they aren't enough just the way they are (the potential downside of process-praise).

Besides, in the busyness of daily life, parents need a clear, workable strategy they can easily use. Are you really going to step back in each moment and think: *This is an achievement moment, so I'll use process-praise.* Or: *This is a moral development moment, so I'll use person-praise.* Not likely.

My workshops with parents and teachers have given me a lot of insight into praise. First, there was the mother in Hong Kong whose son's demotivation showed how process-praise can backfire. Then there's what I call the "yet" story.

A few years ago, I was asked to moderate a panel for a group of schools that were using positive psychology in their classes. One teacher on the panel spoke of the emphasis her school had put on using process-praise and the big push on using the word *yet* to indicate that learning could always improve and to encourage growth mindsets in students. For example, when a student in art or in physical education class said, "I can't do it," the teacher would reply, "Yet." When a student said, "I'm no good at this," the teacher would reply, "Not yet." Many of the teachers on the panel agreed that process-praise had been successful in their schools.

Then a teacher in the audience lifted her hand to ask a question. "I'm confused," she said. "Isn't it OK for a student not to be good at some things? Do students always have to persist in what they can't 'yet' do? If you're asking them to improve on everything, doesn't this mean you're *not* playing to their strengths? I'm wondering whether process-praise might diminish students' sense of their strengths, which do, in fact, have to do with them as a person."

She had a point. I decided that the real downside of praise comes from binary thinking—one of the mental habits we discussed in Chapter 2 that needlessly narrows our view—in this case, the idea that there's only one best way to praise kids. Generic praise, process-praise (including the "yet" model), and person-praise each have their positives and negatives, but the negatives are most likely to kick in when we use one to the exclusion of the others. I vote for a "balanced diet" of praise that sensibly blends them—and I suggest we throw strength-based praise into the mix.

Strength-based praise combines the best of both worlds by connecting a child with his strengths (person-praise) and then praising him for how he uses those strengths (process-praise) to be a good person or perform well. It says two things to kids:

1. *It acknowledges action: "Here's what you did."* Acknowledging action helps the child understand what worked so she can repeat those actions in the future to replicate her success. This is the process-praise part.

2. *It acknowledges strengths: "Here are the strengths you have that helped you."* Acknowledging ability, talent, skills, and positive personality traits recognizes the inner assets the child brought to bear on the situation. This is the person-praise part of the equation. Better yet, because you're showing her *how* her strengths work, not just what they are, you're showing her that strengths are dynamic and can grow. This means that she won't develop a fixed mind-set and let her self-worth get so tied up in a strength that she'll limit herself for fear of failing.

Used this way, strength-based praise encourages both achievement *and* good character by connecting kids with the positive forces they unleash through the combined power of their strengths and their actions.

So how does it look in practice?

Strength-based praise for the child who brings home a painting or a good test grade might sound like this:

- "You really used your creativity [strength] to put in so many colors [action]."
- "There is so much detail in this painting [action]. I can see how you used your ability to observe [strength] to create a lifelike piece of art."
- "You've used your persistence [strength] to stick to the task of reviewing for this test every night last week [action], even when you were tired and wanted to play computer games."
- "I really admire how you drew on your planning skills [strength] to ask for extra help from the teacher [action]— and it has paid off with a better score."

Interestingly, when Dr. Dweck took her research into the homes of families,[17] spending dinnertimes with them to analyze how many times parents used person-praise versus process-praise with their young kids, and then testing the mind-sets of the kids five years later, she found that person-praise didn't lead to a fixed mind-set in those kids. I believe this is because in the more natural setting of the home, where parents likely use a mix of praise over a period of years as kids pass through various phases of identity formation and skills development, it's the *blend* of praise that happens dynamically and organically over time that constructs a growth mind-set.

Here's how one child internalized his mom's strength-based praise over the years to the point where it positively shaped his identity and his decision about how he could contribute at school:

Tom is a very organized kid. When he was younger, he'd pack his older sister's schoolbag and put it at the front door each morning before school. When I asked him why he did this, he said he did it because it was easy for him to do—and it helped to make sure that no one (particularly him!) was late for school. I have always reinforced how helpful being organized is for him and others with comments like, "I reckon

*that being organized makes life feel easier and more enjoyable for you,"
and, "You are the best helper when we need to get things organized."
Tom now prides himself on his ability to remember things that need to
be done and says things like, "Tell me what we need to do, Mom; you
know I won't forget."*

*A couple of weeks ago when I was washing Tom's school cap, I saw
that he had written inside the cap: "throw your hat in" and "organized." When I asked him what this was about, he told me that they
had done an activity in school where each child had to throw his hat
into the center of their circle and share a strength that he would be
known for and would contribute to the class this year. Tom said his
strength was "being organized."*

*Tom told me that he uses this strength to contribute to the class by
reminding kids when things are due and what activities are planned
for the next day. Knowing that he has this ability has given Tom something valuable and unique to contribute to his peers—which he does in
an authentic way and feels proud and good about doing.*

Strength-based praise can also remind a child that he has abilities
on those days—and we all have them—when he doubts he has any:

*The other morning Paddy [age ten] climbed into bed with me and cud-
dled up close. After a while he let out a deep sigh and said, "None of my
talents are useful." Fortunately I was really listening at the time and
was able to engage him in a chat. He told me he thought his talents
were running and playing the guitar but he couldn't see how these offered anything and wouldn't help him "be good at school." We spent
some time talking about how these talents had been useful for him already: He could win running games at school and get out of doing jobs
because he had to do guitar practice. I asked him how he thought his
talents could be useful to the world. It took him some time to generate
answers, but he did, including: It's fun to watch fast runners in the*

Olympics, so maybe he can make other people feel happy when they watch him run fast.

I then told him a bit about Thomas Edison and his invention of the lightbulb. I made Paddy guess how many times Edison failed before he succeeded. Then I told Paddy how, as an eight-month-old, he had mastered climbing out of his bed before he could even walk because he was so determined to find me.

He and Edison "have the characteristic of persistence in common," I said, noting that both of them are good at solving problems others can't see.

I felt my little boy's body grow, just a little bit, as it unfolded right next to me, and I watched him jump out of bed. Talk over. The whole chat probably took less than ten minutes, but it completely changed how he saw himself for that day. Reminding him of his abilities was my little "magic moment" with my young son and a positive-thinking gift I could give him.

Strength-based praise can also remind kids that their unique mix of abilities will help them live out a life story that only they can tell:

We have two great sons. Anthony is now twenty-two and in the honors program at a prestigious science university, and James, nineteen, is taking a gap year after completing the first year of a business degree.

When Anthony was in high school, he was an academic achiever who scored high on tests.

When it was James's turn to prepare for senior year in school, he felt pressured by his older brother's outstanding academic achievements. I remember one conversation in the car where he voiced his concerns about the year ahead: "I can't do what Anthony did!" I realized that he was feeling anxious and replied that I understood his concerns, but then I said, "Be happy for Anthony, but know that that is his story. You are writing your story, the 'James' story." I encouraged him to draw on his hope and perspective to look forward to his journey through this year, along with the kindness and social intelligence that he shows to others. Happily, he completed a successful year filled with study, good friends, and basketball. His final grades resulted in his being offered admission to his preferred college.

Make a list of the things you tend to say to your child when praising her. How would you make them over into strength-based praise of her actions and/or abilities? Here are a few I've made up to get you started:

"OLD" PRAISE: "You did your best and aced the test. Great job!"

STRENGTH-BASED PRAISE: "You're a hard worker [strength] who is naturally curious [strength] and you put in the hours needed to prepare for this test [action]. Let's celebrate your hard work paying off!"

"OLD" PRAISE: "You're great at making friends. You'll be fine at the new school."

STRENGTH-BASED PRAISE: "You know how to build rapport with others because you're kind [strength] and funny [strength] and because you care about others [strength]. Remember when you started at your old school and didn't know anyone? Now you have lots of friends. Let's talk about the things you did to get to know your classmates [action]."

"OLD" PRAISE: "You've got a good head on your shoulders. I'm so proud of you for working out this problem."

STRENGTH-BASED PRAISE: "I've seen you exercise good judgment [strength] and clear thinking [strength] and once again you've made a decision you can be proud of. You asked questions, got the facts, and made a list of pros and cons. Those are all excellent strategies for sound decisions [action]."

"OLD" PRAISE: "You stuck through the hard part of adjusting to sleepaway camp. Good for you!"

STRENGTH-BASED PRAISE: "You were resilient and recovered quickly when things weren't going your way [strength], and you were reliable [strength] because you took personal responsibility for building the team's campfire [action]. I'm sure the team really valued your contributions."

"OLD" PRAISE: "Wow, you've rearranged your bedroom. The new layout is great."

STRENGTH-BASED PRAISE: "The way you take pride [strength] in your bedroom is a reflection of your strength as an improver [strength]. You're always looking for ways to do things better, and the new arrangement you've created [action] gives your bedroom a whole new look, with better lighting near your desk and your favorite posters where you can see them when you wake up in the morning."

"OLD" PRAISE: "Thanks for waiting until I calmed down."

STRENGTH-BASED PRAISE: "I appreciate that you used your social intelligence [strength] and compassion [strength] to let me calm down before you continued this discussion [action]. You waited until you saw I was no longer angry [action], which means you were really thinking about how I felt in this situation [strength]. Thank you for doing that."

Now try adding your own, based on your knowledge of your child's strengths.

EXERCISE: | Write Your Child a Strengths Letter

One way to praise your child is to write your child a strengths letter. For one week, keep notes on the strengths you see in your child each day. Also think back to big events or important times in her life. Write all of these together in a strengths letter and give it to her. You can do the same thing for your spouse, friends, business partner, and coworkers. In my university program I have my students, all mature professionals, write strengths letters for the team they work with. They report that this simple letter has a transformative effect on the team dynamics. Remember to use a blend of the different types of praise. Below is how one parent approached writing her letter to her teenage son prior to his senior year of high school:

> *I wrote to Josh of the things that I had seen him accomplish and of his growth into a young man. I acknowledged his strength of perseverance as he applied himself without complaint to his athletic training and to his studies, aiming to do his best. For this he was rewarded with officer of the school, captain of cross-country, and sportsman of the year for his final year.*
>
> *In these leadership roles, and in general, Josh applied his strength of empathy by supporting the team, often running alongside the last runner(s) despite having finished in the top three for his school, encouraging and spurring his fellow teammates on. He also modeled and applied this skill daily with his youngest brother, who joined our family from foster care.*
>
> *I wrote of his strength of courage as he deliberately looked for opportunities to address his fear of heights, such as choosing rappelling as his last school camp.*

I also encouraged Josh to build on the strengths of curiosity and social intelligence. To look outward and be tolerant of others. To be open to hearing the voices of those around him.

Josh later told me that the letter meant a great deal to him. He keeps it in his bedside table and I hope he will reflect on it with a warm heart.

A year later, I wrote a strengths letter to my second son, and I plan to do so for my two younger children when they're older.

I have found that focusing on my children's strengths is a great way to celebrate what they do well and softly draw attention to opportunities to grow.

I like to think of strength-based praise as a relationship builder between parent and child, helping them rise above the criticism loop that families tend to fall into.

Spotting strengths in kids is also about catching them doing good things. Strengths conversations really are elevating conversations, as opposed to conversations that are about catching kids doing something wrong or misbehaving.

I've devoted a full chapter to praise because it's such an important part of the parent-child relationship, yet it often gets pushed aside in the rush of daily life. Let's all make a pact to be more mindful of opportunities to praise not only our children but also all the important people in our life. This parent captured it well:

> I love the "reframe" that strengths allow. My partner, Gary, is strong in prudence, and a core strength of mine is kindness. Seeing this helped to reframe our conversations and to see each other's point of view. When we built a house together, I was able to understand that his need to inspect everything came from that strength and that it was often necessary and helped get the job done well, while I might have let things go to be "kind." Our relationship has improved a great deal, thanks to this new lens. Our children, too, are learning to see that we all have different strengths. The ability to see value in the way we are has helped our family become a team.

If you're already practicing savoring and gratitude (see Chapter 5), you're probably already becoming more aware of what you appreciate about others. And if you're practicing mindfulness, too (Chapter 6), you'll be in the moment and present so you can see the strengths as they unfold in action. I hope you'll soon find, as I have, how quickly strength-based praise can improve your relationships. What better feeling is there than to know that your words have put a smile of delight on someone's face?

Of course, our conversations with kids consist of more than just giving praise. A big part of my work with parents is to help them re-frame how they interact with their children when dealing with challenges, from misbehavior to sibling spats and more. And that's where we'll turn in the next chapter.

CHAPTER 9

Strength-Based Living in the Real World

As I mentioned in Chapter 7, saying no and setting limits is part of our responsibility as strength-based parents to help our children learn self-control. When my children misbehave or need to work on a weakness, I remind myself, "Here's a moment where we can do some attention training together." The more I build my kids' capacity to focus their attention and override their impulses, the stronger they'll get at handling this challenge and others, too.

Strength-based parents still need to discipline their children. The difference is that they approach misbehavior from a constructive, growth-oriented perspective that gives kids a clear idea of the strengths that can be used to change for the better.

Strength-based discipline is based on the premise that by nature we are motivated to self-develop.[1] Negative patterns or behaviors signify a block in our drive toward strength-based growth. Strength-based discipline is about working with a child to discover what's blocking his progress and helping him get back on track. That's what this chapter will help you do, coupled with the tools you've learned in previous chapters. Strength-based discipline can break the cycle of nagging/ criticism/confrontation that quickly becomes unproductive. Once you and your child get the hang of strength-based discipline, you may find your child steps up with insights and improvement that will surprise you:

One day in assembly I noticed five sixth-grade boys giggling in the back row. I was upset because the first graders were presenting at the time, and it was important that the older students model good audience behavior. After assembly, I asked the boys to meet me the next day and to bring the VIA Surveys they'd completed as part of the school's strengths project. They looked a bit worried—and I was happy to give them time to reflect on their behavior.

Five of the six boys had humor as their greatest strength. When we met, I asked what they thought this might mean. Immediately one answered that they were allowing their strength of humor to take over. I asked what they planned to do to make sure that their humor didn't dominate them at inappropriate times in the future. They were full of ideas and agreed that it would help to couple their humor with another strength to moderate it. One chose kindness; others teamwork; another self-regulation. The last boy said his strength was humility. The others asked him to remind them to consider others if their humor took over again. Their self-awareness and goal setting were so mature that I asked them to share their learnings with the other students. They became the speakers at the next assembly.

EXERCISE: | Your Discipline Style

Despite what you might think (and what kids themselves might say), most children understand that rules are necessary. Even teenagers do, if there's room for negotiation. Children and teens routinely report that they'll follow rules, provided the rules are reasonable, consistent, and fair.[2]

It's in how the rules are enforced—in other words, how we discipline our children—where the conflicts tend to arise.

Many of us equate discipline with punishment: being made to suffer for our actions. But the Latin origin of the word is "to provide instruction or knowledge." We can use discipline to teach our children the values and attitudes of society, right and wrong, how to get along in life, and how to get along with others.[3] Punishment breaks a child down. Discipline can help to build a child up.

How do you commonly discipline your child? Look at the options below in Table 2 and check which ones you're "likely" or "unlikely" to use.[4]

	LIKELY	UNLIKELY
1. Point out how your child's behavior makes others feel.		
2. Tell your child that you are surprised that she has acted like that; it's not like her.		
3. Punish her for what she has done.		
4. Give your child the cold shoulder.		
5. Ask your child to think about how he would feel if someone else had acted the way he did.		

	LIKELY	UNLIKELY
6. Express your disappointment in your child's actions and remind him that he can do better.		
7. Withdraw a privilege or ground your child.		
8. Tell her you are ashamed of her.		
9. Ask her to put herself in someone else's shoes.		
10. Remind your child of times when he has behaved better.		
11. Yell at him.		
12. Make a point of ignoring them.		

Table 2: Discipline Style

The options above represent four different discipline styles identified by psychologists in the late 1960s that continue to be researched today.[5] Although you may use a range of them, research shows that each of us probably has a prevailing style. Review the descriptions below to learn which discipline style you tend to rely on:

- *Other-oriented induction* (options 1, 5, 9) involves communicating with the child about the consequences of her behavior, teaching and reasoning with her, and helping her think about the impact of her behavior on others.
- *Expressing disappointment about expectations* (options 2, 6, 10) involves expressing disappointment with your child's behavior (not with the child) because you know he's capable of better. It teaches your child about your

expectations for good behavior and implies that you know he can make good choices, but that, in this instance, he has fallen short.

- *Power-assertive responses* (options 3, 7, 11) involve controlling the child through physical size/power and control over material resources. This includes physical intimidation, physical punishment (e.g., spanking), yelling, the removal of privileges, grounding, or punishing the child through actions such as assigning extra chores.
- *Love withdrawal* (options 4, 8, 12) involves punishing the child by removing emotional support; ignoring, isolating, turning one's back on, or refusing to speak to the child; explicitly expressing dislike for the child or telling her you're ashamed of her. These actions are intended to make the child feel so bad that she won't do the objectionable thing again.

Power-assertive responses and love withdrawal are forms of *punishment*. They're aimed at making the child *suffer*. They send messages of disapproval and rejection: "I have the power to cut you from the team."

Other-oriented induction and expressing disappointment about expectations are forms of *discipline*. They're aimed at helping a child *learn*. They send messages of responsibility and possibility: "We're in this together, and I'm going to help you learn the right thing to do."

Punishment induces shame, which is destructive to a child's sense of self. Discipline engenders uncomfortable but constructive feelings of guilt that encourage prosocial behavior. Shame and guilt are often confused, but they are very different. Let's take a closer look at each.

Shame versus Guilt

Essentially, there are two broad approaches to correcting your childrens' behavior: by inducing shame or by inducing guilt.

Shame makes a person feel bad about *who they are*. It is deeply rejecting because it rejects the person as being, in essence, bad. Shame-inducing statements might sound like this:

- "How could you be so stupid?"
- "You are rude."
- "You are selfish."

In contrast, guilt makes a person feel bad about *what they did*. It rejects the person's actions but not the person.[6] Guilt-inducing statements might sound like this:

- "That's the third time this week that you've left your math assignment at home. That is not good planning."
- "What you just said to your sister was not kind."
- "Cutting in line isn't fair to others."

Remember the psychological process of projection that we looked at in Chapter 2? I believe that most parents who use shame as a form of punishment are doing so because of projection. They see a quality or behavior in their children that they themselves have and are ashamed of. Instead of dealing with their own shame they project it onto their children so as to avoid discomfort. But you need to think twice if you are doing this, because shame leads to self-doubt, anxiety, and depression.[7] What's more, it's not even an effective form of punishment. When a child feels shame, he will withdraw from others. Shame is so deeply painful that the child's only choice is to avoid (i.e., ignore) whatever caused the shame; thus, no learning can take place.

Shame is damaging, but guilt, while uncomfortable, serves a purpose.[8] Guilt is a powerful part of our evolutionary wiring. Guilt leads to regret and empathy. When a child feels guilt, he can amend and repair. His regret and empathy motivate him to act differently in the future. Guilt is, in a word, prosocial: It fosters bonding within a group, helping us know when we've done something wrong toward someone else and causing us to feel bad about it so that we will repair it and not do it again. Thus, it sends a developmental message that promotes improvement, or development, of our higher capacities: the self-control, good judgment, and kindness needed for appropriate behavior as part of the human family (and our own families).

Far from telling a child he is bad, guilt can be a powerful way to communicate to your child that he is *better* than his bad behavior: "I'm disappointed to hear that you teased the new student in your class. I wouldn't have expected that of you. I know you can do better."

But how will the child figure out what "better" is? Here's where strength-based parenting takes discipline to the next level.

Seeing Behavioral Challenges from a Strengths Perspective

I think the moments when our children make poor choices and get into trouble provide opportunities to talk to them about where they forgot to use their strengths or what strengths they need to call forward. It can be an opportunity to build social intelligence.

I couldn't say it better than this parent. Whereas guilt-based discipline tells children what *not* to do, strength-based discipline goes a step further, letting our kids know what they *can* do—reminding them of strengths they possess to address the problem. We show them how to reach within to find the resources for change, rebound from setbacks, focus their attention on repairing the problem, and move in a more positive direction.

If this sounds like we're helping kids become mindful of their actions and building their ability to activate their nervous system's pause-and-plan mode, which can stand between them and their impulsiveness or lapses in judgment the next time around, you're absolutely right. That's the kind of discipline our children really need.

Five Questions for Diagnosing Strength Breakdowns

For all of the reasons above, I often talk with parents about reframing children's challenging behaviors as lapses in strength or as strength breakdowns. Rather than thinking, *This kid is a problem*, it's about thinking, for example, *This challenging behavior is happening because she forgot to use her strengths of fairness and kindness.* Rather than punishing your child, it's a time to teach her how to better use and fine-tune her strengths. Reframing in this way keeps you from shaming your child *and* makes both you and your child feel that this is something the child is capable of fixing.

Here are five questions you can ask yourself to diagnose a child's strength breakdown:

Question #1: Is It Strength Overuse?

Humor and playfulness are among my husband Matt's top strengths. When I met Matt in college, he had a way of lifting my heavy heart with his quick wit, big laugh, and ability to see the lighter side of life. To this day, he still lifts my heart and makes me laugh—big belly laughs—regularly. I'm not the only one who appreciates his humor and playfulness. He's regularly asked to be master of ceremonies at his friends' functions, and Nick is proud that his friends think he has a funny dad at school.

Everyone enjoys Matt's humor.

Well, almost everyone. He tells me that it used to get him in trouble with the teachers at school. What was an appropriate display of this strength in the schoolyard was not appropriate in the classroom. In one context, Matt's playfulness was appreciated; in another, it was viewed as disrespect. Understanding the social landscape is important in deciding when and exactly how much humor to let out to play. Many strengths are like that. Curiosity can be viewed as overstepping into nosiness; persistence can be seen as stubbornness; planning and forethought can show up as rigidity; kindness can become subservience.

We've all been guilty of misusing a strength and getting into trouble. When we look at behavior this way, it constructively changes how we respond.

A strength-based parent taking a child to task for overplaying humor could say, "You've got a great sense of humor, but when you overplay it, you get out of control and it's not a strength anymore. It leads to bad outcomes. What can you do to fix this situation and make sure your humor doesn't get out of control next time?"

Looking at misbehavior from this perspective teaches kids strengths flexibility: how to switch gears between strengths depending on the situation they're in and the people they're with. We tend to fall into the habit of over-relying on our core strengths. This doesn't sound so bad, but it can lead to negative consequences.[9] Even virtuous qualities like forgiveness can be overplayed and lead to negative outcomes, as this mom explained:

I have a strained relationship with my own mom. She can say and do things that are extremely hurtful. It's always been like this, and my dad has always asked me to forgive my mom so we can mend things. I have a forgiving nature, so I'm the one who makes the peace. When my daughter was born, my mom continued to do hurtful things, but this time toward my daughter. My husband pointed out that the downside of my forgiveness was that I was not setting clear boundaries, which allowed my mom to keep being hurtful. Forgiveness only works if the other person is prepared to change their negative behavior. So I decided to work more through fairness and courage to let me be brave and stand up to my mom and let her know that it wasn't right for her to be so hurtful toward me or my daughter. Things will always be strained, but my new approach has helped to move things forward for us.

Is strength overuse causing problems for your child? This parent noticed that her son's overuse of persistence was leading to frustration:

Ben has always loved building with Lego—a process he approaches very methodically, always studying the pictures on the box, reading the instructions, and, as he says, "preparing his build area" before he starts. When he was about ten, I asked him why he thought he was such a good Lego builder. He said it was because he just stuck with things until he got them done.

Ben used to try to complete his Lego building in one session and wouldn't take a break or stop until it was finished. Toward the end of a build, he often got tired and frustrated if he made a mistake. I saw this as an overuse of his perseverance. I began telling him that he knew he would always finish building because of his perseverance—but he needed to take a break to refresh himself.

This seems to have developed into some effective study habits: He always completes his work, and he paces himself with short breaks.

In another situation, strength overuse affected a child's test performance:

Zoe's top strength is appreciation of beauty and excellence. She was struggling to complete math tests in the time frame allocated, until we figured out that she was handing in the neatest, most beautifully written test papers, but not the fastest. She was focusing too much on the "beauty" of her presentation, to the point of not meeting the time requirements. This was a great insight in helping her improve (although she still hates rushing her work!).

This parent's strength-based reframing helped her work with her teenage son to repair a situation with an angry teacher:

I was just about to leave for work when my son Alex's math teacher called me. She didn't sound happy. I asked how I could help her.

"Alex needs to learn a thing or two about manners and stop talking back to me in class," she snapped.

I felt my indignation rise in defense of my son, but instead of retorting, I said I was just leaving for work and suggested we discuss the issue at a more appropriate time, and after I'd spoken to Alex.

That night, the teacher's words were still ringing in my ears as I asked Alex what happened. While he recounted the situation, I kept in mind that his top strength is fairness.

After listening to Alex's version of the story and seeing it through his lens of fairness and justice, what had transpired made a lot of sense to me. Speaking to his strengths, I told him I understood why he would have felt unjustly targeted. That gave both of us perspective on the situation. I then used his fairness to help him see the situation from his teacher's point of view. After all, it's only fair to see both sides of the story. Using fairness as the anchor for our conversation, we talked about a more constructive way for him to communicate his ideas to the teacher. The next day he was able resolve the issue with her without rancor.

It was a parent-child conversation I was proud of. In the past, I might have simply started with his teacher's accusations, laced with my own disappointment. Coming at this difficult conversation from a strengths perspective made all the difference.

Question #2: Is It Strength Underuse?

Asking your child whether she might be underusing or underplaying a strength is a much more positive way to help her reflect on her behavior than fixating on what she did wrong. Consider these contrasts in parent-child conversation:

Shame based: "I heard you were teasing the new student at school. I'm so humiliated that everyone knows about this. Typical of you to be mean. When will you ever change?"

Strength based: "I'm disappointed that you were teasing the new student at school. I see kindness and generosity in you so many other times. Last week you got up from watching TV to help your grandmother up the stairs and carry in her packages. I was so touched and proud to see how you noticed she needed help and you stepped forward. Your kindness is such a good quality in you. Is there a reason why you aren't using it with the new student?"

Or:

Guilt based: "Why did you quit the team after you lost the game? That's not like you. You know that's poor sportsmanship."

Strength based: "I'm curious what made you decide to quit the team after you lost the game. That just doesn't seem like you. What do you think might have happened if you had brought forward some of your strengths of perspective, teamwork, or fairness?"

Helping children see where they might be underusing their

strengths builds their mindfulness about their behaviors. It's also empowering: Kids realize that it's not a matter of their being "bad" but rather that their best self was not present in a particular situation: *I didn't do this because I'm a bad person. I just forgot to bring in certain strengths. I know I have those strengths inside of me. If I bring them in next time, this situation won't happen again.*

Strength underuse, like overuse, becomes easier to address the more you become a strength-based parent. As your child begins to see that she has many strengths available to her, the two of you will find endless combinations of how she can use her strengths to stay out of trouble and move forward positively in all sorts of situations.

Question #3: Is It the Flip Side or Shadow Side of a Strength?

Sometimes what we see as a problem is really the flip side, or what psychologists call the "shadow side," of a strength.[10] In those situations, we need to help our kids learn new ways to regulate or express their strengths:

Mia asks questions incessantly. It can be exhausting. While I want her to learn, grow in wisdom, and always be curious, at times I just want some peace and quiet! I have been speaking to Mia about how much I love her curiosity and the way she is interested in so many things. I suggested to her that it would also be good to be curious in other ways— without talking. She could be curious about people and what is around her. Together we have worked on showing curiosity about people's body language, i.e., how to tell when someone is looking distracted or, let's face it, getting annoyed with all the questions.

Mia now sees that her curiosity about people and their body language could help her to know when it is a good time to ask questions and when it is best to stay quiet. When it isn't a good time, she chooses to feed her curiosity in other ways, using her other senses. This has helped her to become more aware and know when quiet is required.

Even what we might consider highly challenging behavior might be better handled if we can flip our view to see it through a strength lens, as this teacher discovered:

I thought I knew my eleventh graders pretty well—I had known them for their entire lives at school and taught some of them at some stage. However, talking with them about their strengths surveys allowed me to see them in different ways. For example, we teachers often found one girl challenging. She would do anything to get out of things she didn't want to do, and her mom backed her up all the way, which was frustrating. She always questioned things, challenged school rules, asked why she had to do things, et cetera. She wasn't nasty, just obstructive and needed careful handling, otherwise she could get very argumentative and sometimes rude.

But looking at her strengths and discussing them with her enabled me to understand where she was coming from, and to have a conversation about some of the things that had gotten in the way of our relationship. Her top strength, by far, was curiosity. Her second was fairness. Her third was honesty. She wasn't challenging; she was curious. She wasn't obstructionist; she was honest. If she felt she, and other students, weren't being treated fairly, she was going to tell us!

It was as if scales had dropped from my eyes. In our conversation, I could also express my frustration that she got out of things by using notes from home and how I felt that wasn't fair. She took that on board and, honestly, it hasn't happened since.

Sometimes it's our children who focus on the shadow side of their strengths and need our help to see themselves more positively:

Annalise was a little embarrassed at having appreciation of beauty and excellence as her top strength. She thought it sounded "flaky." That changed in ninth grade, when the students were told they had to conduct research (including generating new data) and produce a "product" based on their findings.

Annalise was interested in the relationship between music and emotions. She developed a product called the "Positivity Playlist," a playlist of ten songs she selected for their positive impact on mood. She surveyed students to identify what genres of music they listened to and then spent a lot of time assembling a playlist that met her criteria for genres, tempos, lyrics, and continuity within the playlist. She took a beautiful photo of yellow daisies for the playlist cover and used it as a brand image on all of her supporting materials, wrote an excellent report, and got an A for her efforts!

In talking about the experience with Annalise, I said that her strengths of appreciation of beauty and excellence and her creativity were evident in the originality of the idea and the care she put into getting just the right look and feel for the playlist and accompanying materials. Many students and teachers had commented on her creativity and attention to detail. She felt really proud of her work.

This very positive experience has led to some fantastic learning developments: This year she's taking a course called History of Aesthetics and is loving it! She's at the top of the class and was singled out for the quality of one of her essays. Her academic confidence is overflowing into other subjects, too. So many positives—and it started with honoring her strengths.

Question #4: Could It Be a Blocked Strength?

A blocked strength can cause a strong emotional response. When we can't live in a way that feels authentic to us, it feels wrong and we get angry. How many of us have been hard to live with at home when we feel undervalued or underutilized at work?

Remember the story I told in Chapter 3 about my writer friend who had tantrums because she didn't yet know how to read? Not everyone feels the depth, richness, magic, and joy of playing with words, but that child had an inborn strength she was struggling to cultivate, and her strength was blocked because she grew up in an era when kids weren't taught to read before first grade. If your child is acting out, ask yourself if his strengths are being frustrated or blocked in some way.

Question #5: Could It Be Forced Overuse of a Weakness or of a Learned Behavior?

It's almost a cliché in the business world: A talented achiever gets promoted into a management position that's a far cry from the original tasks in which she excelled and from which she derived great satisfaction. Even if she's a good manager, she's miserable because her new job forces her to constantly use learned behaviors rather than work from the energizing flow of her strengths. And if management skills are weaknesses for her, let's just say that she won't be the only one who's miserable on the job. Being forced to use weakness or learned behavior could lead to bad behavior.

It's exhausting and stressful to be in a situation where we must constantly use a weakness. Also depleting is being repeatedly required to use a learned skill that we know how to do—and may even perform well and be praised for—but that doesn't energize us and isn't balanced by the opportunity to flex our strengths. If it's hard for us as adults to handle this, imagine how a child, lacking the coping skills of a mature adult, might feel and react in such situations. If your child's behavior is frequently challenging, look at what his typical days are like. Perhaps the bad behavior is a result of him having to over-rely on weaknesses or learned behavior.

Putting Strength-Based Discipline into Practice

It takes only a few minutes to think through the questions above and get a sense of how your child's strengths are playing out (or not) in a given situation. Once you've got a handle on what might be happening, here are four tactics to try:

Tactic #1: Use Circuit Breakers to Reestablish the Strength Connection

You learned about these in previous chapters. They can really help us and our kids replenish self-control by calming the nervous system and shifting thinking from the emotion-driven limbic system to the rational frontal lobe, a driver of self-control. You can still let your child know his behavior was unacceptable, but the discussion will be more effective if you use these tactics to downshift to a calmer mode before addressing the situation:

- *Take some downtime.* Say, "I need time to think about this before we talk about it." Then go do a good goofing-off activity that settles your emotions. Perhaps suggest your child do the same.
- *Do a two-minute breathing exercise.* There's almost always time, even in a tough situation, to take a few deep, steadying breaths. This, too, calms the nervous system.
- *Spend some time feeling grateful.* Bad things happen, but that doesn't mean there's nothing in life to enjoy and appreciate. Find something to be grateful for. Be grateful that you even have a kid to argue with in the first place. Depending on your child's mood, the two of you might do this together. Maybe

try petting the dog together, taking a time-out for a snack, or walking around the block. It may calm the brain's limbic arousal and help both of you get a better handle on feelings.

Tactic #2: Suggest Dialing Up or Dialing Down a Strength

I introduce the idea of dialing up and dialing down strengths to the teachers and parents I work with. It's effective in the classroom and one-on-one.

Basically, you suggest to the child that she needs to turn up or turn down the "volume," or intensity level, on her strengths to address specific issues she's dealing with. You'll discover which strengths need to be dialed up or down by asking yourself Questions 1 and 2 above about strength overuse or underuse. Doing this with your child helps her learn to regulate herself and understand that different situations call for different behaviors:

> *Claire and I spoke about what a wonderful strength bravery is, but how, if overplayed, it could make her too bossy with her sisters and result in clashes. We talked about how she could turn this strength down if she felt it wasn't serving her so well. We also talked about other times she gets to do things her sisters can't because she's "brave." And we talked about how she is someone who sticks with things—and that sometimes that's good, but at other times it's dialed up too high and becomes stubbornness.*

You might even find that your child eventually turns the tables on you!

> *Henry is a social, rambunctious five-year-old with a boundless enthusiasm for life. We ask him to dial up or down his strengths in situations—e.g., kindness when he has hurt another, forgiveness when*

another has hurt him, patience when he needs to wait for what he wants—almost every day! One day when he noticed me impatiently flicking the radio stations in the car, he informed me that I needed to use more of my strength of patience!

Tactic #3: Encourage a Strength versus Fixating on the Negative Behaviors

This tactic can create constructive dialogue around even serious behavior problems, as this school psychologist explains:

A tenth-grade boy at our school was getting into trouble, socializing with the wrong people, and he had just been caught shoplifting. He had already been suspended a few times and we were not expecting him to complete tenth grade. He and I did the VIA Survey of Character Strengths and identified, among other things, that leadership was one of his signature strengths. This discovery and our conversation about it proved pivotal. First, I think it was the first time he had ever received feedback that he had all of these good qualities inside. He was so touched to hear about them that he cried. Secondly, we were able to focus on fostering his leadership strength in healthy ways. We learned that outside of school he was a great rugby player and was the captain of his team. We were able to cultivate his leadership strength in school, and he successfully finished the year.

This family made a ritual of celebrating achievement rather than nagging about who was falling short:

We reward achievement and results with a family celebration dinner. We give our sons their favorite meal and include a special cake. At the dinner, the effort and achievement of our sons are honored. This tradition acts as a motivator.

Tactic #4: Substitute or Swap in a Strength

A friend of mine is a remedial massage therapist who always starts by working with the healthy tissue before she addresses the inflamed and injured area. If she starts directly on the injured tissue, her patients become rigid and the healing isn't effective. Similarly, if you go straight for your child's weakness, your child will naturally become defensive. You can help your child work on her weaknesses more effectively by starting first with her "healthy tissue"—her strengths. When Nick or Emily comes to me with a problem, I've trained myself to swap in a strength and ask: "What is a strength you have that can help you fix this?"

I wasn't always so quick to take this approach. Emily would be the first to admit that impatience is a weakness of hers. When she was in the first grade, her teacher told me Emily was talking too much in class. It turns out Emily was finishing her work more quickly than her classmates and became impatient waiting, so she talked to her friends as they were trying to finish their work. I spoke to Emily a number of times about this and asked her to wait patiently. She didn't exactly take my advice to heart. When she was sent to the school principal, I needed a new tactic.

I realized that I was framing the issue in terms of her weakness—the fact that she lacks patience. Instead of trying to minimize a weakness, I decided to maximize a strength. So I turned on my Strength Switch and thought about the positive feedback I'd gotten from her teacher at the parent-teacher conference the previous semester, when the teacher had praised Emily's cooperative nature, her love of learning, and her kindness. Emily has been kind ever since she was very young, when she would share her toys, include people in her games, and go out of her way to make others feel good. Kindness is one of her core strengths.

I talked to Emily about how she could show kindness to her friends by letting them finish their work because it would make them feel good to have that sense of accomplishment, just as she felt good about her own love of learning. I also suggested that she could show kindness and cooperation to her teacher by not disrupting the class.

As soon as I turned on my Strength Switch and reframed the situation through her strengths of kindness and cooperation rather than harping on her weakness of impatience, Emily immediately understood what she needed to do, and her classroom behavior improved.

Use the Three Ps to Work with Weaknesses

There are times, of course, when you've got to confront weakness head-on. Maybe your child struggles in an academic subject but needs to achieve a certain grade in order to meet his educational goals. I wasn't good at math, but I had to do well enough to get into graduate school for psychology, survive statistics, and get my PhD, so I set about getting extra tutoring. Or maybe your child is impatient like Emily and needs to learn to manage those feelings better. After all, we all have weaknesses. Matt and I think patience is such an important trait that we are working on it directly with Emily.

The key to working with weaknesses is to make sure your focus doesn't become too deficit oriented. Remember the clay-modeling exercise we did in Chapter 1? Use gratitude, mindfulness, and self-control to ensure that your attention hasn't been overly drawn to the holes in the clay. Do what needs to be done to address the weakness so that it's not getting in the way of goals, good behavior, or performance, but don't expect your child to turn a weakness 180 degrees into a strength.

At home and in my work with parents, I find that a three-pronged approach I call the Three Ps—priming, present-moment, and post-mortem—can be effective in working with weakness.

Priming

What it is: In priming, you give the child a heads-up that he's going into a situation where he will need to work with a particular weakness.

Success tips: Be calm and matter-of-fact. Life happens and we all sometimes have to deal with things we don't like to do or aren't good at. Ask the child what strengths he can draw on to manage his feelings. Suggest some circuit breakers the child can use if he starts to feel stressed. If possible, do your first priming processes in low-stakes, low-pressure situations, when both of you are feeling even-keeled and rested, so your child's self-control—and yours—is likely to be strong.

EXAMPLES

- *Emily's impatience:* "This is going to be a long car drive. It's going to take us at least an hour. There's a lot of traffic. I can't do anything about it. I understand it's annoying. It's annoying for me, too. This is one of those situations where your being impatient is not going to get us there any faster. It's just going to make you feel restless and annoyed and anxious. So be mindful of this as we go into the situation. What are some things we can do to help you feel less impatient during the car ride?" (To this, Emily will often suggest bringing a book, some artwork to do, or her finger puppets to play with.)
- *Improving a sports skill:* "You would be a lot harder to beat in basketball if you could learn to shoot outside the key. You're great at shooting under the basket, but everyone expects you to miss outside the key, so no one defends you there. You're wide open to make the shot if you can build that skill. This

week, let's practice making it more automatic to stop and shoot outside the key. I know it's not your favorite shot to take, but it will really expand your offense and it'll get better with practice."

- *Improving an academic skill:* "You know this material well, but your test scores don't reflect it. I think you're letting yourself down through poor exam preparation leading up to the test, and I wonder also if you're getting nervous during the test and that is stopping you from thinking clearly. This month, before we get into the hectic period of finals week, we're going to work on exam prep and strategy, from how you sleep and study to how you use your time and calm your nerves efficiently during the test."

Present Moment

What it is: There are two levels to choose from. Level One is simple mindfulness—flagging the issue for the child as the situation is happening to help the child prepare. Level Two is actively working on the weakness in the moment. The more your child practices addressing her weakness in present-moment situations, the less dominant it becomes.

Success tips: Ideally, practice Level Two at a time when you and your child are feeling rested and able to practice mindfulness, unlikely to lose your tempers.

EXAMPLES

- *Emily's impatience, simple mindfulness:* "This is one of those times when I see your patience is being tested."
- *Emily's impatience, working on the weakness in the moment:* "Now's the time to take a couple of deep breaths and think about a different way of responding. Let's look at it from

another perspective. Is being impatient going to make the
car drive any faster? Is it going to make the legal system
change the speed limits? Is it going to make the other cars
on the road get out of the way because there's an impatient
nine-year-old in the backseat of the car? Nope, impatience is
not going to change things."

- *Improving a sports skill:* Direct the child to do the shot in the
  game, with prompts or corrections called out or given during
  time-outs.

- *Improving an academic skill:* Obviously you won't be in the
  exam, so you can't help the child in the moment. But you can
  coach him while he takes practice exams at home. Here you
  can be in the present moment, coaching him to take deep
  breaths, keep track of the time, highlight the key aspects
  of each question, and ask questions if needed. This way,
  when the moment does arise, your child will be prepared to
  overcome the poor exam technique that has limited him in
  the past.

Postmortem

What it is: Here you talk with your child after the fact to identify what
happened, discuss how things went, look at what needs improvement,
and agree on steps for getting there. A postmortem might happen a
few minutes, hours, or days later (when everyone's feeling cooler):
"OK, let's talk about what just happened/this morning's test/the game
last night/what happened the other day."

Success tips: The goal here is to help the child become mindful about
how events unfolded, how she was feeling, how she acted/reacted, and
what she can do differently next time: "What was it about that situation that made you feel this way/do or say what you did? What
strengths do you think might help you manage better? Is there a

strength that needs to be dialed down or up? What do you think we could try so things might go better next time?"

EXAMPLES

- *Emily's impatience:* As well as drawing on Emily's kindness to address her talking in class, I also spoke with her about her impatience and asked her to tell me what thoughts and feelings she was having when she finished her work and looked around to find others still working. I suggested she use the time to review her work and make sure there were no errors, or make her work look better/prettier. This last idea really appealed to her creative and artistic side, and she learned that there were ways to not listen to her impatient thoughts.

- *Improving a sports skill:* With skills, postmortems are usually about determining next steps for improvement via additional resources and practice. It starts with looking at what went right and what didn't: "You nailed the shot here and here, but there were missed opportunities here and here." "This shot fell short because your body wasn't lined up properly." Then, together, lay out an approach for skill improvement. Be sure to talk about mind-set issues that may be holding the child back.

- *Improving an academic skill:* Here, too, it's about agreeing on the needed resources and practice, based on recent events: "Let's talk about last week's test. You knew your stuff, so do you think the test score matches how much you knew?" "How did you calm yourself down? Did you do some deep breathing?" "How did it go with timing on the test? Did you get stuck for too long in some sections? How could you do better with keeping time?" "Did you ask your teacher to explain if you were unsure about the instructions?" You might talk about arranging for tutoring, setting up study or test prep schedules, doing timed test run-throughs, or other processes to address specific issues in systematic, achievable steps. Also talk about the child's thoughts and feelings to see if these may be undermining the child on some level.

Shifting the Trajectory: The Game-Changing Gifts of Strength-Based Parenting

I've only gone skiing once in my life, but when I did, I learned an interesting fact. I remember standing at the top of the mountain, snow sparkling all around. In front of me were two runs down the mountain. One side of the mountain was flatter and smoother. It would be a slower, more scenic, and, in my novice opinion, more enjoyable ski run. The other side of the mountain was distinctly steeper. It provided a faster, bumpier, and more dangerous ride. The distance between the two? About ten centimeters. All I needed to do was point my ski tips ten centimeters in a different direction to have a very different experience of that mountain.

Strength-based parenting is about angling your ski tips just a little differently at the start of the run. As you practice SBP, it's not as though misbehavior will go away or that life challenges won't continue to happen for you and your child. You still have to make it down the mountain, but you're navigating a very different path through those challenges—one that I think will be smoother and will open up beautiful vistas for both of you. What's more, you can access these powerful experiences through the small moments of parenting we encounter every day.

Imagine having a child who can draw on her courage to make a series of small adjustments to her actions and ultimately form a different circle of friends—a huge life lesson in setting boundaries, knowing one's own worth, and stopping disrespectful treatment from others:

> *Eva has bravery as one of her top strengths. When she was eight, she was having trouble with friends who were being bossy, not taking turns, and excluding her. Initially I asked Eva to reflect on whether there was anything she was doing that might not seem fair to the others. Then I told her she had a choice: She could give the power of her happiness to that group of friends to control, or she could take control of it herself and try a new group.*
>
> *First she decided to use her bravery to tell her friends how she felt when they weren't being fair. Things didn't really improve, and Eva often cried after school. Then one day she fell and cut herself. One friend went to get help, but two others stood around discussing what game to play next and did not help her.*
>
> *After that, Eva decided to use her bravery to make new friends. The new friends she wanted to make liked to play a Harry Potter game. She read the books to learn the characters, learned the new game and rules, and used her bravery to join the new group.*
>
> *She's never looked back and is one of the happiest ten-year-olds I know. She now feels a great sense of empowerment and connection to her top strength and has a much bigger group of friends because of it.*

Imagine a kind and sensitive child who also knows how to change the direction of his skis just a fraction so that he can feel deeply, yet still manage his emotions:

> *Benny is seven and one of the sweetest boys you'll come across. He can be oversensitive sometimes, getting upset at things other boys his age don't. I want him to retain his kind soul, so I make sure to acknowledge his strength of kindness, but when he feels overwhelmed by emotions,*

I've helped him learn to take some deep breaths and to walk away if he needs to. We've also worked on how to use this time to figure out what he is upset about and how to let others know what is going on. I didn't want him to just toughen up, but to be able to use his strengths of kindness, love, and social intelligence with wisdom while also feeling strong and confident.

. . . and children who know how to dial up their appreciation of their parents:

During one family vacation when our sons complained about having to share a room, I explained, "Dad has worked very hard for us to be able to have this trip, and we could draw on our gratitude that we have this great opportunity." The boys really changed their attitude after that.

Imagine children who step up to new roles and responsibilities during life transitions:

When Daniel's little brother was born, we pointed out to Daniel how kind and loving he was when he did things to help with his new brother, e.g., grabbing the pacifier off the floor, cuddling and feeding his brother, or offering his newborn brother his own snuggly toy for comfort when he was crying. We also praised and pointed out in four-year-old-speak when he displayed patience, self-control, and teamwork. We feel this approach helped Daniel bond with his new brother and take on the role of being a big brother, probably reducing the resentment he felt about no longer being the center of attention.

. . . children who learn how to lead, a little at a time:

Sarah has always thrown herself into everything. A very high achiever, her core strengths are love, leadership, fairness, judgment, and kind-

ness. Sarah experienced some social challenges in tenth and eleventh grades when school awards, leadership positions, and competitive natures led to some jealousies and conflicts with her classmates.

We discussed leadership—some people don't like to be led; some hard decisions hurt some people; friendship and leadership can be hard to reconcile: "If you want to lead, Sarah, maybe you will need to accept that you will sometimes have conflicts with others; how might you better handle those conflicts?"

Sarah came to understand that competing for leadership roles would mean that, from time to time, friendships could be compromised. So she worked with love and kindness on developing friendships with people she was not in competition with, and practiced kindness toward people with whom she was competing.

Sarah enjoyed her year as student body president and is now a sophomore in college, doing well in her studies, and volunteering two days per week with an organization that tackles global poverty. She hopes to one day hold an executive role in a similar organization. She continues to keep in touch with her high school friends.

As a parent, I found strengths very useful to help a smart and self-motivated teenager through some challenging times on her own terms.

. . . children who know how to say "I'm sorry":

We were at my brother's house for a family event, and Samuel (thirteen) pulled out the chair on his older brother, Ethan (sixteen), causing Ethan to fall to the floor. While Ethan wasn't hurt, all of his uncles saw this and laughed, causing him some embarrassment. While normally Ethan and Sam are fierce friends, Ethan refused to speak to Sam afterward. For three days I kept telling Sam he needed to apologize to Ethan, but Sam wouldn't budge and the house remained fairly chilly.

After taking a step back, I realized that Sam hates to do anything wrong and has quite a strong shame response if he gets in trouble, so asking him to show humility might be tough for him. I thought about Sam's strengths. Without question, he's known for his kindness: Little children love him; he is gentle and patient and so generous with his kindness. I approached Sam again and talked about repairing his relationship with his brother, as it was the kind thing to do. Incredibly, less than thirty minutes after that conversation, he mended fences with his brother.

. . . and children who cope with tribulations by sharing their learnings with others:

An eighth grader in our school was diagnosed with chronic fatigue that she symbolically described as a combination of an anchor and a cloud. We talked with her about how she could use her strengths to help her cope with the anchor and cloud. Her top strengths were creativity and kindness, so she decided to create a children's book about her experience in the hope of helping others.

Moment by moment, strength-based parenting creates small and achievable shifts that can positively change your child's trajectory through life. I have seen many transformational outcomes in families in my years of developing and teaching SBP. My hope for you and your child is a future fueled by strengths and filled with inspiring journeys of growth, adventure, and joy.

CHAPTER 10

Strong Selves, Strong Families, Strong Communities, Strong World

Becoming a parent transforms you in profound ways. Everything changes—your priorities, your relationships, your routines, and, most fundamentally, you. The world you knew before is forever changed.

But what if you could use what you now know about strengths to change the world?

The first chapter of this book is titled "Standing for Strength in a World Obsessed with Weakness." I hope that by the time you have read these words, you have the tools for doing exactly that.

What kind of world would it be if we could fill the earth with people who know and operate from their strengths and help others do the same, like the strengths I mentioned in chapter 1?

I think it would be more positive, more powerful, more productive, more beautiful, and more fun.

The good news is it's already starting to happen.

In the previous chapter, we saw how small, moment-by-moment applications of strengths awareness can positively change your child's trajectory through life. But it can also sustain us through major life events and adversities—and then some. Here's how two moms, Giselle Marzo Segura and Lisa Honig Buksbaum, called upon their own and their child's strengths in times of great challenge, and then went on to spread strength awareness in their communities:

Starting in third grade, my daughter attended a special school in our area for children with dyslexia and related language-based learning difficulties. The many years of psychological testing we went through leading up to her move to a special school made me feel as if I was forced to point to everything that is "wrong" in a person I love so much.

We don't want someone we love to have to struggle, so we tend to focus on fixing what seems broken. This trap affects all of the relationships in the family. In such stressful conditions, it can be tough to see each other with appreciation. For a time, my marriage was under overwhelming stress; we were exhausted.

Three months into the sixth grade, she was struggling, and I was told: "We're afraid we cannot help your daughter anymore. We suggest you homeschool her."

I had never considered homeschooling, but we had to try a new way. The first few months were extremely difficult. It was the middle of the school year, and I had to put my career in marketing and design aside to work with my daughter.

I've always known that one of my top strengths is creativity, particularly solving problems through design. I realized I had the unique opportunity to turn around our situation by redesigning our daughter's education.

I worked on finding a balance between subjects that naturally motivated her in supporting her strengths and interests—music and art—which we pursued in group classes to provide social interaction, and those that were challenges—which we pursued one-on-one. To fulfill the standard academic requirements, we did things like learn science by attending a weekly marine biology class with a local home-school group and learn about marine life by participating in nature.

I incorporated the VIA strengths language into her homeschooling. It worked so well that, using my design strength, I wondered: Could a visual model help us use this language of appreciation to connect as a family?

That's how I developed Strengths Clusters™, a holistic visual map and tools featuring the VIA Classification of Character Strengths. I'm using it to help families, schools, and workplaces learn about their strengths. My daughter, who is now fourteen, and I have even teamed up to teach diverse groups and corporate clients how to understand, see, and connect with each other through a lens of strengths!

When I answered my cell phone from the trade show floor in Las Vegas, just moments before my marketing communications firm was to launch the largest telecommunications company at the largest telecom trade show in the world, I had no idea my world was about to change.

"Lisa, it's about Jonathan." Instantly my husband, Jacob, had my full attention. "He's catastrophically ill. You have to come home immediately."

Back in New York City, our ten-year-old son had strep throat and had been on antibiotics for ten days. The symptoms grew into rheumatic fever that caused heart and neurological damage.

For four months, he was heavily medicated to prevent seizures. He had to be carried to the bathroom. He slept often and was very scared. We were all very scared.

The head of pediatric neurology said, "I think you should take him and be by the sea." We rented a beach cottage near Coney Island and lived there for four months. Each night, I slept in Jonathan's bed because he'd wake up shouting in pain from cramps in his legs. I'd massage his limbs, comfort him, and help him fall back to sleep. Everyone was exhausted and frazzled, especially me as the mom (Jonathan's younger brother, Josh, was four at the time).

Each morning at 5:30, before my family awoke, I'd walk the beach, praying, singing, and crying as the sun rose. This precious time helped me connect with my strength and find my center.

During one walk, the name Soaringwords came to me. I stopped and took it in. Tears streamed down my face. I walked back to the cottage feeling a powerful sense of purpose. I scribbled Soaringwords onto the idea pad on my night table. Then I bathed and dressed for another long day of caregiving.

Every couple of weeks the three of us met with Jonathan's neurologist and cardiologist. We dreaded those visits: the waiting rooms crowded with parents looking so sad; the children leaning into their parents, eyes closed. In those silent rooms, I heard the calling of Soaringwords growing stronger.

When I learned that one out of five children in the United States— 22 million—have serious, catastrophic, or chronic illness such as asthma, diabetes, or cancer, I knew I had to do something to connect those children and their families to their inner strength, resilience, and hope.

I'd always been able to find creative ways to help Jonathan see the positive during his illness. Every day I made a different sign with positive slogans from sports or popular sayings and hung it next to his bed. Jonathan had a great sense of humor, so I included funny videos and stories in our activities.

When Jonathan started being able to sit up and then walk for longer periods of time, we made a big deal about how much progress he was making. He was excited about riding his bicycle, so we used that as a goal for him to work toward. He loved playing basketball and soccer, so we talked about how much fun he would have playing with his friends. Finally, his doctor gave Jonathan a clean bill of health. He walked into fourth grade and has been healthy ever since.

One year later, in 2001, I closed the successful marketing communications firm I had run for eleven years and started working on the business plan for Soaringwords. I wanted to share with other parents all of the positive encouragement and activities that I used to help my son Jonathan tap into his strengths. Over the past fifteen years, Soaringwords has helped more than 250,000 ill children and their families to NEVER GIVE UP. Soaringwords reaches ill children and their families in person (through more than 196 hospitals) and online, providing fun, creative, and educational modules based on positive psychology concepts that enhance well-being in the midst of serious illness.

Soaringwords also inspires ill children to pay it forward and do something kind for another person. When children create expressive arts projects to support other children, they are taking positive action that fosters altruism and reciprocity, resilience, empathy, and hope. It is a wonderful way to connect them to their creativity, sense of humor, and joy.

Today Jonathan is twenty-six years old. He's six foot one, played basketball throughout high school and college, works in commercial real estate, and cochairs the Young Leadership Board of Soaringwords. I believe his experiences with illness have made him a more empathetic friend, son, and grandson, and given him a greater appreciation for the gift of health, vitality, and life itself. While no one wishes for illness to happen, through it we experienced many blessings that made us stronger individually and as a family.

Both of these moms discovered the power of strengths in helping their kids overcome a serious life challenge and, upon discovering this, committed themselves to bringing strengths to others. My own story, too, is one of using strengths to heal and then committing myself to bringing strengths to the wider community.

We're starting to see evidence of strengths gaining momentum in society. More than 13 million people have taken strengths tests like the Gallup StrengthsFinder, Realise2, and the Values in Action (VIA) Survey, which have been translated into more than twenty languages and used in more than one hundred countries. The VIA Youth Survey has been taken by close to half a million children all over the world and is now available in twenty languages.

Tiffany Shlain, celebrated U.S. filmmaker, has found a novel way to spread knowledge about the VIA character strengths through the not-for-profit organization she cofounded with Sawyer Steele and Makenzie Darling, Let it Ripple: Mobile Films for Global Change. Their cloud films *The Science of Character*, *Adaptable Mind*, and *The Making of a Mensch* have formed the backbone of World Character Day, an annual global initiative where schools, families, and organizations premiere the films and discuss character strengths on the same day in a simultaneous online video conversation. World Character Day is supported by the U.S. State Department with screenings in Washington, DC, and embassies around the world, including Egypt and Vietnam. In 2016, more than 90,000 schools, families, and organizations participated from across 123 countries. Talk about a ripple effect.

Strength-Based Strides in Education

In schools, the strengths movement is growing. The leadership program I developed in partnership with the public education system when I first transferred to the Melbourne Graduate School of Education has trained 100 public school leaders and teachers in strengths. Those leaders and teachers took this learning back to 8,000 teachers and 30,000 students. The ripple effects continue as they move to other schools in the public system and transform those into strength-based schools. Here's feedback from some of the students:

Knowing I can train myself to be a more optimistic person is inspiring, and knowing I can do this through my strengths makes it achievable. What I found most interesting was the fact that strengths are not things that you simply do or don't have. They are learnable, flexible, and forever changing as we change.

I have come away from this semester's course with a stronger ability to be positive about the future. I use this when I have to do something I am not particularly excited about. I now can bring an "imagine how good it will feel when you've finished" attitude to these tasks.

I used to let negative obstacles such as stress and anxiety build and eventually consume my thoughts. No more! Now I accept that they're a part of life and have learned to identify the cause of the problem and look for ways to address it.

Before searching for the negatives in something, I seek out the positives. The "what went well" exercise encourages me to do this. My family and I share three "what went wells" each night. My mom even uses it at work!

Learning my strengths has been helpful to me, making me more conscious of them. It gave me a different perspective on how to handle situations and made me actually think about my moods and how I can improve them to be a better person.

I now think about my strengths in day-to-day situations. I will see even blades of grass and tap into my appreciation of beauty and excellence. I feel so much more gratitude. I'm much more conscious of my own mind and my own qualities.

Now multiply these sentiments by 30,000 and add the ripple effect.

This year I've worked with MAPP alumna Lela McGregor to develop the Positive Detective program for schools and families, based on my TEDx Talk. In my talk I spoke about why we should avoid the nightly news and why, instead, we should spend our time looking for the good in others and sharing this positive news on social media. There's actual data supporting the effects of this. Did you know that posting something positive on social media triggers happiness in 64 percent of your network?[1] What's more, this happiness spreads through social networks by up to three degrees.[2] Your good news positively influences your friends, who in turn positively influence their friends. With one positive post, you can brighten the day of someone you've never met.

Lela and I turned the idea of seeing the good and sharing positive news into an online program for schools and also for families to help children and teens see strengths in themselves and others. Our Positive Detective programs are having a ripple effect across many schools and families in the United States, Canada, the United Kingdom, Mexico, Finland, Ghana, Singapore, China, Hong Kong, Indonesia, Australia, and New Zealand.

In the United States, there's KIPP (Knowledge Is Power Program), a charter of schools started in 1994 "to help children develop the knowledge, skills, character, and habits they need to succeed in college and build a better tomorrow for their communities."[3] The program, which focuses on kids in educationally underserved communities, takes strengths so seriously that it actually assesses seven key strengths along with academics in the students' reports: zest, grit, optimism, self-control, gratitude, social intelligence, and curiosity. At this writing, the program is in twenty states and in the District of Columbia, comprises 183 schools, and reaches almost 70,000 students.

Strength-based education has also made its way to India. Recently I connected with Steve Leventhal, executive director of CorStone, a nonprofit that develops and provides evidence-based resilience programs in the United States and worldwide for marginalized youth and young parents. CorStone takes a strength-based approach to developing well-being in adolescent girls in developing countries, viewing them as critical change agents in their communities.

I was particularly moved by CorStone's Girls First and Youth First programs in urban slums and remote rural and tribal areas of India. The typical girl in these programs is from a "low" caste, minority, or tribal community; the first generation in her family to attend school; at high risk for sexual exploitation and trafficking; and likely to have few, if any, positive employment prospects beyond menial or household labor. Most are at risk for marriage and pregnancy at fourteen to sixteen years of age. They've rarely been told they have strengths.

CorStone's strengths-based resilience training has been well documented. Results from a 2013–2014 large-scale randomized controlled trial of the Girls First program involving 76 schools and 3,400 adolescent girls living in rural poverty in Bihar, India, found significant improvements in emotional resilience, health knowledge, gender attitudes, and clean water behaviors, as well as reductions in early marriage and improvements in school engagement.

Trials involving more than 50,000 high school students in 330 schools in Bihar are now under way with students attending weekly one-hour training sessions in which they learn their VIA character strengths and other health and well-being skills. The hope is that this program will be adopted widely by thousands of government schools serving millions of impoverished youth.

CorStone has rolled out the program elsewhere in India as well. In Surat, a city with more than 500 slums, CorStone has trained more than 100 local women to facilitate a strength-based resilience program for approximately 2,000 low-caste girls. You can learn more about this inspiring program by watching a video at http://corstone .org/girls-first-surat-india. (Warning: It made me cry.)

Steve told me about the "ripple effect" that is happening in the communities where the programs are being run. "When you invest in the health and education of a girl, you improve not only her well-being, but also the well-being of her family and her children," he says. "As these girls learn for the first time that they have specific character strengths and that they can successfully apply these strengths to advocate for their health and education, their right to delay marriage, and their right to self-sufficiency, we are witnessing them making an inspiring first step toward moving not only themselves but—over time—whole families and communities from simply surviving to truly thriving."

As I write this, the newly formed International Positive Education Network is about to host a global conference with more than 1,000 delegates from its 3,700 members across North America, Central America, South America, the United Kingdom, Europe, the Middle East, Africa, Asia, Australia, and New Zealand. I have the honor of presenting my work on . . . you guessed it: SBP.

On my side of the world, the Positive Education Schools Association helps schools across the Austral-Asian region to share best practices for teaching strengths to students. Some schools are partnering with the Centre for Positive Psychology at the University of Melbourne, where over the past five years we've measured the strengths and well-being of more than thirty thousand school students.

Strength-Based Strides in Business

In 2013, I dipped my toe back into the corporate world. A friend asked me to consult with her organization, a large bank. She said, "You know, Lea, if you work with our leaders, you'll be working with many parents. They'll take this approach home with them." I thought back to that holiday party where the wives of the alpha males at the invest-ment firm had told me how much better their husbands were as dads and partners since adopting a strengths focus at work, and I figured she had a point. So together with my colleague from the School of Business and Economics, Adam Barsky, who, like me, has a PhD in organizational psychology, we put together a two-day positive leader-ship executive education program based on strengths.

Since then, we've introduced strengths to senior- and middle-level managers in business, retail, manufacturing, sports, health, conserva-tion, not-for-profit, humanitarian, and the food sectors. These execs share many stories of how they're using their new approach at work and at home. The two words I hear most often: *renewal* and *transfor-mation*. It's as true for them as it was for me: Strengths help us discover new things about ourselves—and when we connect to our true best selves, we transform our own and other people's lives.

Experiencing the success of face-to-face teaching to executives in Melbourne and at the same time seeing the widespread impact of the online Positive Detective program in schools and families across twelve countries ranging five continents got me thinking: *Could I create an online strength-based program for organizations that could have the same widespread impact?* I called up my collaborator Lela McGregor and we've spent the last year designing the Strengths Switch program for organizations. Putting it online makes the program accessible and affordable for com-panies across the world, and it's our way of spreading the strengths as far and wide as we can. The program for organizations has been such a hit that we developed a Strengths Switch program for parents and families, too (you can check out both programs at strengthswitch.com).

We're not the only ones who are using online avenues to bring strengths to the workplace. The Gallup Institute, the VIA Institute, and the Centre of Applied Positive Psychology have clients on their lists such as Facebook, Harley-Davidson, British Broadcasting Com-mission, HSBC Bank, Lendlease, and Aviva insurance.

Following the face-to-face facilitation model, David Cooperrider, PhD, at Case Western Reserve University, has famously developed a strength-based approach to change management in organizations called Appreciative Inquiry. It starts with identifying the strengths in the system such as good communication, high team morale, good-quality equipment, loyal clients, and so on, and then uses these strengths to create change. David has worked with U.S. presidents and Nobel laureates. Appreciative Inquiry has been used in a wide variety of organizations including Apple, Verizon, Johnson & Johnson, Walmart, American Red Cross, Cleveland Clinic, and United Way.

I am honored to be an affiliate researcher at the Center for Positive Organizations, Ross School of Business, University of Michigan.[4] Michigan Ross was named a 2016 Top 30 Executive Education Provider by the *Financial Times*, and I believe that this is due in part to the pioneering strengths work being done at the Center for Positive Organizations on ways to bring strengths (e.g., compassion, honesty, forgiveness, respect, creativity), positive leadership practices, and mindfulness into the workplace. Each year, hundreds of thought leaders, executives, and academics gather at Michigan Ross for the Positive Business Conference, and then they take strength-based approaches back to their workplaces in national and multinational companies, spanning industries from health care to manufacturing.

These are just a few examples of the exciting ways that strengths are being implemented in workplaces. Could yours be next? Maybe it's time to have a talk with your boss.

Toward a Strength-Based Society

In Chapter 4 we explored the idea of scaffolding: the technique of providing children with resources and support in growing their strengths until they can provide empowerment to themselves. I believe that together we can build a scaffold to grow our strengths collectively as a society. Tall order? Not necessarily.

There are plenty of strength-based ways for each of us to look at situations with family and friends, in our communities and workplaces, in our school systems, among religious groups, and when addressing political issues locally and globally. As I showed in my TEDx Talk, you can even take a strength-based approach in the virtual world through social media. The key is to form the habit of swapping the question "What needs to be fixed?" with "What strengths are needed to handle this situation?" In other words, the key is to turn on your Strength Switch.

When you think about it, doesn't it just seem like common sense to seek strength-based solutions to our biggest problems? After all, our strengths evolved with us because they *work*.

We might not be there today, but we can start with our daily interactions and expectations of ourselves, our children, and others to build the scaffold and growth mind-sets that can get us there.

Just as we grow our children's strengths moment to moment, so, too, can we grow strengths in others across our community in our daily interactions. In fact, you almost can't help the ripple effect: strength awareness spilling over into your marriage, friendships, work relationships, and other connections. Noticing what people are doing right. Commenting on what people are doing well.

In the long-term, strength-based children grow into strength-based adults who inspire strengths development in their partners, colleagues, patients, clients, and others they meet in life. They infuse strength-based systems into community groups and schools. They raise their children in a strength-based way—reversing the rising trend of anxiety and depression among our youth—and those children will, in turn, do the same. In time, we'll reach a tipping point in society where we can access the deep well of collective strengths among us all. I truly look forward to that day.

Let It Begin with You

There's no time like the present. Start today to let strength awareness sustain and sweeten your relationship with your child:

> *I love to watch Will's quiet confidence when he methodically tackles problems. It's the little things that become available in our relationship. That moment of eye contact and the almost imperceptible nod he gives me to say, "I've got this," and my nod back that says, "I know, you're on to it; enjoy the process." The way my husband, Brad, acknowledges and respects Will's strengths by giving him room to work on a problem. The way Brad's gentle support and encouragement show his strength of perseverance—encouraging Will to get the job done.*

Once kids internalize the ability to see strengths, they can turn around and see them in others. It's a beautiful way to pay forward strength-based living, knowing you have helped your child make this world a stronger, more supportive place:

> *We did a strengths profile of our family and put it on the fridge so we could see the patterns of strengths in the family. I like to create opportunities for the kids to use their strengths at home. I ask Olivia and Jackson to use their zest to welcome guests and show them around, while Elijah's judgment is used to create caution and rein in risk. The kids have come to know and understand how to play to each other's strengths within the family.*

|||||||||||

> *Michael is able to spot strengths in others. While watching his brother play baseball in a new team where he had to step up his game, his*

comment was, "Wow, Mom, Tim is really playing like he's got hope now." I love that he has the language and insight to identify strengths and understand the importance of them.

Last year, the students were asked to identify strengths in their teachers. These were displayed on screens at the start of school assemblies and in our staff areas. It was an excellent practice for students to identify "strengths in action," and it was lovely for staff to see the students' insights displayed, as such acknowledgments aren't common in day-to-day school life. Some examples:

- *Perseverance: "Ms. Suss told me it was her mission to get me to love and understand math. She continues to ask if I am OK and if I need help. I am starting to really like math."*
- *Kindness: "Whenever I see Ms. O'Neill, she has the biggest smile on her face and always says hello. She never passes without asking me how I'm doing."*
- *Forgiveness: "Ms. Ferdinands doesn't hold grudges. She forgives people and moves on."*
- *Curiosity: "Mrs. Bennett is always thinking deeper than the obvious about things and always engrosses us in the discussion."*
- *Love of learning: "Mr. Rossiter always comes to class prepared and involves all members of the class each lesson. He has a contagious attitude toward learning."*

Last but certainly not least, strength awareness helps us accept ourselves. I cannot imagine what my life, and therefore the lives of Nick and Emily, would be like today had I not learned how to apply strength awareness. If someone had connected me to my strengths at a younger age, I might have had a different, more positive mental and physical health trajectory. Perhaps only when we have this special kind of awareness—first for ourselves and then for others—can we truly begin to change the trajectory toward standing for strength in humanity:

> *Focusing on strengths has helped me let go of the things I'm not so good at and just acknowledge them, find workarounds, or ask others who have that strength—even just little things, like asking my son to re-member where we parked the car in the parking lot! He will remember that detail; I won't.*

It seems fitting to end with the beautiful strength of a child. Below is an excerpt from a student's essay of a high school I worked with. It's on the power of focusing on the positive. To me it says everything important about how strengths can help the generations to come find their way on the path of life—and in the process, bring us all a little closer to our highest destination:

> *In Steven Spielberg's movie* Lincoln *there is a quote:*
> *"The compass always points due north, but it does not tell you what chasms, swamps, and other natural phenomena lie between . . . due north is essential."*
> *This got me thinking:*
> *Perhaps positivity is due north—it is essential. You always strive to be positive, just as the compass always points due north, but you must be prepared to compromise sometimes and be patient. Eventually you will find your way across the chasms, swamps, and other natural phe-nomena if you persist. The rewards will be great and as long as you refer to the compass you will never stray far enough to become lost.*

ACKNOWLEDGMENTS

There are three extraordinary women who acted as midwives for *The Strength Switch*. Catherine Drayton, agent, who helped me fine-tune my book proposal and guided me, a first timer, through the entire journey. You have so many strengths that I'm thankful for, including your honesty, humor, strategic thinking, and passion for publishing. I loved our many conversations about motherhood and the glimpse you gave me into what it's like to parent late teen/early adult boys. Caroline Sutton, editor in chief: I was beyond thrilled to work with you. Thank you for your belief in big ideas and the power of science to change lives. I appreciate your strengths of curiosity, open-mindedness, intellect, and warmth. Toni Sciarra Poynter, consulting editor: We were meant to work together—no doubt. Thank you for helping me to clarify my ideas, give voice to the science, and have the courage to tell my own story. I greatly admire your kindness, creativity, work ethic, organizational skills, and quirky humor.

To the team at Inkwell Literary Agency, especially Richard Pine, William Callahan, Eliza Rothstein, and Lindsey Blessing for giving me confidence and for always being so helpful. I'm still pinching myself that I'm part of the Inkwell family. Thanks to the entire team at Avery, with a special mention to Brianna Flaherty, Alexandra Bruschi, and Lindsay Gordon for their good advice and prompt replies to my e-mails.

I'm lucky to be part of a vibrant and supportive academic community. My thanks go to Martin Seligman for inspiring me to do the strength-based parenting research in the first place. I am grateful to a number of key scholars in the field—Roy Baumeister, Fred Bryant, Scott Barry Kaufman, and Ryan Niemiec—who generously answered my questions about their research areas and sent me scientific studies to read for my book. This also goes for Jane Dutton, who read my book proposal and sample chapters. My research assistants at the University of Melbourne—Saghar Zandi, Dan Loton, Jessie Sun, and Hayley Jach—found me the latest studies and were always interested in the progress of this book. Judy Hewwett and Dee Compson were wonderful editors of the first draft of this book.

To my academic mentors—Kate Moore, Marita McCabe, Maggie Abernethy, and Douglass Tim Hall—thank you for shaping me as a researcher.

There are many academics who inspire me: Barbara Frederickson, Sonja Lyubomirsky, Carol Dweck, Angela Duckworth, Brené Brown, Jane Dutton, Emily Heaphy, Laura Morgan Roberts, Susan Ashford, Gretchen Spreitzer, Carol Ryff, Sara Algoe, Shelley Gable, Amy Wrzesnieski, Sophie Havighurst, Acacia Parks, Dianne Vella-Brodrick, Peggy Kern, Emma Seppala, Sarah Pressman, Veronika Huta, Martin Seligman, Ryan Niemiec, Dacher Keltner, Alex Linley, Shane Lopez, Richard Davidson, Roy Baumeister, Chris Peterson, Scott Barry Kaufman, Kim Cameron, Fred Bryant, Robert Vallerand, James Pawelski, Mathew White, Robert Emmons, Jeffrey Froh, Robert Biswas-Diener, Jon Briscoe, and Michael Steger.

The University of Melbourne provided me with quality research training dating back to my studies as a psychology undergrad in the late 1980s. I'm proud to have worked at the University of Melbourne for over 20 years. Field Rickards has my sincere respect for transforming education training in Australia and for believing in the Centre for Positive Psychology. I have an amazing team of colleagues at the

Centre for Positive Psychology who are living embodiments of the field: Dianne Vella-Brodrick, Lindsay Oades, Kathy Racunica, Grace Fiore, Peggy Kern, Tan Chyuan Chin, Gavin Slemp, Dan Loton, Christine Siokou, Amanda Ng, Lara Mossman, Paige Williams, Jiaying Jiang, Kent Patrick, and Alexandra Johnston. You rock!

My sincere gratitude goes to the board members of the Centre for Positive Psychology for their time, support, and advice: John Higgins, Bruce Parncutt, Chris Tipler, Michael Hewwit-Gleeson, Michael Georgeff, Jane Burns, Field Rickards, and Tim Brabazon. A special mention goes to John Higgins for sponsoring the Gerry Higgins Chair in Positive Psychology, which I am so proud to hold.

Thanks go to my PhD students, most recently Rueben Rusk, Kelly Allen, Paige Williams, Tom Brunzell, and Laura Allison for offering your amazing contributions to positive psychology science—my positive energizers!

Thank you to my amazing Master of School Leadership (MSL) students and the Master of Applied Positive Psychology (MAPP) students with whom I've had the pleasure to teach and from whom I've had the pleasure to learn. I'm excited to see the wonderful impact you're all having on the world.

Thanks to the parents, teachers, and students who contributed stories: Sharon Garro, Rosanna Pingitore, Judy Hilton, Lara Mossman, Laura Allison, Andrew Bailey, Adriane Lack, Rachel Colla, Trina Cummins, Marie McCleod, Roz Rimes, Kathy Tanner, Jo Murray, Claire Fortune, Nathalie Briand-Hickling, Saraid Doherty, Tom Brunzell, Sally Cain, Peta Sigley, Dianne Vella-Brodrick, Fiona Trembath, Alison McClean, Caroline Miller, Giselle Marzo Segura, Rob Painter, Lisa Baylis, Lisa Buksbaum, Charlotte Holland, Rebecca Lewis, Rhiannon McGee, Sally Lawson, Annabelle Knight, Steve Leventhal, and those who preferred to remain anonymous.

I am grateful to the hundreds of schools I've worked with who have helped me develop my strength-based approach. There are four schools that deserve particular mention for being important training grounds to me: the Peninsula School, St. Peter's College Adelaide, the Chinese International School, and Kambrya College. The teachers and parents at Kingswood College have my gratitude for their excitement and encouragement about the book.

Caroline Miller, Emiliya Zhivotovskaya, Lela McGregor, and Claire Fortune encouraged me to extend the ideas in this book and build on-line programs that spread to families, schools, and workplaces across the world. Thanks for being smart, strong, and caring women. To my gifted career coach, John Roberts, for being a skilled strengths helper.

I've had three gifted therapists who, inch by inch, have helped me to come closer to being my full and true self: Oliver, Eric, and Nigel. Words have no adequate description for your profound role in my life.

Thanks to my friends—Genevieve, Sal, Susan, Anita, Su, Nicola, Cass, Ann, Michelle, Natalie, Anne, Adele, Danai, Yve, Karla, Laura, Helen, Fiona, Judy, Virginia, Adam, Noah, Steve, and Andrew—for always holding up a positive mirror.

I'm so lucky to be a member of the Scholes clan (spread across Australia and U.S.). Thank you for welcoming me into your family twenty-five years ago and for the hundreds of loving and fun family times. To Jenny and Rob, thanks for being hands-on grandparents and for passing on your love of art, tennis, football, and birds to Nick and Emily.

To my beautiful sister, Colleen, an amazing social worker who has used her strengths of courage, persistence, and compassion to help thousands of people, including the homeless, the disabled, foster children, and prison inmates. You have made such a positive difference to the world.

To my talented brother, Dan, award-winning songwriter and musician, who has used his strengths of creativity, intelligence, and storytelling to make music that helps people understand themselves. You are an important part of my journey—near or far.

To my parents, Mike and Lynn Waters. Thank you for role modeling the strengths of persistence, work ethic, and citizenship. Thank you for making the decision to move to the countryside to raise us. Growing up on five acres and dirt roads gave us rural freedom—a priceless gift. Thank you for giving me the opportunity to care for animals and for encouraging my studies.

Finally, to Matt, Nick, and Emily for being a perpetual source of joy, energy, and inspiration. You are my biggest healers and truest loves. This book is for you.

Further Resources and Reading

Find Lea Waters, PhD, Online

Lea's Online Programs
Strength-based parenting *(http://www.strengthswitch.com)*
Strength-based work teams *(http://www.strengthswitch.com)*
Strength-based classrooms *(http://www.strengthswitch.com)*
Positive Detective for schools *(http://www.positivedetective.com)*
Positive Detective for families *(http://www.positivedetective.com)*
Positive Detective for workplaces *(http://www.positivedetective.com)*

Lea's Websites
Lea Waters *(http://www.leawaters.com)*
The Strength Switch *(http://www.strengthswitch.com)*
The Strengths Exchange *(http://www.the-strengths-exchange.com.au)*
Positive Detective (http://www.positivedetective.com)

Lea's TEDx Talk
"Warning: Being Positive Is Not for the Faint-Hearted" *(https://www.youtube
.com/watch?v=80U__KwX0iU)*

Lea's YouTube Talks
"Gratitude at Work: Hearts, Minds, and the Bottom Line" *(https://www.youtube
.com/watch?v=KMI27cwZABw)*
"Growing Brains: Capacity, Intelligence, and Resilience"
(https://www.youtube.com/watch?v=roP-aOKcxWs)
"Positive Education: Trends, Evidence, and Advancement" *(https://www.youtube
.com/watch?v=2UABRP73t7A)*

Stay Connected with Lea Waters, PhD

Facebook
@ProfLeaWaters

Twitter
@ProfLeaWaters

Instagram
@ProfLeaWaters

Strengths Surveys

Adult Strengths Surveys
Values in Action Institute *(http://www.viacharacter.org)*
Centre of Applied Positive Psychology *(http://www.cappeu.com)*
Gallup Institute *(http://www.gallupstrengthscenter.com)*

Youth Strengths Surveys
Values in Action Institute *(http://www.viacharacter.org)*
Gallup Institute *(http://www.strengths-explorer.com)*
Gallup Institute *(http://www.strengthsquest.com)*

Websites
1 Giant Mind *(http://www.1giantmind.org)*
1000 Awesome Things *(http://1000awesomethings.com)*
Any.do *(http://www.any.do/anydo)*
Authentic Happiness *(https://www.authentichappiness.sas.upenn.edu)*
Calm *(https://www.calm.com)*
Character Day *(www.letitripple.org/characterday)*
Center for Positive Organizations *(positiveorgs.bus.umich.edu)*
Centre for Positive Psychology *(education.unimelb.edu.au/cpp/home)*
CorStone *(www.corstone.org)*
GoStrengths! *(www.gostrengths.com)*
Greater Good Science Center at the University of California at Berkeley *(www.greatergood.berkeley.edu)*
Growing with Gratitude *(http://www.growingwithgratitude.com.au)*

Happify *(www.happify.com)*

Headspace *(https://www.headspace.com)*

Hoogalit *(www.hoogalit.com)*

International Positive Education Network *(http://www.ipositive-education.net)*

International Positive Psychology Association *(http://www.ippanetwork.org)*

Knowledge Is Power Program (KIPP) *(http://www.kipp.org)*

Laboratory for the Study of Meaning and Quality of Life *(www.michael-fsteger.com)*

Let It Ripple *(www.letitripple.org)*

Mayerson Academy *(www.mayersonacademy.org)*

Pocket Lists *(http://www.pocketlistsapp.com)*

Positive Education Schools Association *(https://www.pesa.edu.au)*

Positive Psychology Center *(ppc.sas.upenn.edu)*

Smiling Mind *(http://smilingmind.com.au)*

Soaringwords *(www.soaringwords.org)*

Strengths Challenge *(http://strengthschallenge.com)*

Strength Clusters *(http://www.strengthclusters.com)*

The Appreciative Inquiry Commons *(https://appreciativeinquiry.case.edu)*

The Character Lab *(https://characterlab.org/measures)*

The Flourishing Center *(http://theflourishingcenter.com)*

The Quiet Revolution *(www.quietrev.com)*

The Wake Up Project *(www.wakeupproject.com.au)*

Todoist *(https://en.todoist.com)*

VIA Institute on Character *(www.viacharacter.org)*

Articles

Greater Good in Action at the University of California at Berkeley (n.d.). "Gratitude letter." Accessed August 14, 2016, http://ggia.berkeley.edu/practice/gratitude_letter.

Huffington Post (May 20, 2013). "Meditation in action: Turn your walk into a mindful moment." Accessed August 14, 2016, http://www.huffingtonpost.com/2013/05/20/meditation-in-action-walking-meditation_n_3279958.html.

Kaplan, J. S. (February 13, 2009). "Subway meditation: No cushion required," *Psychology Today*. Accessed August 14, 2016, https://www.psychologytoday.com/blog/urban-mindfulness/200902/subway-meditation-no-cushion-required.

Marsh, J. (November 17, 2011). "Tips for keeping a gratitude journal," *Greater Good in Action at the University of California at Berkeley*. Accessed August 14,

2016, http://greatergood.berkeley.edu/article/item/tips_for_keeping_a_grat itude_journal.

"Mindfulness in everyday life" (n.d.). Black Dog Institute. Accessed August 14, 2016, http://www.blackdoginstitute.org.au/docs/10.MindfulnessinEveryday Life.pdf.

"Mindfulness tips" (n.d.). *Mindful Moments*. Accessed August 14, 2016, http://www.mindful-moments.co.uk/pages/mindfulness-tips.php.

"Printable mandala coloring pages for free," Education.com. Accessed August 14, 2016, http://www.education.com/worksheets/mandalas/.

Books

Baumeister, R. G. and J. Tierney. *Willpower: Rediscovering the Greatest Human Strength*. New York: Penguin, 2011.

Biswas-Diener, R. *The Courage Quotient: How Science Can Make You Braver*. San Francisco: Jossey-Bass, 2012.

Brooks, D. *The Road to Character*. New York: Random House, 2015.

Brown, B. *Daring Greatly: How the Courage to Be Vulnerable Transforms the Way We Live, Love, Parent, and Lead*. New York: Penguin, 2012.

Cain, S., G. Mone, and E. Moroz. *Quiet Power: The Secret Strengths of Introverts* (a guide for kids and teens). New York: Dial Books for Young Readers, 2016.

Damon, W. *The Path to Purpose: How Young People Find Their Calling in Life*. New York: Free Press, 2009.

Duckworth, A. *Grit: The Power of Passion and Perseverance*. New York: Simon & Schuster, 2016.

Dweck, C. S. *Mindset: The New Psychology of Success*. New York: Ballantine Books, 2008.

Eades, J. M. F. *Celebrating Strengths: Building Strengths-based Schools*. Coventry, UK: Capp Press, 2008.

Fredrickson, B. *Positivity: Top-Notch Research Reveals the Upward Spiral That Will Change Your Life*. New York: Crown, 2009.

———. *Love 2.0: How Our Supreme Emotion Affects Everything We Feel, Think, Do, and Become*. New York: Avery, 2001.

Froh., J., and G. Bono. *Making Grateful Kids: The Science of Building Character*. West Conshohocken, PA: Templeton Press, 2014.

Greenland, S. K. *The Mindful Child: How to Help Your Kid Manage Stress and Become Happier, Kinder, and More Compassionate*. New York: Simon & Schuster, 2010.

Hirsh-Pasek, K. and R. M. Golinkoff. *Einstein Never Used Flash Cards: How Our Children Really Learn—and Why They Need to Play More and Memorize Less.* Stuttgart: Holtzbrink Publishers, 2004.

Kabat-Zinn, M. and J. Kabat-Zinn. *Everyday Blessings: The Inner Work of Mindful Parenting.* New York: Hyperion, 1997.

Kashdan, T. *Curious? Discover the Missing Ingredient to a Fulfilling Life.* New York: Harper Perennial, 2009.

Kaufman, S. B. and C. Gregiore. *Wired to Create: Unravelling the Mysteries of the Creative Mind.* New York: Perigee, 2015.

Keltner, D. *Born to Be Good: The Science of a Meaningful Life.* New York: W. W. Norton, 2009.

Linley, A. *Average to A+: Realising Strengths in Yourself and Others.* Coventry, UK: CAPP Press, 2008.

Linley, A., J. Willars, and R. Biswas-Diener. *The Strengths Book: Be Confident, Be Successful, and Enjoy Better Relationships by Realising the Best of You.* Coventry, UK: CAPP Press, 2010.

Lopez, S. J. *Making Hope Happen: Create the Future You Want for Yourself and Others.* New York: Simon & Schuster, 2013.

Lyubomirsky, S. *The How of Happiness: A New Approach to Getting the Life You Want.* New York: Penguin, 2008.

———. *The Myths of Happiness: What Should Make You Happy, But Doesn't, What Shouldn't Make You Happy, But Does.* New York: Penguin, 2013.

McGonigal, K. *The Willpower Instinct: How Self-Control Works, Why It Matters, and What You Can Do to Get More of It.* New York: Penguin, 2011.

McQuaid, M. and E. Law. *Your Strengths Blueprints: How to Be Engaged, Energized and Happy at Work.* Albert Park, VIC: Michelle McQuaid Pty Ltd., 2014

Medina, J. *Brain Rules for Baby, Updated and Expanded: How to Raise a Smart and Happy Child from Zero to Five.* Edmonds, WA: Pear Press, 2014.

Miller, C. *Getting Grit: The Evidenced-Based Approach to Cultivating Passion, Perseverance, and Purpose.* Lovisville, Colorado: Sounds True, 2017.

Mischel, W. *The Marshmallow Test: Mastering Self-Control.* New York: Little, Brown, 2014.

Niemiec, R. M. *Mindfulness and Character Strengths: A Practical Guide to Flourishing.* Boston: Hogrefe, 2013.

Niemiec, R. M. and D. Wedding. *Positive Psychology at the Movies: Using Films to Build Virtues and Character Strengths,* 2nd edition. Boston: Hogrefe, 2014.

Peterson, C. and M. Seligman. *Character Strengths and Virtues.* New York: Oxford University Press, 2004.

Polly, S. and K. H. Britton. *Character Strengths Matter: How to Live a Full Life.* New York: Positive Psychology News, 2015.

Race, K. *Mindful Parenting: Simple and Powerful Solutions for Raising Creative, Engaged, Happy Kids in Today's Hectic World.* New York: St Martin's Griffin, 2014.

Rath, T. *StrengthsFinder 2.0.* New York: Simon & Schuster, 2007.

Reckmeyer, M. and J. Robison. *Strengths Based Parenting: Developing Your Child's Inner Talents.* New York: Gallup Press, 2015.

Reivich, K. and A. Shatte. *The Resilience Factor: 7 Keys to Finding Your Inner Strength and Overcoming Life's Hurdles.* New York: Harmony, 2003.

Seligman, M. E. *Authentic Happiness: Using the New Positive Psychology to Realize Your Potential for Lasting Fulfillment.* New York: Simon & Schuster, 2004.

———. *Flourish: A Visionary New Understanding of Happiness and Well-Being.* New York: Simon & Schuster, 2012.

———. *Learned Optimism.* New York: Knopf, 1991.

———. *The Optimistic Child: A Proven Program to Safeguard Children Against Depression and Build Lifelong Resilience.* Boston: Mariner Books, 2007.

Siegel, D. J. and T. P. Bryson. *The Whole-Brain Child: 12 Revolutionary Strategies to Nurture Your Child's Developing Mind.* London: Constable & Robinson, 2012.

Siegel, D. J. and M. Hartzell. *Parenting from the Inside Out: How a Deeper Self-Understanding Can Help You Raise Children Who Thrive.* New York: Tarcher, 2004.

Steinberg, L. *Age of Opportunity: Lessons from the New Science of Adolescence.* Boston: Houghton Mifflin Harcourt, 2014.

Tarragona, M. *Positive Identities: Narrative Practices and Positive Psychology* (The Positive Psychology Workbook Series). USA: CreateSpace Independent Publishing Platform, 2013.

Tough, P. *How Children Succeed: Grit, Curiosity, and the Hidden Power of Character.* New York: Houghton, 2012.

Yeager, J. M., S. W. Fisher, and D. N. Shearon. *Smart Strengths: A Parent-Teacher-Coach Guide to Building Character, Resilience, and Relationships in Youth.* New York: Kravis Publishing, 2011.

ENDNOTES

Chapter 1: Standing for Strength in a World Obsessed with Weakness

1 *positive psychology has grown rapidly*: R. Rusk and L. Waters. "Tracing the size, reach, impact and breadth of positive psychology," *Journal of Positive Psychology* 8, no 3 (2013): 207–221.

2 *Optimism*: C. S. Carver, M. F. Scheier, and S. C. Segerstrom. "Optimism," *Clinical Psychology Review* 30, no 7 (2010): 879–889.

3 *Resilience*: A. Masten. *Ordinary Magic: Resilience in Development*. New York: Guilford Press, 2014.

4 *things that delight you most as a parent*: T. D. Hodges and J. K. Harter. "A review of the theory and research underlying the StrengthQuest program for students," *Educational Horizons* 83, no 3 (2005): 190–201.

5 *"strength-based parenting" (SBP)*: L. Waters. "Strengths-based parenting and life satisfaction in teenagers," *Advances in Social Sciences Research Journal* 2, no 11 (2015): 158–173; L. Waters. "The relationship between strengths-based parenting with children's stress levels and strengths-based coping approaches," *Psychology* 6, no 6 (2015): 689–699.

6 *strength-based science*: Strengths-based science seeks to create change by utilizing strengths and resources that are already present in a person, group, or community. The origins of strengths development go back more than fifty years to the early work of Donald Clifton (1924–2003) during his tenure as professor of educational psychology at the University of Nebraska. He based his research and practice on the question: "What would happen if we studied what is right with people?" The American Psychological Association named Clifton the "father of strengths-based psychology and grandfather of positive psychology." See J. McKay and M. Greengrass. "People," *Monitor on Psychology* 34, no 3 (2003): 87.

Strengths-based science gained momentum in the 1980s and is incorporated in approaches such as asset-based community development, appreciative inquiry, positive youth development, restorative justice, solution-focused therapy, and sustainable livelihoods. It has been studied in a broad range of fields including family therapy, social work, public health, epidemiology, juvenile justice, business, sports coaching education and psychology.

7 *positive psychology*: Positive psychology was launched as a field in 1998 by Professor Martin Seligman, then president of the American Psychological Association. See M. E. P. Seligman. "American Psychological Association 1998 annual report," *American Psych-*

ologist 54, no 8 (1999): 559–562. Positive psychology has a strong, but not exclusive, focus on strengths. See L. G. Aspinwall and U. M. Staudinger, eds. *A Psychology of Human Strengths: Fundamental Questions and Future Directions for a Positive Psychology.* Washington, DC: American Psychological Association, 2003.

8 neurospsychology: S. Trojan and J. Porkorny. "Theoretical aspects of neuroplasticity," *Physiological Research* 48, no 2 (1999): 87–97; N. Doidge. *The Brain's Way of Healing: Remarkable Discoveries and Recoveries from the Frontiers of Neuroplasticity.* New York: Penguin, 2015.

9 examining the question scientifically: M. Csikszentmihalyi and M. E. P. Seligman. "Positive psychology: An introduction," *American Psychologist* 55, no 1 (2000): 5–14.

10 drawing on our most abundant inner resources: P. A. Linley and S. Harrington. "Playing to your strengths," *The Psychologist* 19, no 2 (2006): 86–89.

11 negative bias: See the Ohio State University study in T. A. Ito et al. "Negative information weighs more heavily on the brain: The negativity bias in evaluative categorizations," *Journal of Personality and Social Psychology* 75, no 4 (1998): 887–900.

12 greater levels of happiness and engagement at school: M. E. P. Seligman. "Positive education: Positive psychology and classroom interventions," *Oxford Review of Education* 35, no 3 (2009): 293–311; A. Shoshani, S. Steinmetz, and Y. Kanat-Maymon. "Effects of the Maytiv positive psychology school program on early adolescents' well-being, engagement, and achievement," *Journal of School Psychology* 57 (2016): 73–92.

13 smoother transitions: A. Shoshani and I. Aviv. "The pillars of strength for first-grade adjustment—Parental and children's character strengths and the transition to elementary school," *The Journal of Positive Psychology* 7, no 4 (2012): 315–326; A. Shoshani and M. Slone. "Middle school transition from the strengths perspective: Young adolescents' character strengths, subjective well-being, and school adjustment," *Journal of Happiness Studies* 14, no 4 (2013): 1163–1181.

14 higher levels of academic achievement: In a landmark study conducted in Nebraska's school system, six thousand tenth-grade students were put into three different groups to try new methods for speed-reading. The study found no differences in reading speed across the three different methods. However, researchers did find that improvement in speed-reading was influenced by the students' innate reading ability. This finding makes intuitive sense, but what is surprising was the disproportionate improvement that the above-average-ability group made in comparison to the average group. Those students who had average reading ability went from 90 words per minute to 150. Those students who were already strong in speed-reading went from 300 words per minute to 2,900 words per minute. See J. W. Glock. "The relative value of three months of improving reading—Tachistoscope, films, and determined effort," unpublished PhD thesis, Lincoln: University of Nebraska, 1955. See also A. Duckworth and M. E. P. Seligman. "Self-discipline outdoes IQ in predicting academic performance of adolescents," *Psychological Science* 16, no 16 (2005): 939–944; N. Park and C. Peterson. "Positive psychology and character strengths: Application to strengths-based school counseling," *Professional School Counseling* 12, no 2 (2008): 85–92.

15 happiness at work: C. Harzer and W. Ruch. "The application of signature strengths and positive experiences at work," *Journal of Happiness Studies* 14, no 3 (2013): 965–983.

16 staying at work: L. Eskreis-Winkler et al. "The grit effect: Predicting retention in the military, the workplace, school and marriage," *Frontiers in Personality Science and Individual Differences* 5, no 36 (2014): 1–12.

17 better work performance: C. Harzer and W. Ruch. "The role of character strengths for task performance, job dedication, interpersonal facilitation, and organizational support," *Human Performance* 27, no 3 (2014): 183–205; M. P. Dubreuil, J. Forest, and F. Courcy. "From strengths use to work performance: The role of harmonious passion, subjective vitality, and concentration," *The Journal of Positive Psychology* 9, no 4 (2014): 335–349.

18 *being happy in your marriage*: L. Eskreis-Winkler et al. "The grit effect: Predicting retention in the military, the workplace, school and marriage"; L. G. Cameron, R. A. M. Arnette, and R. E. Smith. "Have you thanked your spouse today?: Felt and expressed gratitude among married couples," *Personality and Individual Differences* 50, no 3 (2011): 339–343.

19 *higher levels of physical fitness*: M. Ford-Gilboe. "Family strengths, motivation, and resources as predictors of health promotion behavior in single-parent and two-parent families," *Research in Nursing & Health* 20, no 3 (1997): 205–217; S. K. Leddy. *Health Promotion: Mobilizing Strengths to Enhance Health, Wellness, and Well-being*. Philadelphia: Davis, 2006; R. T. Proyer et al. "What good are character strengths beyond subjective well-being? The contribution of the good character on self-reported health-oriented behavior, physical fitness, and the subjective health status," *The Journal of Positive Psychology* 8 no 3 (2013): 222–232.

20 *better recovery after illness*: C. Peterson, N. Park, and M. E. P. Seligman. "Greater strengths of character and recovery from illness," *The Journal of Positive Psychology* 1, no 1 (2006): 17–26.

21 *increased levels of life satisfaction and self-esteem*: G. Minhas. "Developing realized and unrealized strengths: Implications for engagement, self-esteem, life satisfaction and well-being," *Assessment and Development Matters* 2, no 1 (2010): 12–16; A. M. Wood et al. "Using personal and psychological strengths leads to increases in well-being over time: A longitudinal study and the development of the strengths use questionnaire," *Personality and Individual Differences* 50, no 1 (2011): 15–19.

22 *reduced risk of depression*: M. E. P. Seligman et al. "Positive psychology progress: Empirical validation of interventions," *American Psychologist* 60, no 5 (2005): 410–421; F. Gander et al. "Strengths-based positive interventions: Further evidence for their potential in enhancing well-being and alleviating depression," *Journal of Happiness Studies* 14, no 4 (2013): 1241–1259.

23 *enhanced ability to cope with stress and adversity*: A. Shoshani and M. Slone. "The resilience function of character strengths in the face of war and protracted conflict," *Frontiers in Psychology* 6 (2016), doi: 10.3389/fpsyg.2015.02006.

24 *we all have specific talents*: See, for example, B. S. Bloom, ed. *Developing Talent in Young People*. New York: Ballantine Books, 1985; P. A. Linley and S. Harrington. "Playing to your strengths," *The Psychologist* 19, no 2 (2006): 86–89; S. B. Kaufman and J. C. Kaufman. "Ten years to expertise, many more to greatness: An investigation of modern writers," *Journal of Creative Behavior* 41, no 2 (2007): 114–124. The Gallup Institute sees talent as a building block of a strength, together with knowledge and skills. It defines strengths as the ability to provide consistent, near-perfect performance in a given activity. See M. Buckingham and D. O. Clifton. *Now, Discover Your Strengths*. New York: The Free Press, 2001. Other researchers consider talent to be a strength. See R. Govindji and A. Linley. "Strengths use, self-concordance and well-being: Implications for strengths coaching and coaching psychologists," *International Coaching Psychology Review* 2, no 2 (2007): 143–153.

25 *positive personality traits*: Dr. Ryan Niemiec defines strengths as "positive characteristics of our personality" and "positive personality characteristics." See R. Niemiec. *Mindfulness and Character Strengths*. Boston: Hofgreve Publishing, 2014.

26 *big-headed narcissism*: L. J. Otway and V. L. Vignoles. "Narcissism and childhood recollections: A quantitative test of psychoanalytic predictions," *Personality and Social Psychology Bulletin* 32, no 1 (2006): 104–116; J. Twenge and K. Campbell. *The Narcissism Epidemic*. New York: Atria Books, 2009.

27 *Diana Baumrind, PhD*: Dr. Baumrind's work was influenced by R. R. Sears, E. E. Maccoby, and H. Levin. *Patterns of Child Rearing*. Evanston, IL: Row Peterson, 1957.

28 *two parenting dimensions*: On profiling the body of work of Dr. Baumrind, Greenspan concluded that "Diana Baumrind's typology of parenting is based on a two-factor model of 'control' and 'warmth' (i.e., nurturance)" (p. 5). See S. Greenspan. "Rethinking 'harmonious parenting' using a three-factor discipline model," *Child Care in Practice* 12, no 1 (2006): 5–12. Bastaits et al. also assert that Baumrind's model consists of two dimensions: support (i.e., nurturance) and control. See K. Bastaits et al. "Adult non-response bias from a child perspective. Using child reports to estimate father's non-response," *Social Science Research* 49 (2014): 31–41.

29 *punitive, permissive, and authoritative*: In Dr. Baumrind's original papers she identified three parenting styles: authoritarian, authoritative, and permissive. I've found in my workshops that the terms *authoritarian* and *authoritative* are confusing and so I use the term *punitive parenting* instead of *authoritarian*. In her later work, Dr. Baumrind identified a fourth parenting style: rejecting-neglecting parents (low control, low nurturance). These parents are low in warmth and control. They are disengaged in their role and provide no structure or support and no warmth. They may also be outright rejecting of the child. See D. Baumrind. J. Brooks-Gunn, R. Lerner, and A. C. Petersen, eds. "Parenting styles and adolescent development," in *The Encyclopedia on Adolescence*, New York: Garland, 1991, 746–758. In another study she identified seven types of parenting styles. See D. Baumrind. "The influence of parenting style on adolescent competence and substance use," *Journal of Early Adolescence* 11, no 1 (1991): 56–95. Despite these newer styles, the three styles most commonly used in research and practice since the 1960s have been: authoritarian (punitive), permissive, and authoritative. All of her work stayed with the two dimensions of control and nurturance.

30 *authoritative parenting*: S. D. Lamborn et al. "Patterns of competence and adjustment among adolescents from authoritative, authoritarian, indulgent, and neglectful families," *Child Development* 62, no 5 (1991): 1049–1065; L. Steinberg et al. "Impact of parenting practices on adolescent achievement: Authoritative parenting, school involvement, and encouragement to succeed," *Child Development* 63, no 5 (1992): 1266–1281.

31 *a strength-based approach boosts student well-being*: L. Waters. "A review of school-based positive psychology interventions," *The Australian Educational and Developmental Psychologist* 28, no 2 (2011): 75–90; L. Waters. "Using positive psychology to foster character strengths and wellbeing in students," paper at the Forward Thinking: Emerging Answers to Education's Big Questions Conference, Australian College of Educators (2013), 28–36; M. White and L. Waters. "The good school: A case study of the use of Christopher Peterson's work to adopt a strengths-based approach in the classroom, chapel and sporting fields," *Journal of Positive Psychology* 10, no 1 (2014): 69–76; L. Waters. "Balancing the curriculum: Teaching gratitude, hope and resilience," in *A Love of Ideas*, H. Sykes, ed. London: Future Leaders Press (2014), 117–124; T. Brunzell, H. Stokes, and L. Waters. "Trauma-informed positive education: Using positive psychology to strengthen vulnerable students," *Contemporary School Psychology* 20, no 1 (2015): 63–83; T. Patston and L. Waters. "Positive instruction in music studios: Introducing a new model for teaching studio music in schools based upon positive psychology," *Psychology of Well-being* 5, no 1 (2015): 1–10; T. Brunzell, L. Waters, and H. Stokes. "Teaching with strengths in trauma-affected students: A new approach to healing and growth in the classroom," *American Journal of Orthopsychiatry* 85, no 1 (2015): 3–9; M. A. White and L. E. Waters. "Strengths-based approaches in the classroom and staffroom," in *Evidence-based Approaches in Positive Education: Implementing a Strategic Framework for Well-being in Schools*, M. White and A. S. Murray, eds. Berlin: Springer (2015), 111–133.

32 lower levels of day-to-day stress: L. Waters. "Strengths-based parenting and life satisfaction in teenagers," *Advances in Social Sciences Research Journal* 2, no 11 (2015): 158–173; L. Waters. "The relationship between strengths-based parenting with children's stress levels and strengths-based coping approaches," *Psychology* 6, no 6 (2015): 689–699.

33 continuing to take care of my ill mother: In my late thirties, following the advice of my the rapist after the birth of my daughter, I stopped away from playing an active care-taking role of my mother.

34 tested them with thousands of other children: L. Waters. "Parent strengths knowledge and use: Relationship to family satisfaction in parents and children," paper at the Fourth World Congress of Positive Psychology, Orlando; L. Waters. "The power of strengths-based parenting," *Early Learning Review*. Accessed February 1, 2015, http://www.ear lylearningreview.com.au/?s=lea+waters; T. Brunzell, L. Waters, and H. Stokes. "Teaching with strengths in trauma-affected students"; L. Waters. "Strengths-based parenting: Modernizing what we know about parenting," paper at the 2nd Annual Positive Education Schools Conference, Mornington, Melbourne, 2016; L. Waters. "Strengths-based parenting," paper at the 3rd Canadian Conference on Positive Psychology, Niagara on the Lake, Ontario, 2016; L. Waters. "Strengths-based parenting: A key piece in positive education," paper at the Festival of Positive Education, Dallas, 2016.

35 positive emotions about their children: Waters, L. and Sun, J. "Can a brief strength-based parenting intervention boost self-efficacy and positive emotions in parents?" *International Journal of Applied Positive Psychology* (2017).

Chapter 2: The Strength Switch

1 didn't even notice the gorilla: C. Chabris and D. Simons. *The Invisible Gorilla: And Other Ways Our Intuitions Deceive Us*. New York: Broadway Books, 2009.

2 "inattentional blindness": T. Drew, M. L.-H. Võ, and J. M. Wolfe. "The invisible gorilla strikes again: Sustained inattentional blindness in expert observers," *Psychological Science* 24, no 9 (2013): 1848–1853.

3 programmed to see what's wrong: R. F. Baumeister et al. "Bad is stronger than good," *Review of General Psychology* 5, no 4 (2001): 323–370.

4 negativity bias happens before we're even aware of it: See the Ohio State University study in T. A. Ito et al. "Negative information weighs more heavily on the brain: The negativity bias in evaluative categorizations," *Journal of Personality and Social Psychology* 75, no 4 (1998): 887–900.

5 "positive-negative asymmetry": G. Peeters and J. Czapiński. "Positive-negative asymmetry in evaluations: The distinction between affective and informational negativity effects," in *European Review of Social Psychology, Vol. 1*, W. Stroebe, and M. Hewstone, eds. New York: Wiley, 1990, 33–60.

6 this bias happens: T. A. Ito, J. T. Cacioppo, and P. J. Lang. "Eliciting affect using the International Affective Picture System: Trajectories through evaluative space," *Personality and Social Psychology Bulletin* 24, no 8 (1998): 855–879.

7 good evolutionary reasons: R. F. Baumeister et al. "Bad is stronger than good," *Review of General Psychology* 5, no 4 (2001): 323–370.

8 "defense mechanisms": P. Cramer. "Defensiveness and defense mechanisms," *Journal of Personality* 66, no 6 (2002): 879–894.

9 Projection, also known as blame shifting: S. Freud. *Case Histories II, Vol. 9*. London: Penguin Freud Library, 1991, 13.

10 Projection is common in everyday life: L. A. Sroufe. "From infant attachment to promotion of adolescent autonomy: Prospective, longitudinal data on the role of parents in development," in *Parenting and the Child's World: Influences on Academic, Intellectual, and*

Social-emotional Development, J. G. Borkowski, S. L. Ramey, and M. Bristol-Power, eds. Abingdon, UK: Psychology Press, 2001.

11 *It leads you to think that weakness and strength are polar opposites*: The philosopher Simon Blackburn defines polar concepts as "concepts that gain their identity in part through their contrast with one another." See S. Blackburn. *The Oxford Dictionary of Philosophy*, 2nd edition. Oxford, UK: Oxford University Press, 2008.

12 *strength and weakness are not polar opposites*: P. B. Warr, J. Barter, and G. Brownbridge. "On the independence of positive and negative affect," *Journal of Personality and Social Psychology* 44, no 3 (1983): 644–651.

13 *Strengths sit along a continuum from high to low*: C. Peterson and M. E. P. Seligman. *Character Strengths and Virtues: A Handbook and Classification*. New York: Oxford University Press, 2004.

Chapter 3: Understanding Strengths

1 *Trait strengths are the positive aspects of our personality*: C. Peterson and M. E. P. Seligman. *Character Strengths and Virtues*.

2 *a key group of positive traits*: K. Dahlsgaard, C. Peterson, and M. E. P. Seligman. "Shared virtue: The convergence of valued human strengths across culture and history," *Review of General Psychology* 9, no 3 (2005): 203–213; N. Park, C. Peterson, and M. E. P. Seligman. "Character strengths in fifty-four nations and the fifty US states," *Journal of Positive Psychology* 1, no 3 (2006): 118–129.

3 *six broad groupings for these positive traits*: C. Peterson and M. E. P. Seligman. *Character Strengths and Virtues*; R. Biswas-Diener. "From the Equator to the North Pole: A study of character strengths," *Journal of Happiness Studies* 7, no 3 (2006): 293–310.

4 *close bonds among families and friends*: R. F. Baumeister and M. R. Leary. "The need to belong: Desire for interpersonal attachments as a fundamental human motivation," *Psychological Bulletin* 117, no 3 (1995): 497–529.

5 *positive traits like empathy . . . are hardwired into our brains*: J. L. Goetz, D. Keltner, and E. Simon-Thomas. "Compassion: An evolutionary analysis and empirical review," *Psychological Bulletin* 136, no 3 (2010): 351–374.

6 *survival of the kindest*: D. Keltner. *Born to Be Good: The Science of a Meaningful Life*. New York: W. W. Norton, 2009.

7 *performance . . . energy . . . high use*: A. Linley, J. Willars, and R. Biswas-Diener. *The Strengths Book: Be Confident, Be Successful, and Enjoy Better Relationships by Realizing the Best of You*. Coventry, UK: CAPP Press, 2010.

Other researchers have found strengths can be classified along similar dimensions. For example, Buckingham and Clifton (2001) identified three elements of a strength: 1) yearnings (can be mapped onto use) such as the desire to learn a new language or the aspiration to create great art; 2) rapid learning (can be mapped onto performance) of a skill or ability such as with a musical instrument or a computer program; and 3) satisfaction (which can be mapped onto energy) derived from using the strength such as delivering an important speech or organizing a major campus event. See M. Buckingham and D. O. Clifton. *Now, Discover Your Strengths*. New York: Free Press, 2001.

Similarly, Subotnik, Olszewski-Kubilius, and Worrell (2011), in the context of developing talents in gifted children, argue that talents are based on 1) ability (can be mapped onto performance); 2) interest (can be mapped onto energy); and 3) persistence (can be mapped onto use). See R. F. Subotnik, P. Olszewski-Kubilius, and F. C. Worrell. "Rethinking giftedness and gifted education: A proposed direction forward based on psychological science," *Psychological Science in the Public Interest* 12, no 1 (2011): 3–54.

8 *Do I see high use?*: A. Linley. *Average to A+: Realizing Strengths in Yourself and Others*. Coventry, UK: CAPP Press, 2008.

9 high use—also known as effort or practice—improves performance levels: Professor Robert Vallerand and colleagues found that passion predicts the amount of practice a person will undertake and, as such, passion predicts expert performance in a range of arenas such as basketball, synchronized swimming, water polo, and classical music. See R. J. Vallerand et al. "On the role of passion in performance," *Journal of Personality* 75, no 3 (2007): 505–533; R. J. Vallerand et al. "Passion and performance attainment in sport," *Psychology of Sport and Exercise* 9, no 3 (2008): 373–392; also see S. Silverman. "Relationship of engagement and practice trials to student achievement," *Journal of Teaching in Physical Education* 5, no 1 (1986): 13–21.

10 assessing whether a particular trait or talent develops: R. F. Subotnik, P. Olszewski-Kubilius, and F. C. Worrell. "Rethinking giftedness and gifted education."

11 "flow": M. Csikszentmihalyi. *Flow: The Psychology of Optimal Experience*, 1st Harper Perennial Modern Classics edition, New York: HarperCollins, 2008.

12 socially or morally valuable: For example, Peterson and Seligman (2004) specify that strengths are (among other criteria) intrinsically considered a moral quality and are qualities that, when used, enhance other people rather than harm them. See C. Peterson and M. E. P. Seligman. *Character Strengths and Virtues*.

13 realized strengths, unrealized strengths, learned behavior, and weakness: A. Linley. *Average to A+: Realizing Strengths in Yourself and Others*; G. Minhas. "Developing realized and unrealized strengths: Implications for engagement, self-esteem, life satisfaction and well-being."

14 overusing learned behaviors: A. Linley, J. Willars, and R. Biswas-Diener. *The Strengths Book*.

15 making the most of our strengths: A. Linley. *Average to A+: Realizing Strengths in Yourself and Others*. Coventry, UK: CAPP Press, 2008: 5 [original emphasis]. Also see R. E. Kaplan. *Internalizing Strengths: An Overlooked Way of Overcoming Weaknesses in Managers*. Greensboro, NC: Center for Creative Leadership, 1999.

16 connect strengths with strengths: Peter Drucker wrote in his 1967 classic: "To make strength productive is the unique purpose of organization. One cannot build on weakness. To achieve results, one has to use all the available strengths . . . These strengths are the true opportunities." See P. Drucker. *The Effective Executive*. London: Heinemann, 1967: 60.

17 Studies on twins and children who have been adopted: S.-A. Rhea et al. "The Colorado Adoption Project," *Twin Research Human Genetics* 16, no 1 (2013): 358–365.

18 altruism, empathy, and nurturance: J. Rushton et al. "Altruism and aggression: The heritability of individual differences," *Journal of Personality and Social Psychology* 50, no 6 (1986): 1192–1198.

19 the genetic contributions to "character strengths": M. Steger et al. "Genetic and environmental influences on the positive traits of the Values in Action classification, and biometric covariance with normal personality," *Journal of Research in Personality* 41, no 3 (2007): 524–539.

20 the development of strengths: J. Barkow, L. Cosmides, and J. Tooby, eds. *The Adapted Mind: Evolutionary Psychology and the Generation of Culture*. New York: Oxford University Press, 1992.

21 Mental strengths like curiosity: S. Mithen. *The Prehistory of the Mind: The Cognitive Origins of Art, Religion, and Science*. London: Thames and Hudson, 1996.

22 humans are naturally motivated to develop strengths: A. Maslow. "A theory of human motivation," *Psychological Review* 50, no 4 (1943): 370–396; K. Horney. *Neurosis and Human Growth: The Struggle Towards Self-realization*. London: Routledge and Kegan Paul (1951); C. Rogers. *On Becoming a Person: A Therapist's View of Psychotherapy*. Boston: Houghton Mifflin, 1961.

23 *known as "neurogenesis"*: G. Kemermann. "Adult neurogenesis: An evolutionary perspective," *Cold Spring Harbor Perspectives in Biology*. New York: Cold Spring Harbor Press, 2015.

24 *after a single activity . . . your brain changes*: S. Trojan and J. Porkorny. "Theoretical aspects of neuroplasticity," *Physiological Research* 48, no 2 (1999): 87–97.

25 *Strength-based experiences shape strength-based networks*: X. Chen et al. "Structural basis for synaptic adhesion mediated by neuroligin–neurexin interactions," *Nature Structural & Molecular Biology* 15, no 1 (2008): 50–56.

26 *"synaptic elimination"*: Also known as neural pruning. See J. Iglesias et al. "Dynamics of pruning in simulated large-scale spiking neural networks," *BioSystems* 79, no 9 (2005): 11–20.

27 *"unfriend" each other*: You can see a video of two neurons breaking free of each other at Dr. Jo Dispenza's website. Accessed February 2, 2016, http://www.drjoedispenza.com /index.php?page_id=Live_Neurons_Connecting_Pruning.

28 *"use it or lose it"*: N. Doidge. *The Brain that Changes Itself: Stories of Personal Triumph from the Frontiers of Brain Science*. New York: Penguin, 2007; N. Doidge. *The Brain's Way of Healing: Remarkable Discoveries and Recoveries from the Frontiers of Neuroplasticity*. New York: Penguin, 2015.

29 *activity in the neural systems associated with compassion*: H. Y. Weng et al. "Compassion training alters altruism and neural responses to suffering," *Psychological Science* 24, no 7 (2013): 1171–1180.

30 *Scott Kaufman, PhD, and Angela Duckworth, PhD*: S. B. Kaufman and A. L. Duckworth. "World-class expertise: A developmental model," *Wiley Interdisciplinary Reviews: Cognitive Science*. Accessed November 26, 2015, http://scottbarrykaufman.com/wp-content/ uploads/2015/09/10.1002_wcs.1365.pdf.

31 *a list of 118 strengths*: The list (see the Strength Switch website) is collated from the work of three major institutes that focus on strengths development: 1) Values in Action Institute (VIA) (www.viacharacter.org); see C. Peterson and M. E. P. Seligman. *Character Strengths and Virtues*. 2) Gallup Institute (www.gallupstrengthscenter.com); see M. Buckingham and D. O. Clifton. *Now, Discover Your Strengths*. New York: Free Press, 2001. 3) Centre of Applied Positive Psychology (CAPP) (www.cappeu.com); see A. Linley, J. Willars, and R. Biswas-Diener. *The Strengths Book*.

Chapter 4: The Ages and Stages of Strength Growth

1 *nothing beats the first three years*: S. Dehaene, G. Dehaene-Lambertz, and L. Cohen. "Abstract representations of numbers in the animal and human brain," *Trends in Neuroscience* 21, no 8 (1998): 355–361.

2 *more neural connections than an adult*: R. K. Lenroot and J. N. Giedd. "Brain development in children and adolescents: Insights from anatomical magnetic resonance imaging," *Neuroscience & Biobehavioral Reviews* 30, no 6 (2006): 718–729.

3 *build their brain fast*: T. Paus et al. "Maturation of white matter in the human brain: A review of magnetic resonance studies," *Brain Research Bulletin* 54, no 3 (2001): 255–266.

4 *Strengths unfold according to a pattern*: B. S. Bloom, ed. *Developing Talent in Young People*. New York: Ballantine Books, 1985; J. S. Renzulli. "What makes giftedness? Reexamining a definition," *Phi Delta Kappan* 60, no 3 (1978): 180–184.

5 *only 5 percent smaller than an adult brain*: J. N. Giedd. "The teen brain: Insights from neuroimaging," *Journal of Adolescent Health* 42, no 4 (2008): 335–343.

6 *the volume and density of the brain grow swiftly*: E. R. Sowell et al. "Longitudinal mapping of cortical thickness and brain growth in normal children," *The Journal of Neuroscience* 24, no 38 (2004): 8223–8231.

7 *"overproduction" phase*: J. Giedd (n.d.). "Interview: Inside the teenage brain," *Frontline*. Accessed November 25, 2015, http://www.pbs.org/wgbh/pages/frontline/shows/teen brain/interviews/giedd.html.

8 *changes that begin in the brain in early to mid-adolescence*: J. N. Giedd. "The teen brain: Insights from neuroimaging."

9 *the brain's gray matter peaks at age twelve and then begins a long decline*: This pattern has been shown for gray matter volume, electrical activity, and density of neurotransmitter receptor sites.

10 *correcting the overproduction phase of late childhood*: E. R. Sowell et al. "Mapping continued brain growth and gray matter density reduction in dorsal frontal cortex: Inverse relationships during postadolescent brain maturation," *Journal of Neuroscience* 21, no 22 (2001): 8819–8829.

11 *long and deep period of neural change*: Ibid.

12 *more interconnected, and more efficient*: T. Paus. "Mapping brain maturation and cognitive development during adolescence," *Trends in Cognitive Sciences* 9, no 2 (2005): 60–68.

13 *determined partly by genes*: Genetic factors are the dominant force in explaining variance in many measures of brain structure throughout the life cycle, but interesting brain region differences have been found. For example, the size and shape of the corpus callosum is remarkably similar among twins. The corpus callosum connects the two halves of the brain and is involved in creativity and higher type of thinking. In contrast, the cerebellums of identical twins are no more alike than nonidentical twins. This part of the brain is influenced by the environment and it's a part of the brain that changes most during the teen years. The cerebellum is involved in the coordination of your muscles, allowing you to be graceful (or not) and is similarly involved in the coordination of your cognitive processes and your social skills. See J. N. Giedd et al. "Structural brain magnetic resonance imaging of pediatric twins," *Human Brain Mapping* 28, no 6 (2007): 474–481.

14 *higher-level functioning*: T. Paus et al. "Maturation of white matter in the human brain: A review of magnetic resonance studies."

15 *"back to front" brain development*: E. R. Sowell et al. "Mapping continued brain growth and gray matter density reduction in dorsal frontal cortex: Inverse relationships during postadolescent brain maturation."

16 *emotion-driven limbic system overrides the logic-driven frontal lobe*: R. Cardinal et al. "Emotion and motivation: The role of the amygdala, ventral striatum and prefontal cortex," *Neuroscience and Biobehavioral Reviews* 26, no 3 (2002): 321–352; A. Etkin, T. Egner, and R. Kalisch. "Emotional processing in anterior cingulate and medial prefrontal cortex," *Trends in Cognitive Sciences* 15, no 2 (2011): 85–93.

17 *emotional behavior, impulsivity, risk taking, and sensation-seeking behaviors*: T. A. Wills et al. "Novelty seeking, risk taking, and related constructs as predictors of adolescent substance use: An application of Cloninger's theory," *Journal of Substance Abuse* 6, no 1 (1994): 1–20; J. J. Arnett. "Sensation seeking, aggressiveness, and adolescent reckless behavior," *Personality and Individual Differences* 20, no 6 (1996): 693–702.

18 *high rates of mental illness in the teenage years*: R. C. Kessler et al. "Age of onset of mental disorders: A review of recent literature," *Current Opinion in Psychiatry* 20, no 4 (2007): 359–364; S. L. Andersen and M. H. Teicher. "Stress, sensitive periods and maturational events in adolescent depression," *Trends in Neurosciences* 31, no 4 (2008): 183–191.

19 *sophisticated, smoother, faster communication*: T. Paus. "Mapping brain maturation and cognitive development during adolescence."

20 *In this phase, the child achieves high performance*: The trajectory of strengths evolution across these three phases differs across domains and is influenced by factors like

physical and intellectual maturation, time needed for a strength to fully develop, and the systems we've set in place to recognize and/or build particular strengths. For example, in music talent, the phases will start earlier for boy soprano than adult vocal artist because these strengths are affected by different physical maturation of the vocal cord. In physical strengths, phases will start earlier for gymnastics because this is when the body is most limber as compared to football, which requires advanced size and speed. For mental talents, signs of precocity in mathematics can be seen in preschool years, whereas strengths for psychology don't occur until late adolescence/early adulthood because the serious study of social science is not taught until later high school and university. See R. F. Subotnik, P. Olszewski-Kubilius, and F. C. Worrell. "Rethinking giftedness and gifted education."

21 *Musical ability is detectable from six months of age*: S. E. Trehub. "Musical predispositions in infancy," *Annals of the New York Academy of Sciences* 930, no 1 (2001): 1–16.

22 *Empathy . . . starts in infancy*: M. L. Hoffman. *Empathy and Moral Development: Implications for Caring and Justice*, Cambridge, UK: Cambridge University Press, 2000; M. Davidov et al. "Concern for others in the first year of life: Theory, evidence, and avenues for research," *Child Development Perspectives* 7, no 2 (2013): 126–131.

23 *respond to the distress of others*: J. Decety. "The neural pathways, development and functions of empathy," *Current Opinion in Behavioral Sciences* 3, no 1 (2015): 1–6.

24 *early signs of sporting ability*: R. S. Masters. "Theoretical aspects of implicit learning in sport," *International Journal of Sport Psychology* 31, no 4 (2000): 530–541; J. Côté and J. Fraser-Thomas. "Play, practice, and athlete development," in *Developing Elite Sport Performance: Lessons from Theory and Practice*, D. Farrow, J. Baker, and C. MacMahon, eds. New York: Routledge, 2008: 17–28.

25 *a glimpse into your child's personality*: J. Block. "Ego-resilience through time," paper presented at the Biennial Meeting of the Society for Research in Child Development, New Orleans, 1993.

26 *more consistent signs of a child's personality*: A. Caspi and P. A. Silva. "Temperamental qualities at age three predict personality traits in young adulthood: Longitudinal evidence from a birth cohort," *Child Development* 66, no 2 (1995): 486–498.

27 *emotion . . . and the appropriate facial expression*: C. Izard et al. "Emotion knowledge as a predictor of social behavior and academic competence in children at risk," *Psychological Science* 12, no 4 (2001): 18–23.

28 *advanced reasoning ability and perspective taking*: J. Piaget. *Judgment and Reasoning in the Child*. London: Kegan Paul, 1926. (Original work published in 1924.)

29 *harmony and tonality*: E. Costa-Giomi. "Young children's harmonic perception," *Annals of the New York Academy of Sciences* 999, no 1 (2003): 477–484.

30 *cognitive capacity expands*: M. H. Bornstein. "Stability in early mental development: From attention and information processing in infancy to language and cognition in childhood," in *Stability and Continuity in Mental Development: Behavioral and Biological Perspectives*, M. H. Bornstein and N. A. Krasnegor, eds. Hillsdale, NJ: Erlbaum (1989), 147–170; P. B. Baltes, U. M. Staudinger, and U. Lindenberger. "Lifespan psychology: Theory and application to intellectual functioning," *Annual Review of Psychology* 50 (1999): 471–507.

31 *Little creativity . . . and daily ingenuity*: J. C. Kaufman and R. A. Beghett. "Beyond big and little: The four C model of creativity," *Review of General Psychology* 13, no 1 (2009): 1–12; S. W. Kleibeuker, C. K. Dreu, and E. A. Crone. "Creativity development in adolescence: Insight from behavior, brain, and training studies," *Perspectives on Creativity Development. New Directions for Child and Adolescent Development* 151 (2016): 73–84.

32 *a "slow burn" strength*: J. D. Webster. "Wisdom and positive psychosocial values in young adulthood," *Journal of Adult Development* 17, no 2 (2010): 70–80.

33 Girls tend to develop wisdom faster than boys: M. Ferragut, M. J. Blanca, and M. Ortiz-Tallo. "Psychological virtues during adolescence: A longitudinal study of gender differences," *European Journal of Developmental Psychology* 11, no 5 (2014): 521–531.

34 a set of beliefs: G. D. Heyman and C. S. Dweck. "Children's thinking about traits: Implications for judgments of the self and others," *Child Development* 69, no 2 (1998): 391–403.

35 two types of mind-set: Dweck, C. S. *Mindset: The New Psychology of Success*. New York: Ballantine Books, 2008.

36 intelligence can grow: L. Blackwell, K. Trzesniewski, and C. S. Dweck. "Implicit theories of intelligence predict achievement across an adolescent transition: A longitudinal study and an intervention," *Child Development* 78, no 1 (2007): 246–263.

37 Children with growth mind-sets do better: Ibid.

38 Since they believe that people are capable of change, they act more prosocially: C. S. Dweck. *Mindset: The New Psychology of Success.*

39 parents' mind-sets about failure: K. Haimovitz and C. S. Dweck. "What predicts children's fixed and growth intelligence mind-sets? Not their parents' views of intelligence but their parents' views of failure," *Psychological Science* 1–11 (2016), doi: 10.1177/0956797616639727.

40 a teen with a growth mind-set is more receptive to strength-based messages: H. Jach, et al. "Strengths and subjective wellbeing in adolescence: Strength-based parenting and the moderating effect of mindset." Journal of Happiness Studies (2017). You can find details of this publication at www.leawaters.com.

41 role modeling: J. P. Rushton. "Generosity in children: Immediate and long-term effects of modeling, preaching, and moral judgment," *Journal of Personality and Social Psychology* 31, no 3 (1975): 459–466.

42 scaffolding: R. Wass, T. Harland, and A. Mercer. "Scaffolding critical thinking in the zone of proximal development," *Special Issue: Critical Thinking in Higher Education* 30, no 3 (2011): 317–328.

43 Lev Vygotsky . . . the zone of proximal development: M. Cole. "The zone of proximal development: Where culture and cognition create each other," in *Culture, Communication, and Cognition: Vygotskian Perspectives*, J. Wertsch, ed. Cambridge, UK: Cambridge University Press, 1985; R. Van der Veer and J. Valsiner. *Understanding Vygotsky. A Quest For Synthesis*, Oxford, UK: Basil Blackwell, 1991.

44 one's level of optimism or pessimism has a big impact on depression: C. S. Carver, M. F. Scheier, and S. C. Segerstrom. "Optimism," *Clinical Psychology Review* 30, no 7 (2010): 879–889.

Chapter 5: Attention, Savoring, Gratitude, and Goofing Off

1 two dimensions: direction and maintenance: A. M. Treisman. "Strategies and models of selective attention," *Psychological Review* 76, no 3 (1969): 282–299; L. Visu-Petra, O. Benga, and M. Miclea. "Dimensions of attention and executive functioning in 5- to 12-year-old children: Neuropsychological assessment with the NEPSY battery," *Cognition, Brain, Behavior* 11, no 3 (2007): 585–608; D. Goleman. *Focus: The Hidden Driver of Excellence*. New Delhi: Bloomsbury, 2013.

2 attention is also built through rest: G. Northoff, N. W. Duncan, and D. J. Hayes. "The brain and its resting state activity—Experimental and methodological implications," *Progress in Neurobiology* 92, no 4 (2010): 593–600.

3 Adults max out at somewhere between twenty to thirty-five minutes: W. H. Teichner. "The detection of a simple visual signal as a function of time of watch," *Human Factors* 16, no 4 (1974): 339–353.

4 after nine minutes or so, our vigilance declines: K. H. Nuechterlein, R. Parasuraman, and Q. Jiang. "Visual sustained attention: Image degradation produces rapid sensitivity decrement over time," *Science* 220, no 4594 (1983): 327–329.

5 back on task again: W. H. Teichner. "The detection of a simple visual signal as a function of time of watch."

6 Most three-year-olds can hold focused attention for approximately three to five minutes: K. E. Moyer and B. V. H. Gilmer. "Attention spans of children for experimentally designed toys," *The Journal of Genetic Psychology* 87, no 2 (1955): 187–201; H. Ruff, M. Capozzoli, and R. Weissberg. "Age, individuality, and context as factors in sustained visual attention during the preschool years," *Developmental Psychology* 34, no 3 (1998): 454–464.

7 *Between the ages of six and twelve there's a developmental spurt*: H. A. Ruff, M. Capozzoli, and R. Weissberg. "Age, individuality, and context as factors in sustained visual attention during the preschool years," *Developmental Psychology* 34, no 3 (1998): 454–464; C. C. H. Lin et al. "Development of sustained attention assessed using the continuous performance test among children 6–15 years of age," *Journal of Abnormal Child Psychology* 27, no 5 (1999): 403–412.

8 around age fifteen, there's another spurt in attention-aiming capacity: J. Giedd et al. "Quantitative magnetic resonance imaging of human brain development: Ages 4–18," *Cerebral Cortex* 6, no 4 (1996): 551–560; V. A. Anderson et al. "Development of executive functions through late childhood and adolescence in an Australian sample," *Developmental Neuropsychology* 20, no 1 (2001): 385–406.

9 sustained attention: R. Parasuraman. "Vigilance, monitoring and search," in *Handbook of Human Perception and Performance, Vol. 2, Cognitive Processes and Performance*, J. R. Boff, L. Kaufmann, and J. P. Thomas, eds. New York: Wiley (1986), 41–49.

10 our attentional ability levels off: A. Berardi, R. Parasuraman, and J. Haxby, J. "Overall vigilance and sustained attention decrements in healthy aging," *Experimental Aging Research* 27, no 1 (2001): 19–39.

11 At age fifteen, that jumps to 96 percent: C. C. H. Lin et al. "Development of sustained attention assessed using the continuous performance test among children 6–15 years of age."

12 adults do about the same: W. J. Chen et al. "Performance of the continuous performance test among community samples," *Schizophrenia Bulletin* 24, no 1 (1998): 163–174.

13 kids with attentional challenges: R. Ylvén, E. Björck-Åkesson, and M. Granlund. "Literature review of positive functioning in families with children with a disability," *Journal of Policy and Practice in Intellectual Disabilities* 3, no 4 (2006): 253–270.

14 June Pimm, PhD: J. Pimm. *The Autism Story*. Markham, ON: Fitzhenry and Whiteside, 2014.

15 Early Start Denver Model: S. J. Rogers, G. Dawson, and L. A. Vismara. *An Early Start for Your Child with Autism: Using Everyday Activities to Help Kids Connect, Communicate, and Learn*. New York: Guilford Press, 2012.

16 positive parenting with children who have ADHD: A. M. Chronis et al. "Maternal depression and early positive parenting predict future conduct problems in young children with attention-deficit/hyperactivity disorder," *Developmental Psychology* 43, no 1 (2007): 70–82; D. M. Healeya et al. "Maternal positive parenting style is associated with better functioning in hyperactive/inattentive preschool children infant and child development," *Infant and Child Development* 20, no 2 (2011): 148–161.

17 the ability to aim and sustain attention: J. G. Randall, F. L. Oswald, and M. E. Beier. "Mind-wandering, cognition, and performance: A theory-driven meta-analysis of attention regulation," *Psychological Bulletin* 140, no 6 (2014): 1411–1431.

18 *Savoring*: F. B. Bryant and J. Veroff. *Savoring: A New Model of Positive Experience*. Mahwah, NJ: Lawrence Erlbaum, 2007.

19 *Savoring . . . boosts happiness, positive mood, and life satisfaction*: F. B. Bryant and J. Veroff. *Savoring*; P. E. Jose, B. T. Lim, et al. "Does savoring increase happiness? A daily diary study," *The Journal of Positive Psychology* 7, no 3 (2012): 176–187.

20 *"reminiscent savoring"*: F. B. Bryant, C. M. Smart, and S. P. King. "Using the past to enhance the present: Boosting happiness through positive reminiscence," *Journal of Happiness Studies* 6, no 3 (2005): 227–260. Also see B. L. Fredrickson. "Extracting meaning from past affective experiences: The importance of peaks, ends, and specific emotions," *Cognition and Emotion* 14, no 4 (2000): 577–606.

21 *Looking ahead*: J. Quoidbach et al. "Positive emotion regulation and well-being: Comparing the impact of eight savoring and dampening strategies," *Personality and Individual Differences* 49, no 5 (2010): 368–373.

22 *gratefulness, as distinct from the social quality of gratitude*: R. Rusk, D. Vella-Brodrick, and L. Waters. "Gratitude or gratefulness? A conceptual review and proposal of the System of Appreciative Functioning," *Journal of Happiness Studies* (2016), doi: 10.1007 /s10902-015-9675-z.

23 *gratitude . . . linked to a host of positive indicators*: A. M. Wood, J. J. Froh, and A. W. Geraghty. "Gratitude and well-being: A review and theoretical integration," *Clinical Psychology Review* 30, no 7 (2010): 890–905.

24 *people who feel grateful . . . fall into slumber more quickly*: A. M. Wood et al. "Gratitude influences sleep through the mechanism of pre-sleep cognitions," *Journal of Psychosomatic Research* 66, no 1 (2009): 43–48.

25 *Gratitude also builds our relationships*: M. E. P. Seligman et al. "Positive education: Positive psychology and classroom interventions," *Oxford Review of Education* 35, no 3 (2009): 293–311; J. J. Froh et al. "Who benefits the most from a gratitude intervention in children and adolescents? Examining positive affect as a moderator," *The Journal of Positive Psychology* 4, no 5 (2009): 408–422; L. Waters and H. Stokes. "Positive education for school leaders: Exploring the effects of emotion-gratitude and action-gratitude," *Australian Educational and Developmental Psychologist* 32, no 1 (2015): 1–22.

26 *gratitude created a bond*: D. Keltner. *Born to Be Good: The Science of a Meaningful Life*.

27 *through words or actions*: S. B. Algoe, B. L. Fredrickson, and S. L. Gable. "The social functions of the emotion of gratitude via expression," *Emotion* 13, no 4 (2013): 605–609.

28 *1000 Awesome Things*: http://1000awesomethings.com.

29 *the power of the gratitude letter*: M. E. P. Seligman et al. 2005. "Positive psychology progress"; J. Froh, W. Sefick, and R. A. Emmons. "Counting blessings in early adolescents: An experimental study of gratitude and subjective well-being," *Journal of School Psychology* 46, no 2 (2008): 213–233.

30 *attention-sharpening benefits of moderate aerobic exercise*: C. H. Hillman et al. "The effect of acute treadmill walking on cognitive control and academic achievement in preadolescent children," *Neuroscience* 159, no 3 (2009): 1044–1054.

31 *in this . . . resting state, our brain is still highly active*: M. H. Immordino-Yang, J. A. Christodoulou, and V. Singh. "Rest is not idleness: Implications of the brain's default mode for human development and education," *Perspectives on Psychological Science* 7, no 4 (2012): 352–64.

32 *ERP improves . . . after people engage in moderate aerobic exercise*: C. H. Hillman et al. "The effect of acute treadmill walking on cognitive control and academic achievement in preadolescent children."

33 *"cerebral congestion"*: F. Jabr. "Why your brain needs more downtime," *Scientific American*, October 15, 2013. Accessed August 14, 2016, http://www.scientificamerican.com /article/mental-downtime.

34 *memory consolidation*: G. Girardeau et al. "Selective suppression of hippocampal ripples impairs spatial memory," *Nature Neuroscience* 12 (2009): 1222–1223.

35 *stepping away from the problem*: A. Dijksterhuis et al. "On making the right choice: The deliberation-without-attention effect," *Science* 311, no 5763 (2006): 1005–1007.

36 *unstructured play-based curriculum*: A. Diamond et al. "Preschool program improves cognitive control," *Science* 318, no 5855 (2007): 1387–1388; A. Diamond and K. Lee. "Interventions shown to aid executive function development in children 4–12 years old," *Science*, 333, no 6045 (2011): 959–964.

37 *Attention is built through rest and play*: D. S. Weisberg et al. "Guided play: Making play work for education," *Phi Beta Kappan* 96, no 8 (2015): 8–13; J. M. Zosh, K. Hirsh-Pasek, and R. Golinkoff. "Guided play," in *Encyclopedia of Contemporary Early Childhood Education*, D. L. Couchenour and K. Chrisman, eds. Thousand Oaks, CA: Sage, 2015.

38 *free time during the week*: Although we hear about the need for downtime, as parents we're sent mixed messages. On one hand, people lament the fast pace of our modern society and yearn for the days when kids could play freely until called for dinner, and on the other hand, it seems everywhere we turn we're being told that we must make every minute count and that we need to be constantly stimulating our child's brains by enrolling them in yet another activity. According to Dr. Kathy Hirsh-Pasek's website (http://kathyhirshpasek.com), playtime has dropped precipitously from 40 percent in 1981 to 25 percent in 1997. See K. Hirsh-Pasek and R. M. Golinkoff. *Einstein Never Used Flash Cards: How Our Children Really Learn—and Why They Need to Play More and Memorize Less*. Stuttgart: Holtzbrink Publishers, 2003. In the last two decades, children have lost eight hours of free playtime per week. Also see D. Elkind. *The Hurried Child: Growing Up Too Fast Too Soon*, 3rd edition. Cambridge, MA: Perseus Publishing, 2001; P. N. Stearns. *Anxious Parents: A History of Modern Child-rearing in America*. New York: New York University Press, 2002; E. Morman. "25 years of parenting: A look back and ahead," *Metro Parent/Daily*, January 8, 2011. Accessed February 2, 2016, http://www.metroparent.com/daily/parenting/parenting-issues-tips/25-years -parenting-look-back-ahead.

39 *building their identity*: M. H. Immordino-Yang, J. A. Christodoulou, and Vanessa Singh. "Rest is not idleness: Implications of the brain's default mode for human development and education," *Perspectives on Psychological Science* 7, no 4 (2012): 352–64.

40 *reduced empathic responses*: P. Trapnell and L. Sinclair. "Texting frequency and the moral shallowing hypothesis," poster presented at the Annual Meeting of the Society for Personality and Social Psychology, San Diego, CA, 2012.

Chapter 6: Mindfulness

1 *mindfulness*: J. Kabat-Zinn. "Mindfulness-based interventions in context: Past, present, and future," *Clinical Psychology: Science and Practice* 10, no 2 (2003): 144–156.

2 *"bare attention"*: J. M. Schwartz. "Mental force and the advertence of bare attention," *Journal of Consciousness Studies* 6, no 2–3 (1999): 293–296.

3 *I don't have to be perfect, I just have to be present*: I take great comfort in Donald Winnicott's idea of "good enough" parenting. That as long as I am here to "hold" the emotional space for my children (be it good or bad emotions), then I am doing a good job. See D. W. Winnicott, *The Child, the Family, and the Outside World*, 2nd edition. Cambridge, MA: Da Capo Press, 1992.

4 *our mood is best when we're present in the moment*: M. A. Killingsworth and D. T. Gilbert. "A wandering mind is an unhappy mind," *Science* 330, no 6006 (2010): 932.

5 large-scale meta-review of mindfulness: L. Waters et al. "Contemplative education: A systematic, evidence-based review of the effect of meditation interventions in schools," *Educational Psychology Review* 27, no 1 (2015): 103–134.

6 increased activity in their left prefrontal cortex: R. Davidson and S. Begley. *The Emotional Life of Your Brain*. New York: Hudson Street Press, 2013.

7 mentally rehearse: A. Pascual-Leone et al. "The plastic human brain cortex," *Annual Review of Neuroscience* 28 (2005): 377–401.

8 The more mindful the parent, the more mindful the child: L. Waters. "The relationship between parent mindfulness, child mindfulness and child stress," *Psychology* 7 (2016): 40–51.

9 become aware of patterns in . . . thoughts and feelings: J. Brefcynski-Lewis et al. "Neural correlates of attentional expertise in long term meditation practitioners," *Proceedings of the National Academy of Sciences* 104, no 27 (2007): 11483–11488; A. Lutz et al. "Mental training enhances attentional stability," *Journal of Neuroscience* 29, no 42 (2009): 13418–13427.

10 mindfulness fosters positive emotions: R. Davidson and S. Begley. *The Emotional Life of Your Brain*.

11 Mindfulness opens the door of awareness: R. Niemiec. *Mindfulness and Character Strengths*.

12 mindfulness is a great way to help your child build resilience: M. D. Keye and A. M. Pidgeon. "An investigation of the relationship between resilience, mindfulness, and academic self-efficacy," *Open Journal of Social Sciences* 1, no 6 (2013): 1–4.

13 emotional complexity: S.-M. Kang and P. R. Shave. "Individual differences in emotional complexity: Their psychological implications," *Journal of Personality* 72, no 4 (2004): 687–726.

14 emotional coaching: J. M. Gottman, L. F. Katz, and C. Hooven. "Parental meta-emotion philosophy and the emotional life of families: Theoretical models and preliminary data," *Journal of Family Psychology* 10, no 3 (1996): 243–268.

15 parents who are emotional coaches: N. Eisenberg, A. Cumberland, and T. L. Spinrad. "Parental socialization of emotion," *Psychological Inquiry* 9, no 4 (1998): 241–273; A.L. Gentzler et al. "Parent–child emotional communication and children's coping in middle childhood," *Social Development* 14, no 4 (2005): 591–612.

16 calmer central nervous system: S. B. Perlman, L. A. Camras, and K. A. Pelphrey. "Physiology and functioning: Parents' vagal tone, emotion socialization, and children's emotion knowledge," *Journal of Experimental Child Psychology* 100, no 4 (2008): 308–315.

17 we . . . learn how to handle emotions from our parents: J. Gottman and J. Declaire. *Raising an Emotionally Intelligent Child: The Heart of Parenting*. New York: Simon & Schuster, 1998; D. J. Siegel and M. Hartzell. *Parenting from the Inside Out 10th Anniversary Edition: How a Deeper Self-Understanding Can Help You Raise Children*. New York: Penguin, 2013.

18 Emotional coaching is a skill you can learn quickly: S. S. Havighurst et al. "Tuning in to kids: Improving emotion socialization practices in parents of preschool children—findings from a community trial," *Journal of Child Psychology and Psychiatry* 51, no 12 (2010): 1342–1350; C. E. Kehoe, S. S. Havighurst, and A. E. Harley. "Tuning in to teens: Improving parent emotion socialization to reduce youth internalizing difficulties," *Social Development* 23, no 2 (2013): 413–431.

19 challenging behaviors: K. Bluth et al. "A stress model for couples parenting children with Autism Spectrum Disorders and the introduction of a mindfulness intervention," *Journal of Family Theory & Review* 5, no 3 (2013): 194–213.

20 mindful parenting: S. Bögels et al. "Mindfulness training for adolescents with externalizing disorders and their parents," *Behavioral and Cognitive Psychotherapy* 36, no 2 (2008): 193–209.

21 *mindfulness-based interventions helped . . . parents*: R. Keenan-Mount, N. Albrecht, and L. Waters. "Mindfulness-based approaches for young people with autism spectrum disorder and their caregivers: Do these approaches hold benefits for teachers?" *Australian Journal of Teacher Education*, 2016.

22 *compulsory mindfulness is an oxymoron*: S. Kaiser Greenland. *The Mindful Child: How to Help Your Kid Manage Stress and Become Happier, Kinder, and More Compassionate*, New York: Free Press, 2010.

23 *relaxation response in the body*: R. Jerath et al. "Physiology of long pranayamic breathing: Neural respiratory elements may provide a mechanism that explains how slow deep breathing shifts the autonomic nervous system." *Medical Hypotheses* 67, no 3 (2006): 566–571.

Chapter 7: Self-Control

1 *self-control helps us overcome internal conflict*: K. McGonigal. *The Willpower Instinct: How Self-Control Works, Why It Matters, and What You Can Do to Get More of It*. New York: Avery, 2011.

2 *Table 1*: This is an adaptation of the Brief Self-Control Scale. See J. P. Tangney, R. F. Baumeister, and A. L. Boone. "High self-control predicts good adjustment, less pathology, better grades, and interpersonal success," *Journal of Personality* 72, no 2 (2004): 271–324.

3 *self-control . . . is often low*: C. Peterson and M. E. P. Seligman. *Character Strengths and Virtues*.

4 *programs to build . . . self-control*: M. Oaten and K. Cheng. "Improved self-control: The benefits of a regular program of academic study," *Basic and Applied Social Psychology* 28, no 1 (2006): 1–16; M. Oaten and K. Cheng. "Longitudinal gains in self-regulation from regular physical exercise," *British Journal of Health Psychology* 11 (4): 717–733; M. Oaten and K. Cheng. "Improvements in self-control from financial monitoring," *Journal of Economic Psychology* 28, no 4 (2007): 487–501.

5 *impulse spending when . . . attention is distracted*: B. Shiv, A. Fedorikhin, and S. M. Nowlis. "Interplay of the heart and mind in decision making," in *Inside Consumption: Frontiers of Research on Consumer Motives, Goals, and Desire*, S. Ratneshwar, and D. Mick, eds. Abingdon, UK: Routledge, 2005.

6 *physiological capacity wired into our nervous system*: S. C. Segerstrom and L. S. Nes. "Heart rate variability indexes self-regulatory strength, effort, and fatigue," *Psychological Science* 18, no 3 (2007): 275–281.

7 *some people have more innate self-control*: S. C. Segerstrom, T. W. Smith, and T. A. Eisenlohr-Moul. "Positive psychophysiology: The body and self-regulation," in *Designing the Future of Positive Psychology: Taking Stock and Moving Forward*, K. M. Sheldon, T. B. Kashdan, and M. F. Steger, eds. New York: Oxford University Press (2011), 25–40.

8 *brain area responsible for self-monitoring*: M. Inzlicht and J. N. Gutsell. "Running on empty: Neural signals for self-control failure," *Psychological Science* 18, no 11 (2007): 933–937.

9 *we cave to our impulses about 60 percent of the time*: W. Hofmann et al. "Everyday temptations: An experience sampling study of desire, conflict, and self-control," *Journal of Personality and Social Psychology* 102, no 6 (2012): 1318–1335; W. Hofmann, K. D. Vohs, and R. F. Baumeister. "What people desire, feel conflicted about, and try to resist in everyday life," *Psychological Science* 23, no 6 (2012): 582–588.

10 *"pause and plan response"*: S. C. Segerstrom et al. "'Pause and plan': Self-regulation and the heart," in *Motivational Perspectives on Cardiovascular Response*, G. Gendolla

and R. Wright, eds. Washington, DC: American Psychological Association (2011), 181–198.

11 taking a moment: R. Jerath et al. "Physiology of long pranayamic breathing"; K. McGonigal. *The Willpower Instinct.*

12 We start to develop self-control even as infants: B. E. Vaughn, C. B. Kopp, and J. B. Krakow. "The emergence and consolidation of self-control from eighteen to thirty months of age: Normative trends and individual differences," *Child Development* 55 no 3 (1984): 990–1004.

13 delayed gratification: W. Mischel, E. B. Ebbesen, and A. Raskoff Zeiss. "Cognitive and attentional mechanisms in delay of gratification," *Journal of Personality and Social Psychology* 21, no 2 (1972): 204–218.

14 developmental spurt in our self-control capacity: C. Hay and W. Forrest. "The development of self-control: Examining self-control theory's stability thesis," *Criminology* 44, no 4 (2006): 739–774.

15 the teenage years: J. N. Giedd. "The teen brain: Insights from neuroimaging."

16 the cortex can put the brakes on . . . impulsivity: J. N. Giedd et al. "Brain development during childhood and adolescence: A longitudinal MRI study," *Nature Neuroscience* 2, no 10 (1999): 861–863; E. R. Sowell. "Mapping continued brain growth and gray matter density reduction in dorsal frontal cortex: Inverse relationships during post-adolescent brain maturation."

17 self-control is more important than IQ: For university students, see J. P. Tangney, R. F. Baumeister, and A. L. Boone. "High self-control predicts good adjustment, less pathology, better grades, and interpersonal success," *Journal of Personality* 72, no 2 (2004): 271–324; for middle-school students, see A. L. Duckman and M. E. P. Seligman. "Self-discipline gives girls the edge: Gender in self-discipline, grades, and achievement test scores," *Journal of Educational Psychology* 98, no 2 (2006): 198–208.

18 It builds confidence and caring behavior and reduces depression and risky behavior: S. Gestsdóttir and R. M. Lerner. "Intentional self-regulation and positive youth development in early adolescence: Findings from the 4-H study of positive youth development," *Developmental Psychology* 43, no 2 (2007): 508–521; A. L. Duckworth, T. S. Gendler, and J. J. Gross. "Self-control in school-age children," *Educational Psychologist* 49, no 3 (2014): 199–217; B. M. Galla and A. L. Duckworth. "More than resisting temptation: Beneficial habits mediate the relationship between self-control and positive life outcomes," *Journal of Personality and Social Psychology* 109, no 3 (2015): 508–525.

19 children with high self-control: W. Mischel, Y. Shoda, and M. I. Rodriguez. "Delay of gratification in children," *Science* 244, no 4907 (1989): 933–939; R. F. Krueger et al. "Delay of gratification, psychopathology, and personality: Is low self-control specific to externalizing problems?" *Journal of Personality* 64, no 1 (1996): 107–128; W. Mischel and O. Ayduk. "Willpower in a cognitive-affective processing system," in *Handbook of Self-regulation: Research, Theory, and Applications*, R. F. Baumeister and K. D. Vohs, eds. New York: Guilford, 2004: 99–129; T. E. Moffitt et al. "A gradient of childhood self-control predicts health, wealth, and public safety," *Proceedings of the National Academy of Sciences* 108, no 7 (2011): 2693–2698.

20 liken self-control to a muscle: M. Muraven and R. F. Baumeister. "Self-regulation and depletion of limited resources: Does self-control resemble a muscle?" *Psychological Bulletin* 126, no 2 (2000): 247–259.

21 we start with strong self-control . . . our ability to apply it diminishes: W. Hofmann et al. "Everyday temptations: An experience sampling study of desire, conflict, and self-control," *Journal of Personality and Social Psychology* 102, no 6 (2012): 1318–1335.

22 *children of strength-based parents experience less stress*: L. Waters. "The relationship between strength-based parenting with children's stress levels and strength-based coping approaches," *Psychology* 6, no 6 (2015): 689–699.

23 *people in positive moods experienced less self-control depletion*: D. M. Tice et al. "Restoring the self: Positive affect helps improve self-regulation following ego depletion," *Journal of Experimental Social Psychology* 43, no 3 (2007): 379–384.

24 *power break*: DeskTime (a time-tracking and productivity app) analyzed user data from adults (5.5 million daily logs) and found that the most productive 10 percent of users worked with purpose for fifty-two minutes and took seventeen-minute breaks where they were completely removed from the work they were doing (entirely resting, not looking at e-mail, etc.). But shorter work times, and thus, breaks, might work better with children and teens. See J. Gifford. 2014. "The secret of the 10% most productive people? Breaking!," *DeskTime*. Accessed August 14, 2016, http://blog.desktime.com/2014/08/20/the-secret-of-the-10-most-productive-people-breaking; J. Gifford (n.d.). "The rule of 52 and 17: It's random but it ups your productivity," *The Muse*. Accessed August 14, 2016, https://www.themuse.com/advice/the-rule-of-52-and-17-its-random-but-it-ups-your-productivity/; http://time.com/3518053/perfect-break.

25 *Dirty Sock Syndrome*: This study was conducted by psychologist Daryl Bem and outlined in R. F. Baumeister and J. Tierney. "Willpower: Why self-control is the secret to success," in *Willpower: Rediscovering the Greatest Human Strength*. New York: Penguin, 2011.

26 *to-do lists*: K. McGonigal. *The Willpower Instinct*.

27 *Self-awareness is fostered and supported by mindfulness*: P. D. Zelazo and K. E. Lyons. "The potential benefits of mindfulness training in early childhood: A developmental social cognitive neuroscience perspective," *Child Development Perspectives* 6, no 2 (2012): 154–160.

28 *breathing exercises can actually reset the nervous system*: R. Jerath et al. "Physiology of long pranayamic breathing"; R. M. Kaushik et al. "Effects of mental relaxation and slow breathing in essential hypertension," *Complementary Therapies in Medicine* 14, no 2 (2006): 120–126.

29 *physiological changes lead to a relaxation response*: Ibid.

30 *there's a purely practical benefit to mindfulness*: H. A. Slagter et al. "Mental training affects distribution of limited brain resources," *Biology* 5, no 6 (2007): e138.

31 *feelings, thoughts, and sensations can arise and pass without requiring our energy*: Y. Y. Tang et al. "Short-term meditation training improves attention and self-regulation," *Proceedings of the National Academy of Sciences* 104, no 43 (2007): 17152–17156.

32 *mindfulness inoculates us against our impulses*: S. Bowen and A. Marlatt. "Surfing the urge: Brief mindfulness-based intervention for college student smokers," *Psychology of Addictive Behaviors* 23, no 4 (2009): 666–671.

33 *electrical activity in people's brains*: M. Inzlicht and J. N. Gutsell. "Running on empty neural signals for self-control failure," *Psychological Science* 18, no 11 (2007): 933–937.

34 *areas of the brain that assist with impulse control*: K. Demos et al. "Correlates of self-regulator depletion in chronic dieters," poster presented at the Society for Personality and Social Psychology Annual Convention, San Antonio, Texas, 2011.

35 *Kathleen Vohs . . . Roy Baumeister*: K. D. Vohs, R. F. Baumeister, and N. J. Ciarocco. "Self-regulation and self-presentation: Regulatory resource depletion impairs impression management and effortful self-presentation depletes regulatory resources," *Journal of Personality and Social Psychology* 88, no 4 (2005): 632–657.

36 *to change a habit can actually enlarge our capacity for self-control*: M. Muraven, R. F. Baumeister, and D. M. Tice. "Longitudinal improvement of self-regulation through practice: Building self-control strength through repeated exercise," *The Journal of*

Social Psychology 139, no 4 (1999): 446–457; R. F. Baumeister et al. "Self-regulation and personality: How interventions increase regulatory success, and how depletion moderates the effects of traits on behavior;" M. Oaten and K. Cheng. "Longitudinal gains in self-regulation from regular physical exercise. *British Journal of Health Psychology* 11, no 4 (2006): 717–733.

37 **strengthen self-control:** R. F. Baumeister and J. Tierney. "Willpower: Why self-control is the secret to success," in *Willpower: Rediscovering the Greatest Human Strength.*

Chapter 8: Communication

1 **parent-teenager pairs guessed wrong:** A. Sillars, A. Koerner, and M. A. Fitzpatrick. "Communication and understanding in parent–adolescent relationships," *Human Communication Research* 31, no 1 (2005): 102–128.

2 **less open communication and more problem communication:** H. L. Barnes and D. H. Olson. 1985. "Parent–adolescent communication and the circumplex model," *Child Development* 56, no 2 (1985): 438–447.

3 **low levels of positive communication may adversely affect a child's brain:** S. Whittle et al. "Positive parenting predicts the development of adolescent brain structure: A longitudinal study," *Developmental Cognitive Neuroscience* 8 (2014): 7–17. For those of you who want to know more about the specific areas in the brain that were affected, positive maternal behavior was linked to reduced growth of the right amygdala and accelerated cortical thinning in left and right orbitofrontal cortices, between baseline and follow up. For boys there was also a thinning in the right anterior cingulate. Reduced growth in the amygdala is associated with a lower fear response, lower emotional reactivity, and higher emotional regulation abilities. Thinning of the orbitofrontal cortices is associated with superior cognitive functioning. Thinning of the orbitofrontal cortices and anterior cingulate cortices is associated with lower levels of internalizing behaviors (e.g., depression and anxiety) and higher temperamental effortful control (i.e., self-regulation and impulse control). Thinning of cortical tissue during adolescence is thought to occur due to the beneficial adaptive changes of synaptic pruning, propagation of glial cells, and increased myelination of previously unmyelinated tissue. These neurological changes make the neurons more efficient, so the brain can "prune"/reduce the amount of neurons required in these areas while still achieving high functioning and, thus, allow for neuronal growth elsewhere in the brain. Also see M. B. H. Yap et al. "Parenting experiences interact with brain structure to predict depressive symptoms in adolescents," *Archives of General Psychiatry* 65, no 12 (2008): 1377–1385; O. S. Schwartz et al. "Observed maternal responses to adolescent behavior predict the onset of major depression," *Behavior Research and Therapy* 49, no 5 (2011): 331–338.

4 **how the parents reacted to their children's display of emotions:** A.L. Gentzler et al. "Parent–child emotional communication and children's coping in middle childhood," *Social Development* 14, no 4 (2005): 591–612.

5 **praise is related to task achievement:** C. M. Mueller and C. S. Dweck. "Praise for intelligence can undermine children's motivation and performance," *Journal of Personality and Social Psychology* 75, no 1 (1998): 33–52; M. L. Kamins and C. S. Dweck. "Person versus process-praise and criticism: Implications for contingent self-worth and coping," *Developmental Psychology* 35, no 3 (1999) 835–847; J. K. Harter, F. L. Schmidt, and T. L. Hayes. "Business-unit-level relationship between employee satisfaction, employee engagement, and business outcomes: A meta-analysis," *Journal of Applied Psychology* 87, no 2 (2002): 268–279; S. R. Zentall and B. J. Morris. "'Good job, you're so smart': The effects of inconsistency of praise type on young children's motivation," *Journal of Experimental Child Psychology* 107, no 2 (2010): 155–163.

6 Praise . . . influences how your child reacts to failure: C. M. Mueller and C. S. Dweck. "Praise for intelligence can undermine children's motivation and performance."

7 effect on a child's mind-set: A. Cimpian et al. "Subtle linguistic cues impact children's motivation," *Psychological Science* 18, no 4 (2007): 314–316; C. S. Dweck. *Mindset: The New Psychology of Success*.

8 these statements . . . don't build the child's strengths: T. Thompson. "Do we need to train teachers how to administer praise? Self-worth theory says we do," *Learning and Instruction* 7, no 1 (1997): 49–63.

9 "Good job" doesn't tell the child what he did that was good: A. Kohn. "Five reasons to stop saying 'good job,'" *Young Children* 56, no 5 (2001): 24–30.

10 generic praise can leave kids in a state of uncertainty: S. R. Zentall and B. J. Morris. "'Good job, you're so smart.'"

11 process-praise: L. Blackwell, K. Trzesniewski, and C. S. Dweck. "Implicit theories of intelligence predict achievement across an adolescent transition: A longitudinal study and an intervention," *Child Development* 78, no 1 (2007): 246–263; A. Cimpian et al. "Subtle linguistic cues impact children's motivation."

12 researchers at the University of Hong Kong: S. Lam, P. Yim, and Y. Ng. "Is effort praise motivational? The role of beliefs in the effort–ability relationship," *Contemporary Educational Psychology* 33, no 4 (2008): 694–710.

13 critical phase of development: J. E. Grusec and E. Redler. "Attribution, reinforcement, and altruism: A developmental analysis," *Developmental Psychology*, 16, no 5 (1980): 525–34.

14 moral strengths: C. J. Bryan et al. "When cheating would make you a cheater: Implicating the self prevents unethical behavior," *Journal of Experimental Psychology: General* 14, no 4 (2013): 1001–1005; A. Grant. "Raising a moral child," *The New York Times*, Sunday Review, April 11, 2014; accessed May 24, 2016, http://mobile.nytimes.com/2014/04/12/opinion/sunday/raising-a-moral-child.html.

15 person-praise . . . likely to lead to a fixed mind-set: C. M. Mueller and C. S. Dweck. "Praise for intelligence can undermine children's motivation and performance."

16 person-praise . . . weakens their resilience: Ibid; M. L. Kamins and C. S. Dweck. "Person versus process-praise and criticism: Implications for contingent self-worth and coping," *Developmental Psychology* 35, no 3 (1999) 835–847; J. H. Corpus and M. R. Lepper. "The effects of person versus performance praise on children's motivation: Gender and age as moderating factors," *Educational Psychology* 27, no 4 (2007): 487–508; E. A. Gunderson et al. 2013. "Parent praise to 1- to 3-year-olds predicts children's motivational frameworks 5 years later," *Child Development* 84, no 5 (2013): 1526–1541.

17 Dr. Dweck took her research into the homes of families: E. A. Gunderson et al. "Parent praise to 1- to 3-year-olds predicts children's motivational frameworks 5 years later."

Chapter 9: Strength-Based Living in the Real World

1 by nature we are motivated to self-develop: A. Maslow. "A theory of human motivation." A. Maslow. *Motivation and Personality*. New York: Harper, 1954; A. Maslow. *Toward a Psychology of Being*. Princeton, NJ: D. Van Nostrand, 1962; K. Horney. *Neurosis and Human Growth: The Struggle Towards Self-realization*. C. Rogers. *On Becoming a Person: A Therapist's View of Psychotherapy*. C. Rogers. *A Way of Being*. Boston: Houghton Mifflin, 1980.

2 they'll follow rules, provided the rules are reasonable, consistent, and fair: E. Nixon and A. M. Halpenny. *Children's Perspectives on Parenting Styles and Discipline: A Developmental Approach*. Dublin: Office of the Minister for Children and Youth Affairs (2010). Accessed November 26, 2015, http://www.dcya.gov.ie/documents/publications/childrens_perspectives_on_parenting_styles.pdf.

3 teach our children about the values and attitudes of society: D. Baumrind. "Parental disciplinary patterns and social competence in children," *Youth & Society* 9 no 3 (1978): 239–276; J. Belsky. "Early human experience: A family perspective," *Developmental Psychology* 17, no 1 (1981): 3; D. Baumrind and R. A. Thompson. "The ethics of parenting," in *Handbook of Parenting, Vol. 5: Practical Issues in Parenting*, 2nd edition, M. H. Bornstein, ed. Mahwah, NJ: Lawrence Erlbaum Associates, 2002, 3–34.

4 How do you . . . discipline your child?: This exercise is an amalgam of those used by M. L. Hoffman and H. D. Saltzstein. "Parent discipline and the child's moral development," *Journal of Personality and Social Psychology* 5, no 1 (1967): 45–57; J. Krevans and J. C. Gibbs. "Parents' use of inductive discipline: Relations to children's empathy and pro-social behavior," *Child Development* 67, no 6 (1996): 3263–3277; R. B. Patrick and J. C. Gibbs. "Parental expression of disappointment: Should it be a factor in Hoffman's model of parental discipline?" *Journal of Genetic Psychology* 168, no 2 (2007): 131–146; R. B. Patrick and J. C. Gibbs. "Inductive discipline, parental expression of disappointed expectations, and moral identity in adolescence."

5 different discipline styles: M. L. Hoffman. "Moral development," *Carmichael's Manual of Child Psychology, Vol. 2*, P. H. Mussen, ed. New York: Wiley, 1970; M. L. Hoffman. "Childrearing practices and moral development: Generalizations from empirical research," *Child Development* 34, no 2 (1993): 295–318; R. B. Patrick and J. C. Gibbs. "Parental expression of disappointment: Should it be a factor in Hoffman's model of parental discipline?" *Journal of Genetic Psychology* 168, no 2 (2007): 131–146.

6 guilt makes a person feel bad about what they did: S. Kim, R. Thibodeau, and R. S. Jorgensen. "Shame, guilt, and depressive symptoms: A meta-analytic review," *Psychological Bulletin* 137, no 1 (2011): 68–96.

7 shame leads to self-doubt, anxiety, and depression: P. Gilbert. What is shame? Some core issues and controversies," in *Shame: Interpersonal Behavior, Psychopathology, and Culture*, P. Gilbert and B. Andrews, eds. New York: Oxford University Press (1998), 3–38; S. Kim, R. Thibodeau, and R. S. Jorgensen. "Shame, guilt, and depressive symptoms: A meta-analytic review."

8 Shame is damaging, but guilt . . . serves a purpose: J. Price Tangey and R. Dearing. *Shame and Guilt*. New York: Guilford Press, 2002; P. Gilbert. "Evolution, attractiveness, and the emergence of shame and guilt in a self-aware mind: A reflection on Tracy and Robins," *Psychological Inquiry* 15, no 2 (2004): 132–135.

9 over-relying on our core strengths: B. Schwartz and K. E. Sharpe. "Practical wisdom: Aristotle meets positive psychology," *Journal of Happiness Studies* 7, no 3 (2006): 377–395; A. M. Grant and B. Schwartz. "Too much of a good thing: The challenge and opportunity of the inverted U," *Perspectives on Psychological Science* 6, no 1 (2011): 61–76.

10 the "shadow side" of a strength: R. Niemiec. "Mindfulness and character strengths."

Chapter 10: Strong Selves, Strong Families, Strong Communities, Strong World

1 posting something positive on social media triggers happiness: L. Rouyon and S. Utz. "The emotional responses of browsing Facebook: Happiness, envy, and the role of tie strength," *Computers in Human Behavior* 52 (2015): 29–38.

2 happiness spreads through social networks: L. Coviello et al. "Detecting emotional contagion in massive social networks," *PLOS One* 9, no 3 (2014): e90315.

3 Knowledge Is Power Program: KIPP. Accessed July 12, 2016, http://www.kipp.org.

4 Center for Positive Organizations, Ross School of Business, University of Michigan: "The top 50 schools," *Financial Times*, 2016, http://rankings.ft.com/businessschoolrankings/executive-education-customised-2016

INDEX

Page numbers in **bold** indicate tables; those in *italics* indicate figures.